VH

It Goes Without Saying

Peanuts at Its Silent Best

Charles M. Schulz

Ballantine Books • New York

Copyright © 2005 United Feature Syndicate, Inc.
Foreword © 2005 Jean Schulz

Published in the United States by Ballantine Books,
an imprint of The Random House Publishing Group,
a division of Random House, Inc., New York.

BALLANTINE and colophon are registered trademarks of Random House, Inc.

The comic strips in this book were originally published in newspapers worldwide.

Library of Congress Cataloging-in-Publication Data

Schulz, Charles M.
  [Peanuts. Selections]
  It goes without saying: Peanuts at its silent best/Charles M. Schulz.
    p.cm.
  Selections form the comic strip Peanuts.
  ISBN 0-345-46414-1 (alk. paper)
    I. Title

PN6728.P4S31923 2005
741.5'973—dc22   2005052063

Printed in the United States of America on acid-free paper

www.ballantinebooks.com

2 4 6 8 9 7 5 3 1

First Edition

Design by Diane Hobbing of Snap-Haus Graphics

It Goes Without Saying

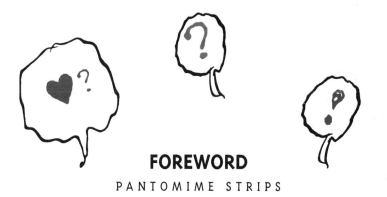

FOREWORD
PANTOMIME STRIPS

That a picture is worth a thousand words is a truism we don't question. The point is made dramatically in this book of very special *Peanuts* strips. In these cartoons Sparky tells a story without dialogue or explanation. Sometimes the joke is so subtle that you have to scour the final panel to get the joke. Sparky became known for his spare style of drawing, and these cartoons are spare to the extreme.

Sparky was always quick to remind colleagues and interviewers who might praise his philosophy and characterization that "cartooning is still about drawing funny pictures." Sparky set the pattern for these sight-gag strips early on. In fact, the third *Peanuts* strip published in October 1950 is indeed a funny picture, and there were seven more sight gags in the first month. Many of them were an extension of the ones he had drawn in *Li'l Folks,* which appeared in *The St. Paul Pioneer Press* from 1948 to 1950.

The pantomime strips continued in abundance in the early years. Often they were gags involving Snoopy, who doesn't talk in any case, but eventually all the characters found their personalities exploited in visual gags.

Without really being aware, readers bring all their senses to bear when they approach a comic strip. One can feel the "POW," "KLUNK," "AAUGH," and "CRASH" of an action strip, and one can get a sense of mustiness when the girls make mud pies in the early strips, so it should be no surprise that readers can become completely engaged in visual strips.

Notice the strips with rain. Sparky said that rain was fun to draw. The Bart Pen Lines Demonstration was one of the lessons in the *Art Instruction School* manual. It was an exercise in making smooth pen lines in three different widths. For fun, the instructors used to have competitions among themselves to draw the best page of lines. Sparky was proud of the way he could produce smooth, even pen strokes. In some of his strips, you could actually *feel* the rain. Rain is noisy, but falling snow is by its nature silent. Sparky also found the snow themes fun to draw and perfect for visual gags.

Music is a universal language and Sparky enjoyed playing visual games with the notes. I think he was fascinated by the silent language appearing on the page. Of course, a musician can read and "hear" the notes, but most of us don't have that talent. As Schroeder and his piano became a standard *Peanuts* theme, so did the strips with musical notes. Sparky always drew his notes from actual piano pieces, and he often received letters from musicians who recognized the compositions.

Emotions don't need words. All the emotions are depicted in these visual strips: the forlorn Charlie Brown watching his train, Snoopy showing his spunk and becoming increasingly opinionated, and often just plain silliness. I can hear Sparky's voice saying that these strips were "just fun to draw." He said that sometimes he would burst into laughter as he was drawing. I can imagine his laughter while he drew Linus stuffing his blanket in his mouth until his cheeks bulged in order to hide it from Snoopy.

Sparky was so prolific with his sight gags that there could be a book solely of Sunday strips with visual gags. It seems to me that it takes a great deal of concentration to plan an entire Sunday page based on a sight gag or a pantomime. The timing has to be perfect, yet Sparky did it over and over.

In later years, Spike became the subject of many of Sparky's visual gags, and when Rerun came on the scene, Sparky returned to some of the humor involving small fry with oversized equipment.

Sparky remarked repeatedly over the years that these visual strips would be a perfect way to introduce *Peanuts* to non-English speaking audiences or preschoolers. I realize that this book is written for the established *Peanuts* audience, but for whatever audience, Sparky would be glad to see his idea come to fruition. A picture *is* worth a thousand words. That is the power behind the *Peanuts* comic strip.

—Jean Schulz
March 2005

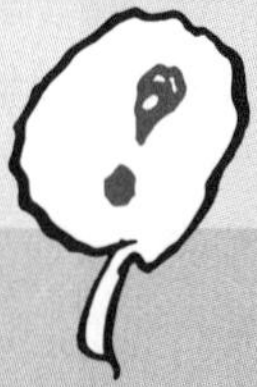

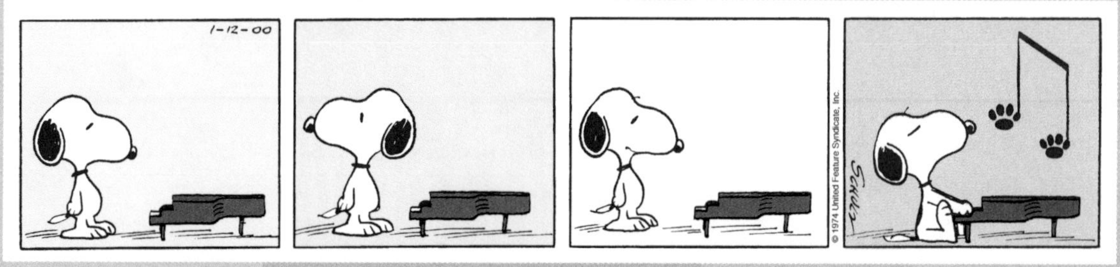
1-12-00
© 1974 United Feature Syndicate, Inc.
SCHULZ

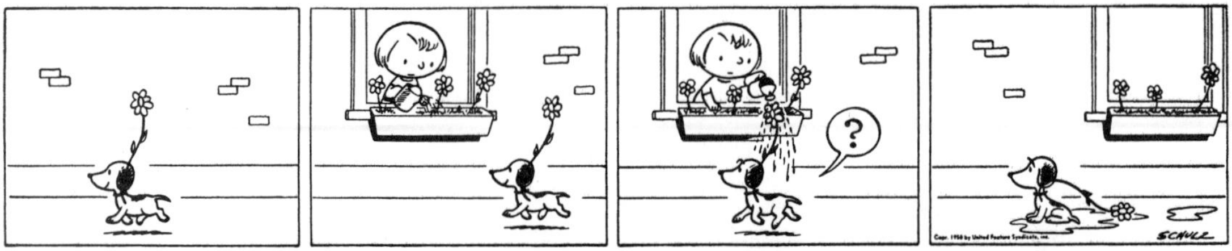
?
Copr. 1950 by United Feature Syndicate, Inc.
SCHULZ

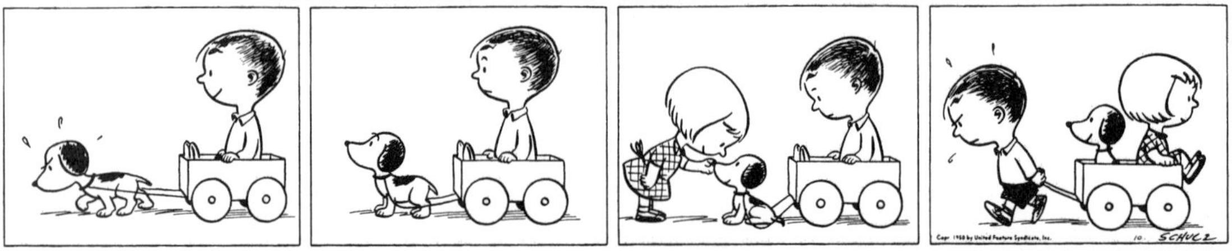
Copr. 1950 by United Feature Syndicate, Inc.
10.
SCHULZ

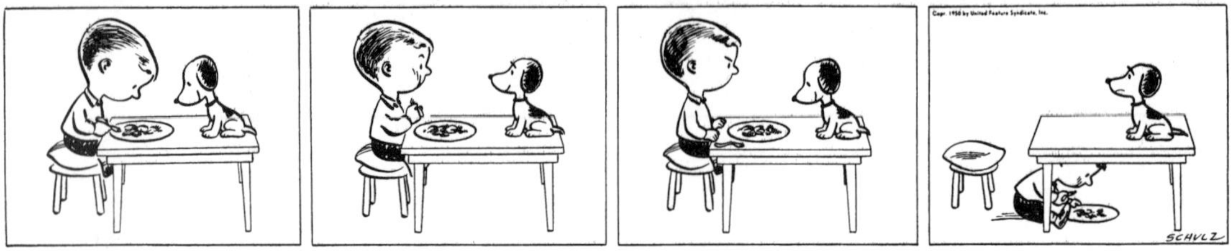
Copr. 1950 by United Feature Syndicate, Inc.
SCHULZ

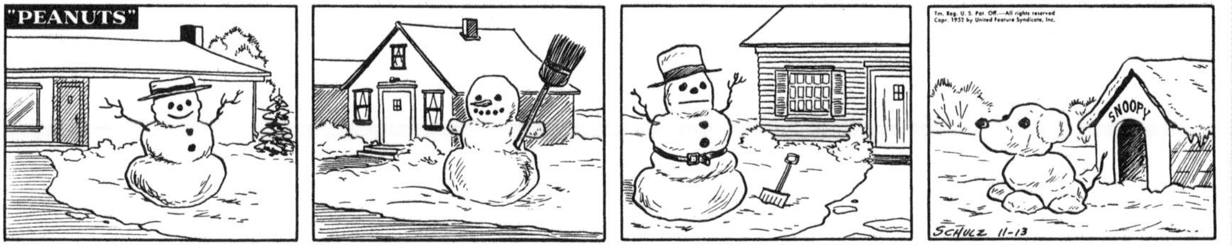
"PEANUTS"
Tm. Reg. U. S. Pat. Off.—All rights reserved
Copr. 1952 by United Feature Syndicate, Inc.
SNOOPY
SCHULZ 11-13

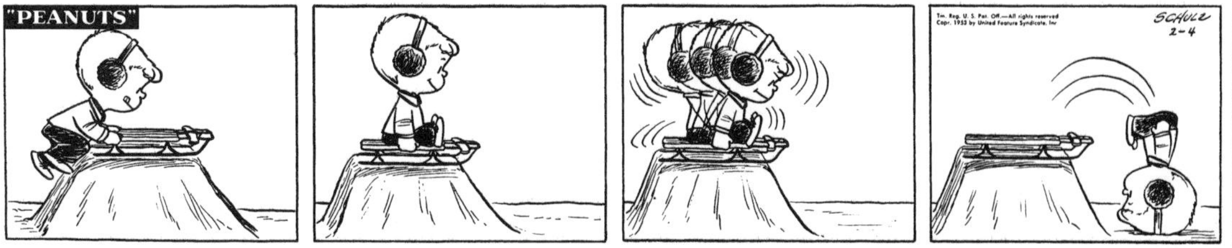
"PEANUTS"
Tm. Reg. U. S. Pat. Off.—All rights reserved
Copr. 1953 by United Feature Syndicate, Inc
SCHULZ 2-4

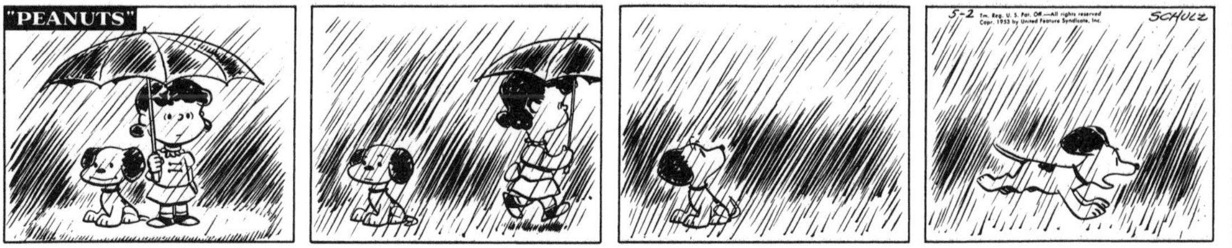
"PEANUTS"
5-2
Tm. Reg. U. S. Pat. Off.—All rights reserved
Copr. 1953 by United Feature Syndicate, Inc.
SCHULZ

"PEANUTS"
?
SCHULZ
5-19
!
Tm. Reg. U. S. Pat. Off.—All rights reserved
Copr. 1953 by United Feature Syndicate, Inc.

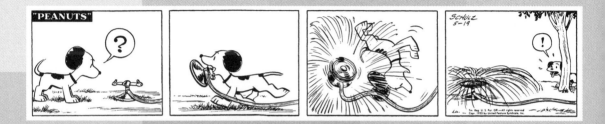

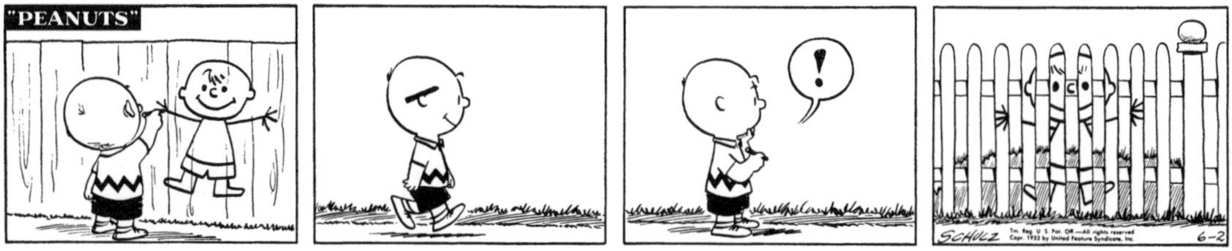
"PEANUTS"
!
SCHULZ
Tm. Reg. U. S. Pat. Off.—All rights reserved
Copr. 1953 by United Feature Syndicate, Inc.
6-2

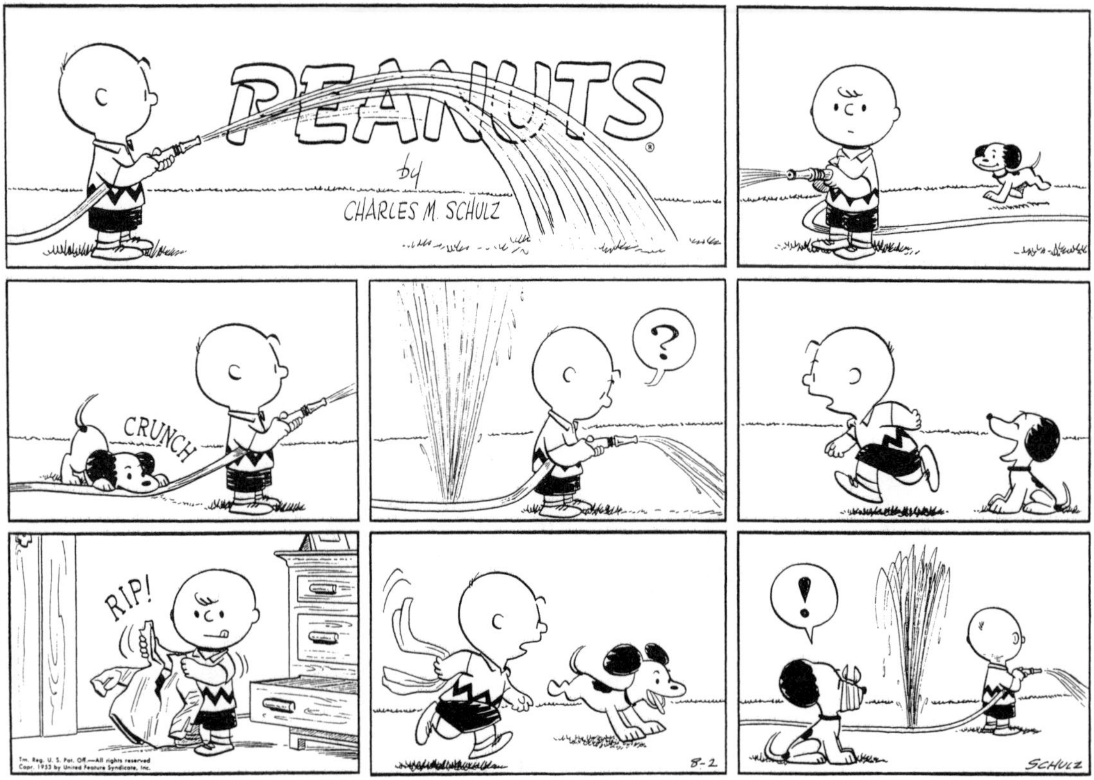
PEANUTS®
by
CHARLES M. SCHULZ
CRUNCH
?
RIP!
Tm. Reg. U. S. Pat. Off.—All rights reserved
Copr. 1953 by United Feature Syndicate, Inc.
8-2
!
SCHULZ

"PEANUTS"
ZZ
?
Z
SCHULZ
8-11

"PEANUTS"
!
8-22
SCHULZ

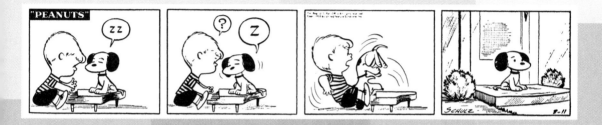

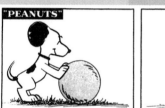

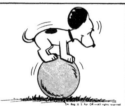

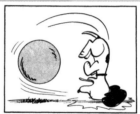

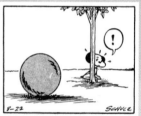

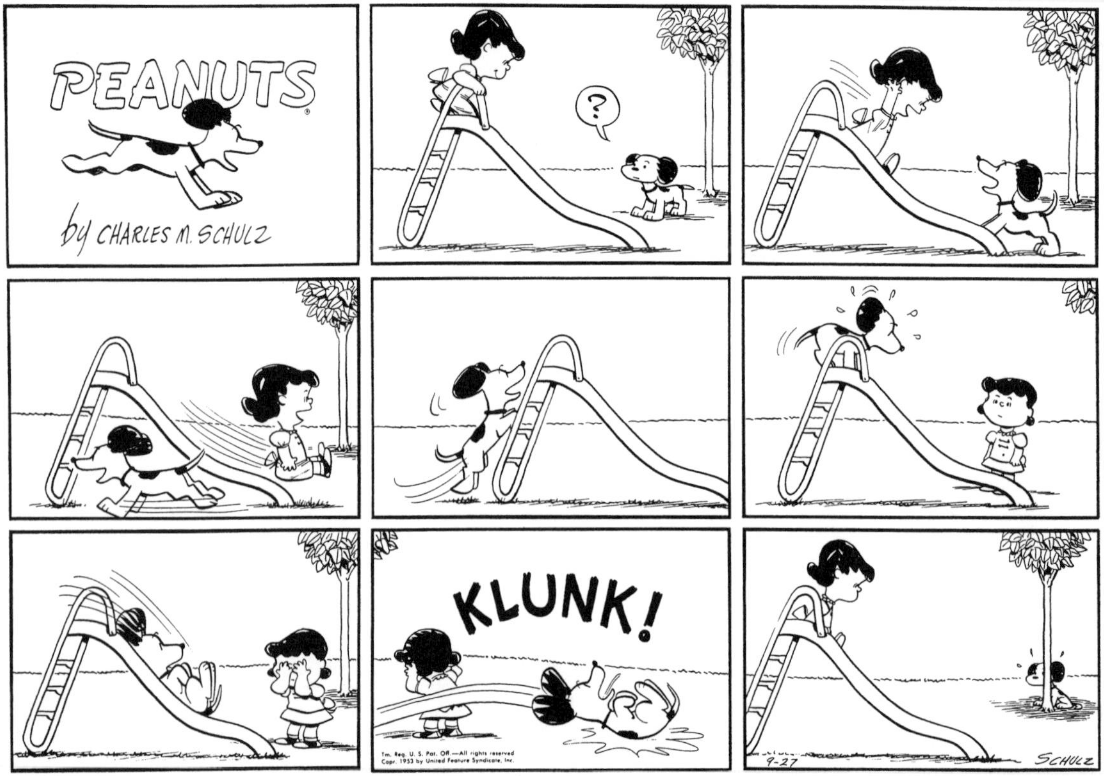
PEANUTS
by CHARLES M. SCHULZ
?
KLUNK!
Tm. Reg. U. S. Pat. Off.—All rights reserved
Copr. 1953 by United Feature Syndicate, Inc.
9-27
SCHULZ

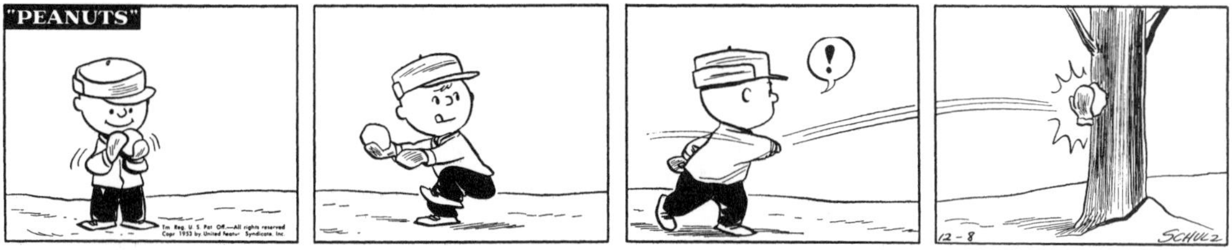
"PEANUTS"
Tm Reg. U. S. Pat. Off.—All rights reserved
Copr. 1953 by United Feature Syndicate, Inc.
!
12-8
SCHULZ

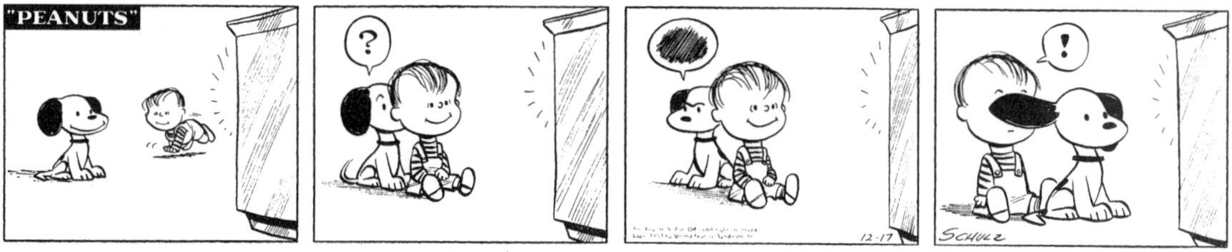
"PEANUTS"
?
12-17
!
SCHULZ

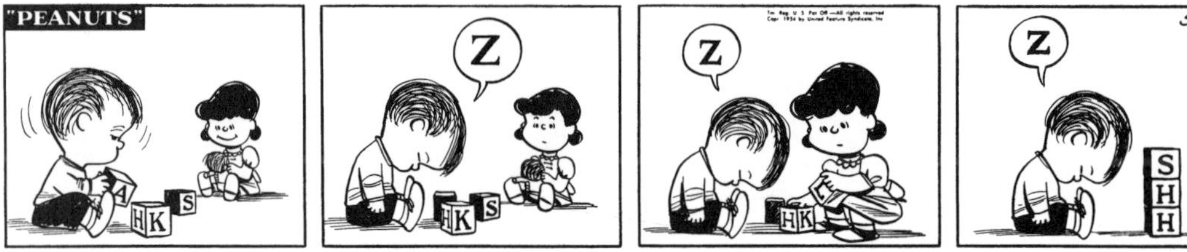
"PEANUTS"
A
H K
S
Z
H K
S
Z
Tm. Reg. U. S. Pat. Off.—All rights reserved Copr. 1954 by United Feature Syndicate, Inc
H K
Z
SCHULZ 1-12
S
H
H

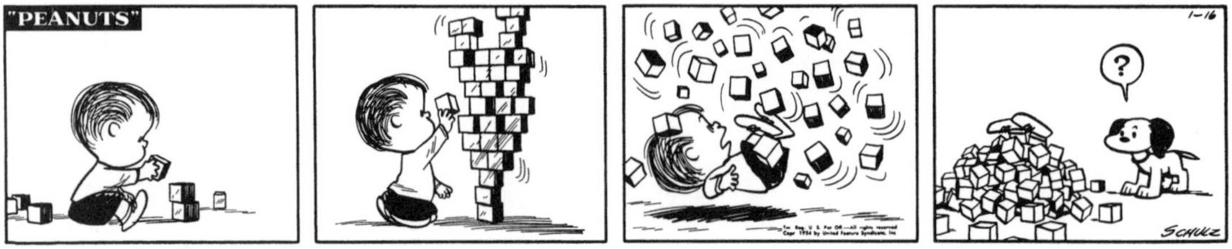
"PEANUTS"
1-16
Tm. Reg. U. S. Pat. Off.—All rights reserved Copr. 1954 by United Feature Syndicate, Inc
?
SCHULZ

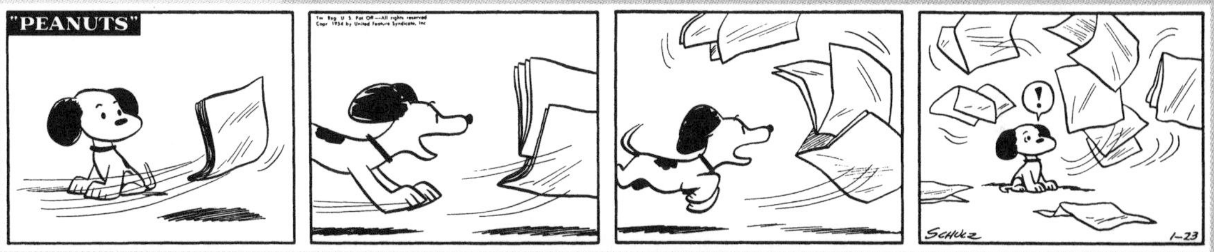
"PEANUTS"
Tm Reg U S Pat Off—All rights reserved
Copr 1954 by United Feature Syndicate, Inc
!
SCHULZ
1-23

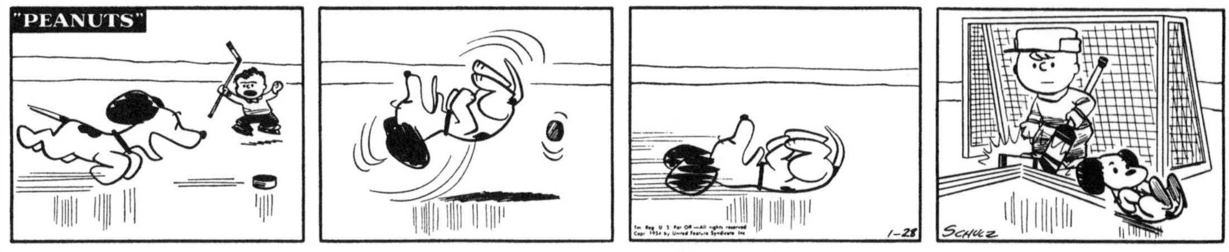
"PEANUTS"
Tm Reg U S Pat Off—All rights reserved
Copr 1954 by United Feature Syndicate Inc
1-28
SCHULZ

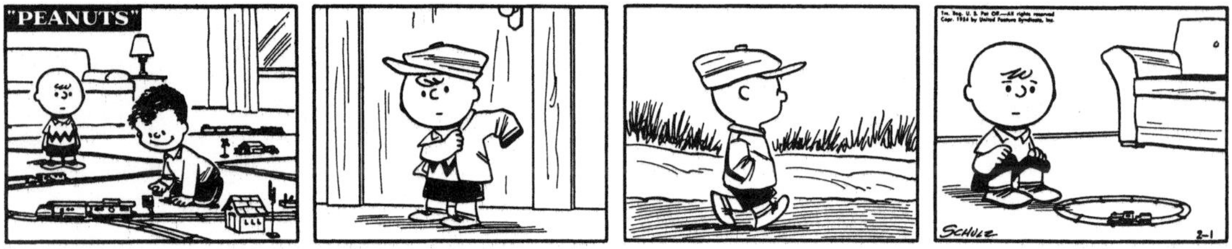
"PEANUTS"
Tm. Reg. U. S. Pat. Off.—All rights reserved
Copr. 1954 by United Feature Syndicate, Inc.
SCHULZ
2-1

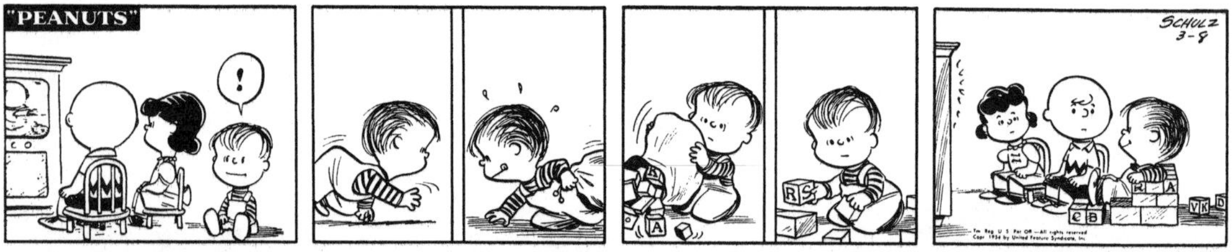
"PEANUTS"
!
SCHULZ
3-8
Tm. Reg. U. S. Pat. Off.—All rights reserved
Copr. 1954 by United Feature Syndicate, Inc.

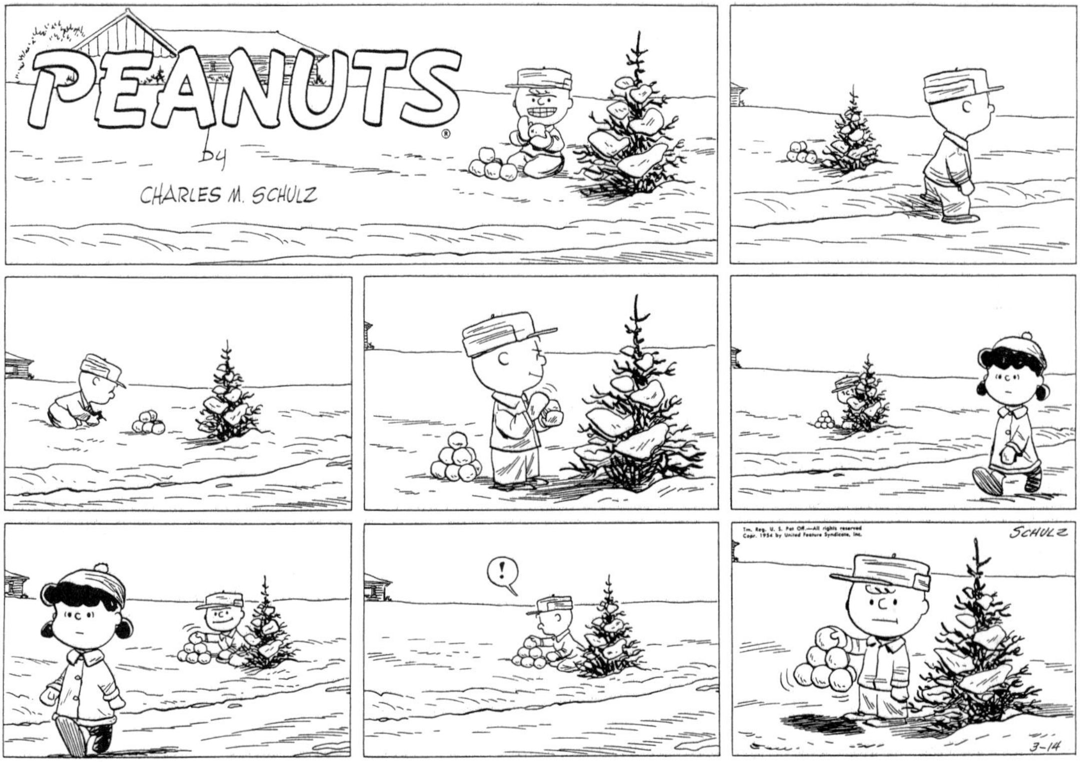
PEANUTS
by
CHARLES M. SCHULZ
!
Tm. Reg. U. S. Pat Off.—All rights reserved
Copr. 1954 by United Feature Syndicate, Inc.
SCHULZ
3-14

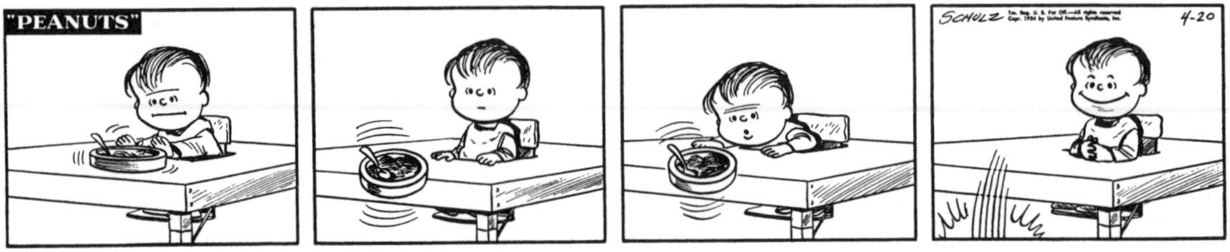
"PEANUTS"
SCHULZ
Tm. Reg. U. S. Pat. Off.—All rights reserved
Copr. 1954 by United Feature Syndicate, Inc.
4-20

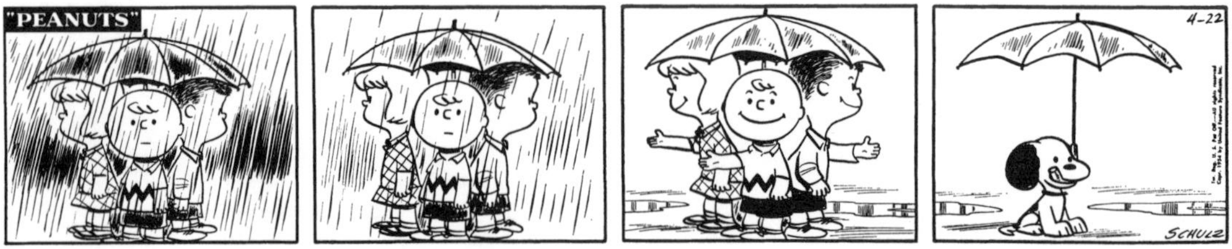
"PEANUTS"
4-22
SCHULZ

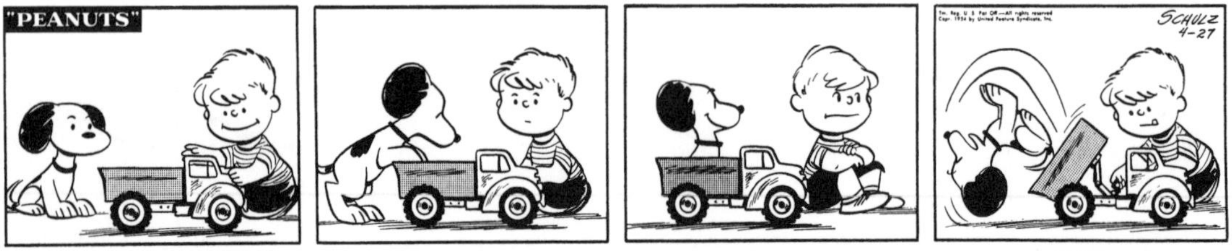
"PEANUTS"
Tm. Reg. U. S. Pat. Off.—All rights reserved
Copr. 1954 by United Feature Syndicate, Inc.
SCHULZ
4-27

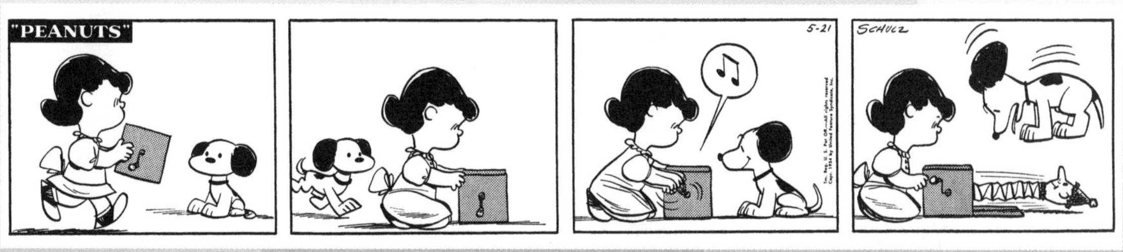
"PEANUTS"
5-21
SCHULZ

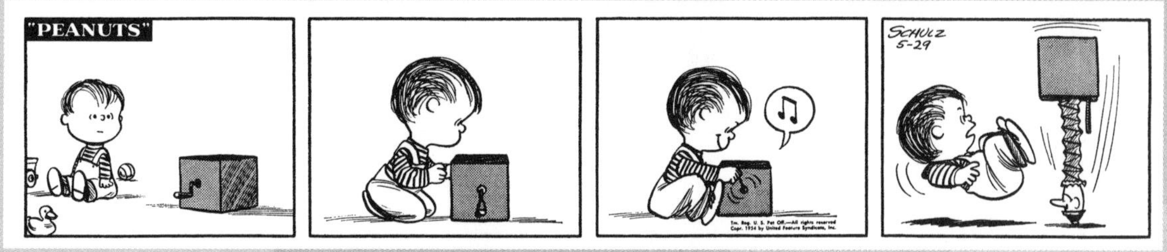
"PEANUTS"
Tm. Reg. U. S. Pat Off.—All rights reserved
Copr. 1954 by United Feature Syndicate, Inc.
SCHULZ
5-29

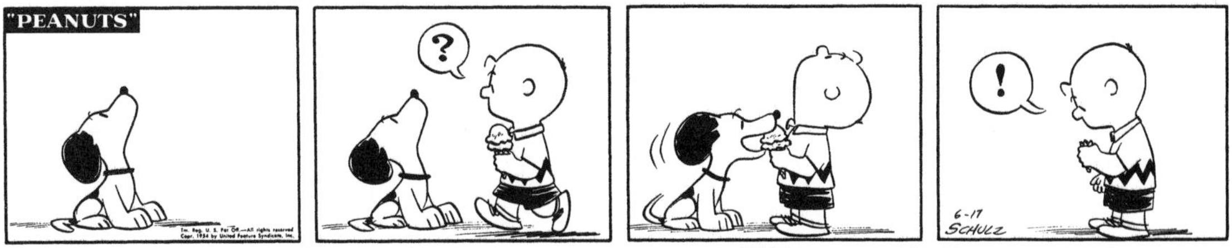
"PEANUTS"
Tm. Reg. U. S. Pat Off.—All rights reserved Copr. 1954 by United Feature Syndicate, Inc.
?
!
6-17
SCHULZ

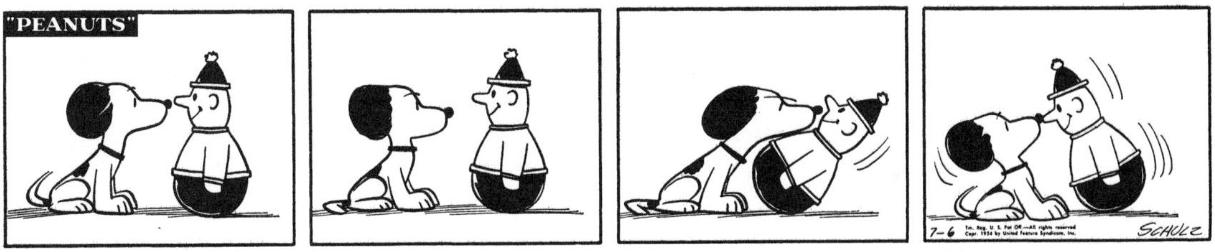
"PEANUTS"
7-6
Tm. Reg. U. S. Pat Off.—All rights reserved Copr. 1954 by United Feature Syndicate, Inc.
SCHULZ

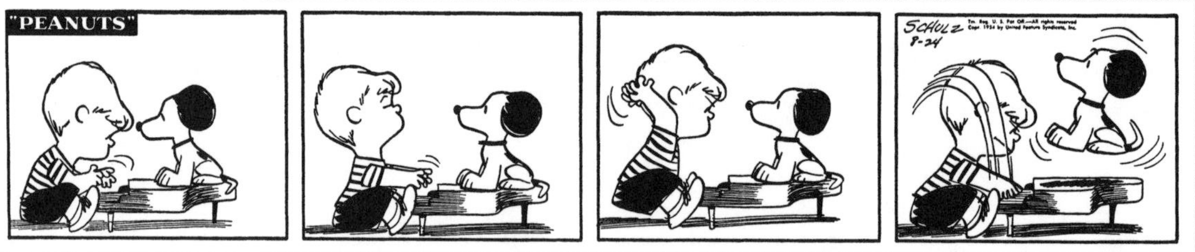
"PEANUTS"
SCHULZ
8-24
Tm. Reg. U. S. Pat Off.—All rights reserved
Copr. 1954 by United Feature Syndicate, Inc.

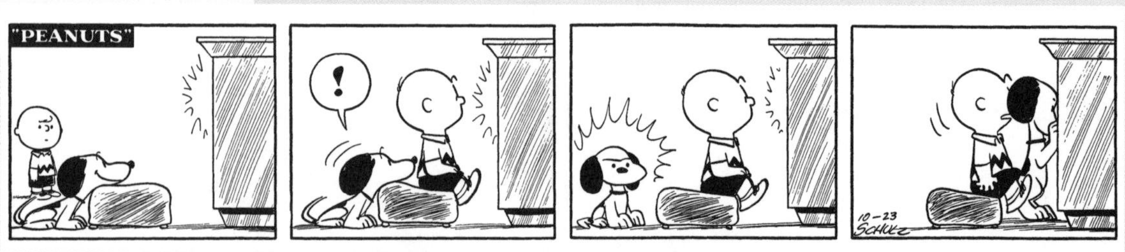
"PEANUTS"
!
10-23
SCHULZ

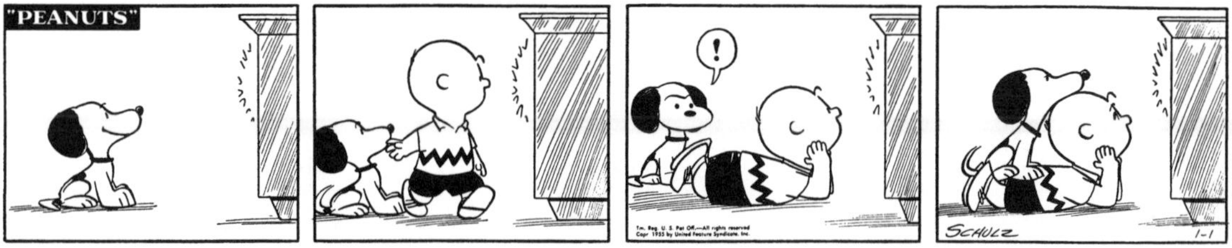
"PEANUTS"
!
Tm. Reg. U. S. Pat. Off.—All rights reserved
Copr. 1955 by United Feature Syndicate, Inc.
SCHULZ
1-1

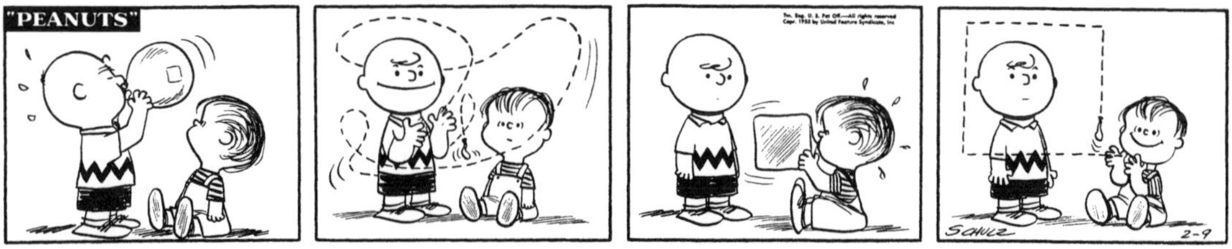
"PEANUTS"
Tm. Reg. U. S. Pat. Off.—All rights reserved
Copr. 1955 by United Feature Syndicate, Inc.
SCHULZ
2-9

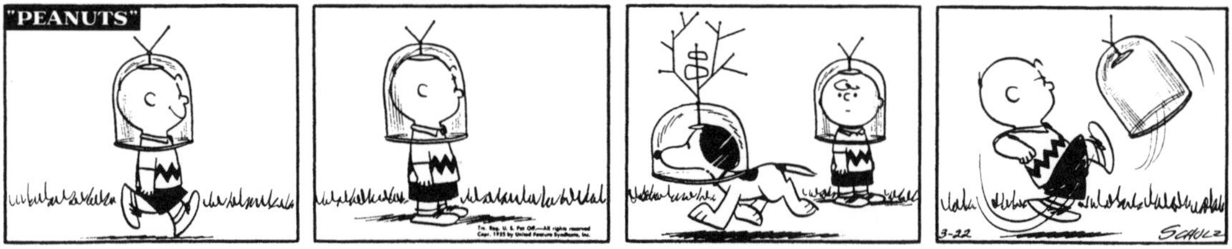
"PEANUTS"
Tm. Reg. U. S. Pat. Off.—All rights reserved
Copr. 1955 by United Feature Syndicate, Inc.
3-22
SCHULZ

PEANUTS
by
CHARLES M. SCHULZ
?
5-1
Tm. Reg. U. S. Pat Off.—All rights reserved
Copr. 1955 by United Feature Syndicate, Inc.
SCHULZ

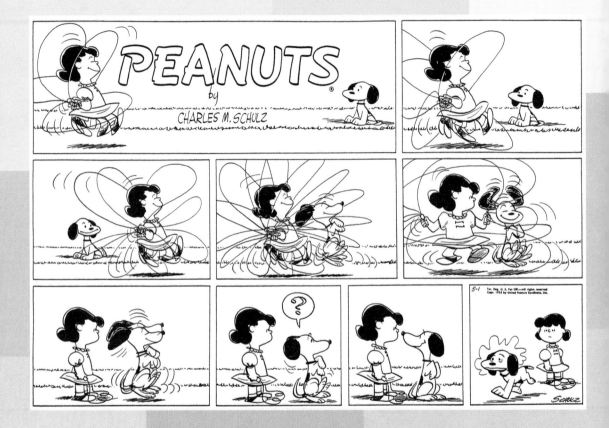

29

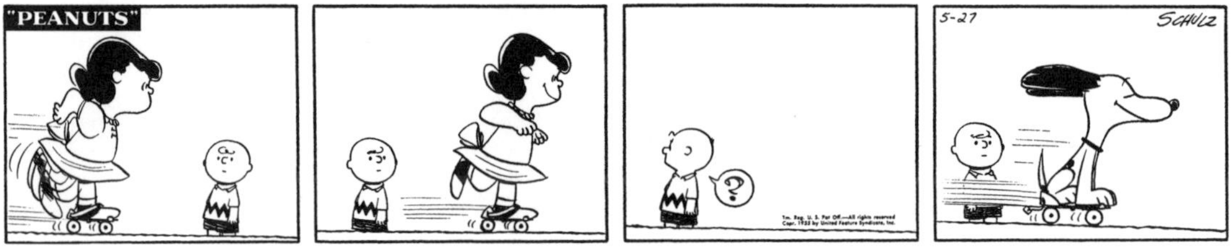
"PEANUTS"
5-27
SCHULZ

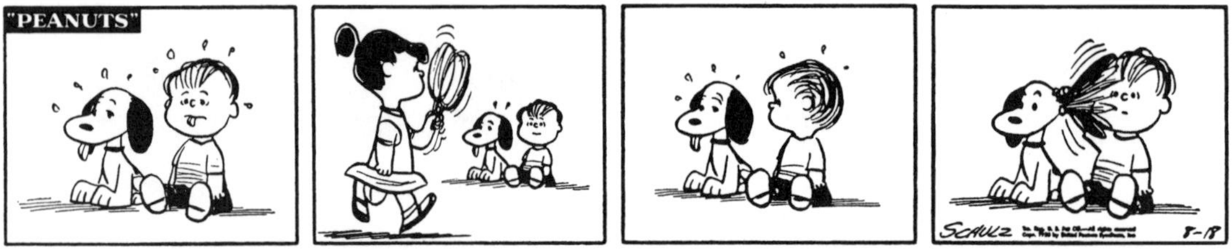
"PEANUTS"
SCHULZ
8-18

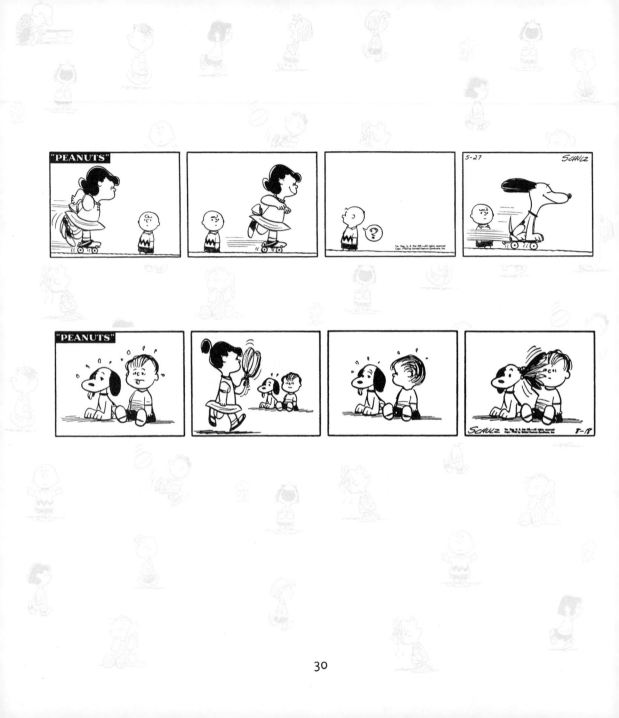

PEANUTS
by
CHARLES M. SCHULZ
?
Tm. Reg. U. S. Pat Off.—All rights reserved
Copr. 1956 by United Feature Syndicate, Inc.
2-12
SCHULZ

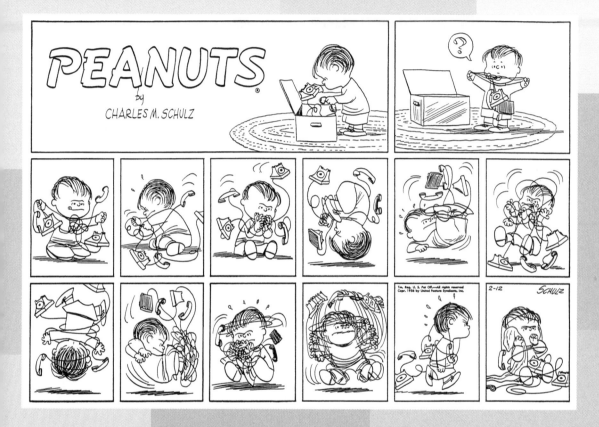

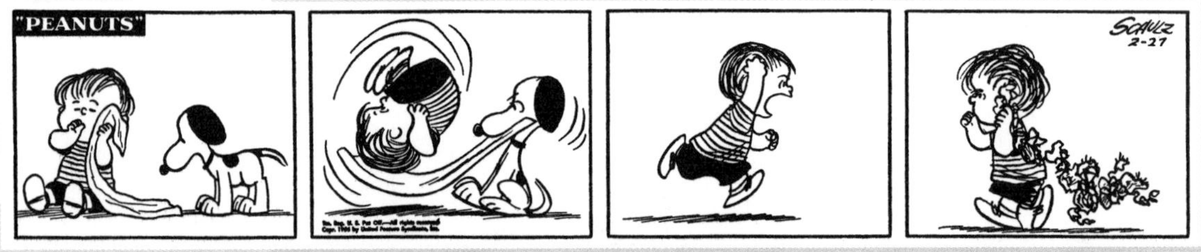
"PEANUTS"
SCHULZ
2-27

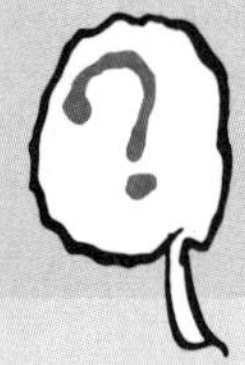
?

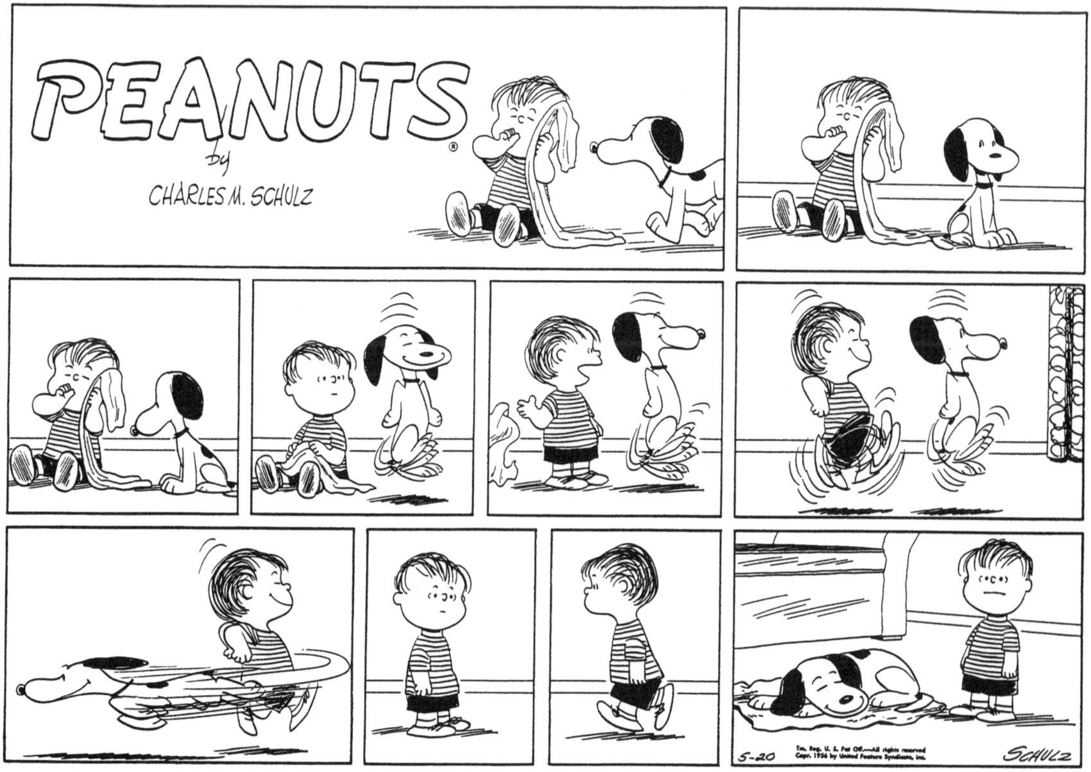
PEANUTS
by
CHARLES M. SCHULZ
5-20
Tm. Reg. U. S. Pat Off.—All rights reserved
Copr. 1956 by United Feature Syndicate, Inc.
SCHULZ

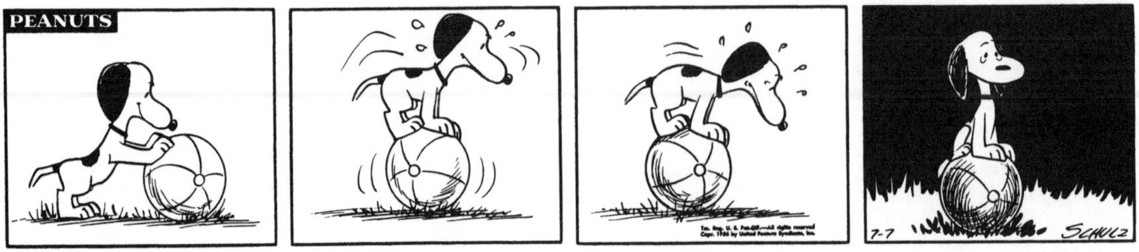
PEANUTS
7-7
SCHULZ

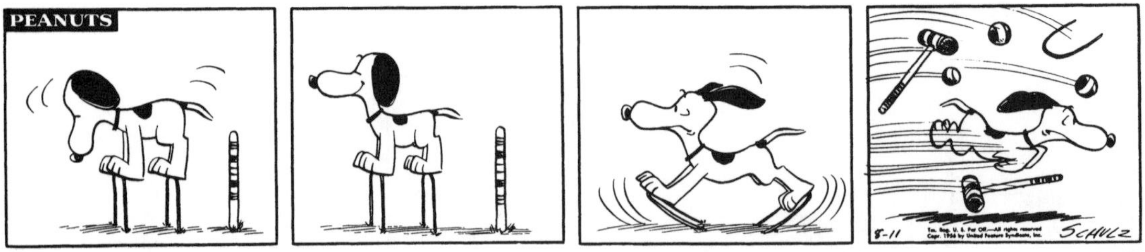
PEANUTS
8-11
SCHULZ

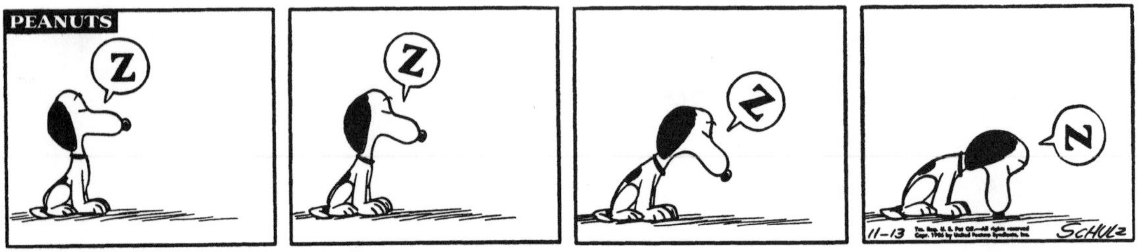
PEANUTS
Z
Z
Z
Z
11-13
SCHULZ

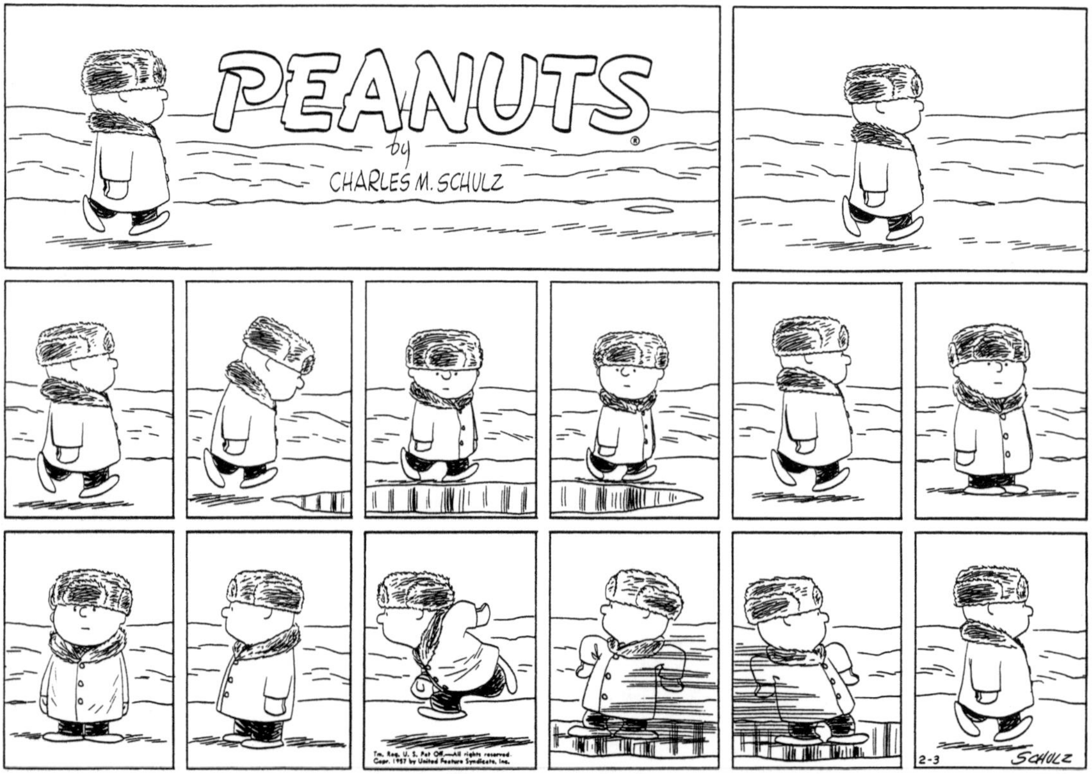
PEANUTS
by
CHARLES M. SCHULZ
Tm. Reg. U. S. Pat Off.—All rights reserved.
Copr. 1957 by United Feature Syndicate, Inc.
2-3
SCHULZ

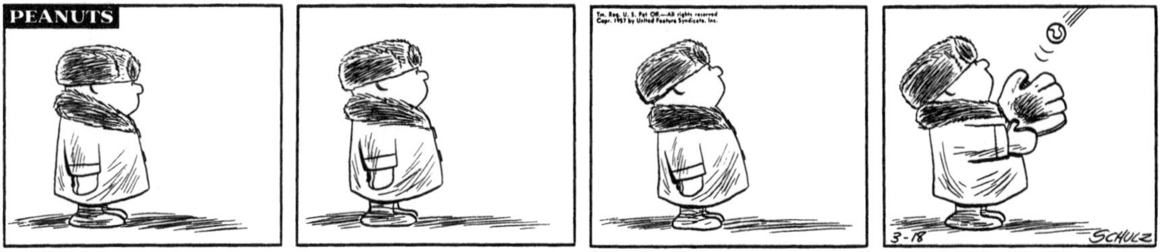
PEANUTS
Tm. Reg. U. S. Pat. Off.—All rights reserved
Copr. 1957 by United Feature Syndicate, Inc.
3-18
SCHULZ

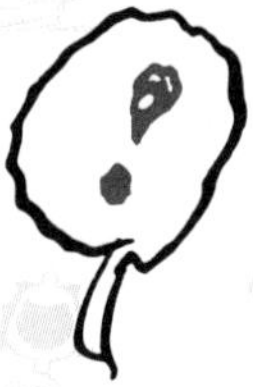

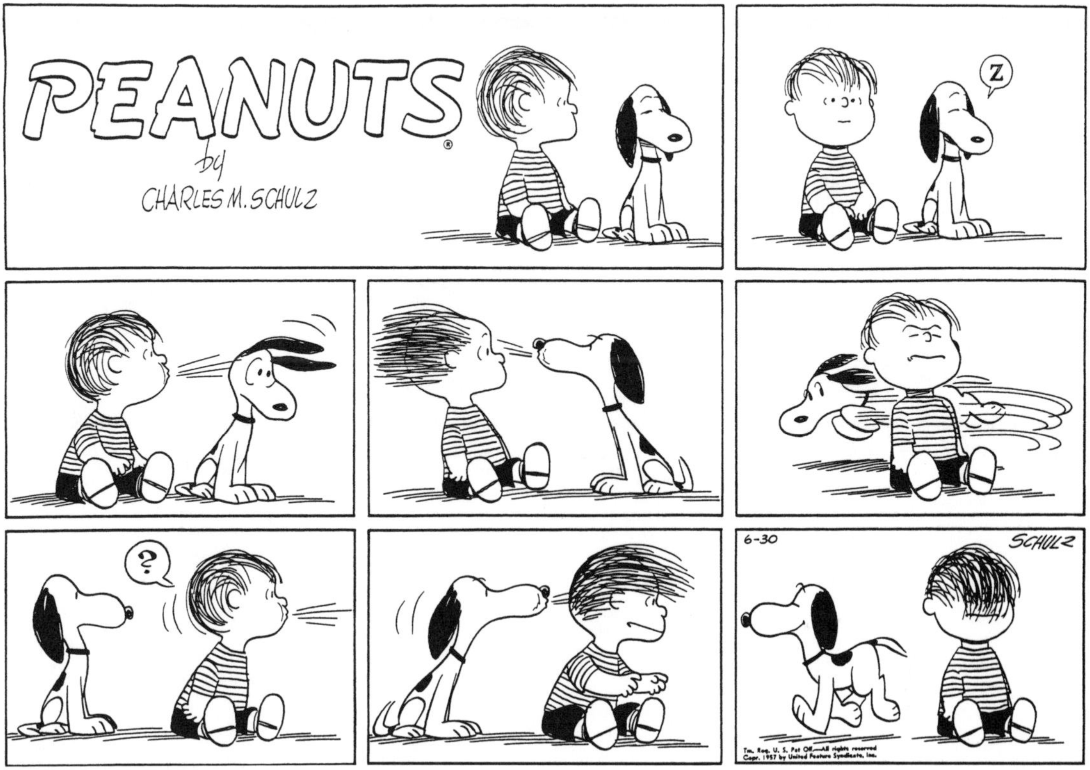
PEANUTS
by
CHARLES M. SCHULZ
Z
?
6-30
SCHULZ
Tm. Reg. U. S. Pat Off.—All rights reserved
Copr. 1957 by United Feature Syndicate, Inc.

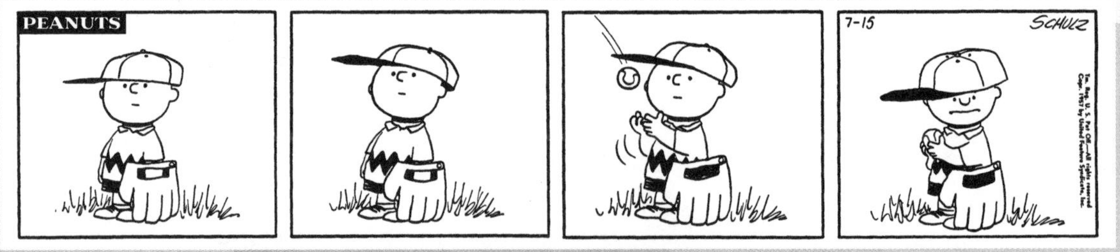
PEANUTS
7-15
SCHULZ
Tm. Reg. U. S. Pat. Off.—All rights reserved
Copr. 1957 by United Feature Syndicate, Inc.

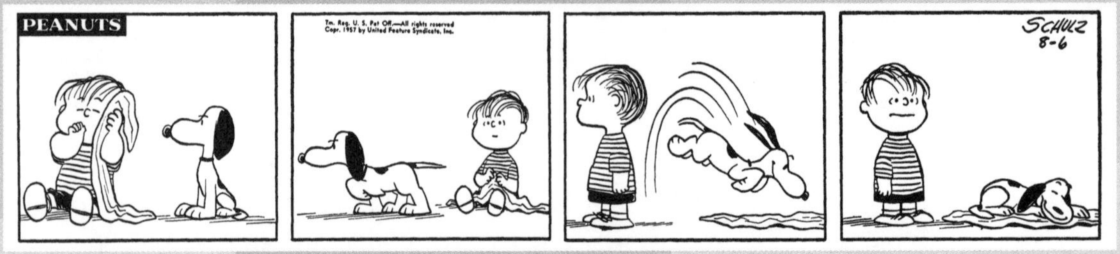
PEANUTS
Tm. Reg. U. S. Pat Off.—All rights reserved
Copr. 1957 by United Feature Syndicate, Inc.
SCHULZ
8-6

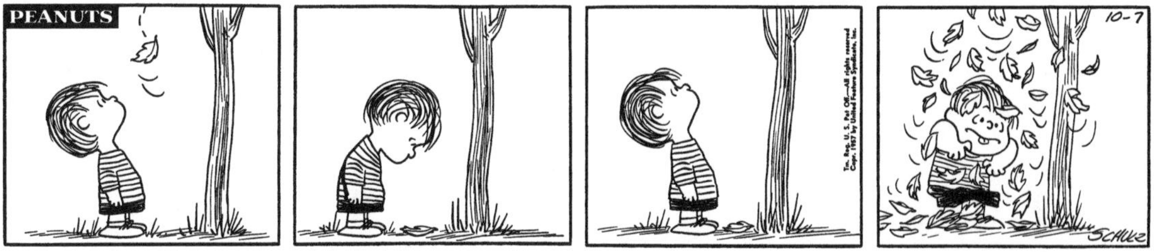
PEANUTS
Tm. Reg. U. S. Pat. Off.—All rights reserved
Copr. 1957 by United Feature Syndicate, Inc.
10-7
SCHULZ

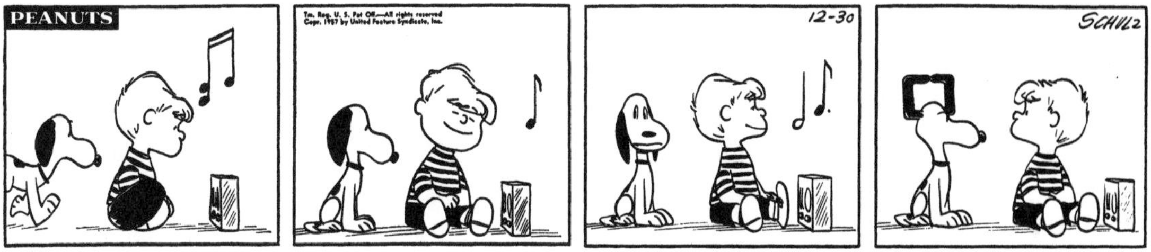
PEANUTS
Tm. Reg. U. S. Pat. Off.—All rights reserved
Copr. 1957 by United Feature Syndicate, Inc.
12-30
SCHULZ

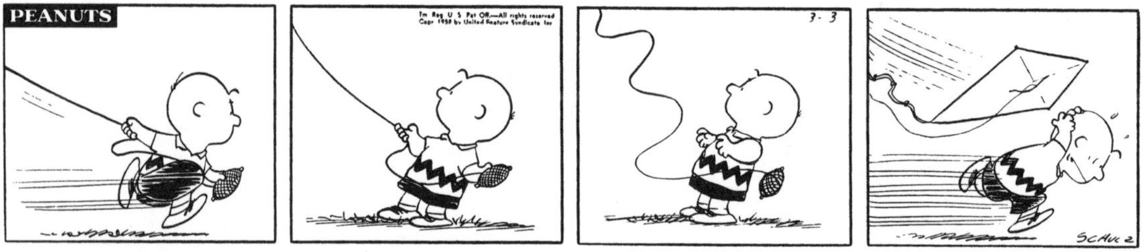
PEANUTS
3-3
SCHULZ

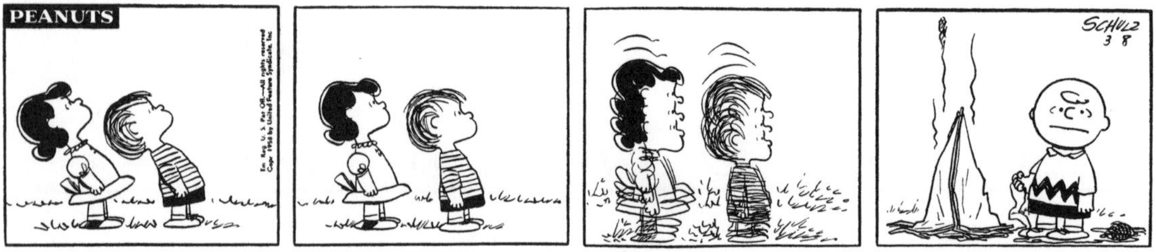
PEANUTS
SCHULZ
3 8

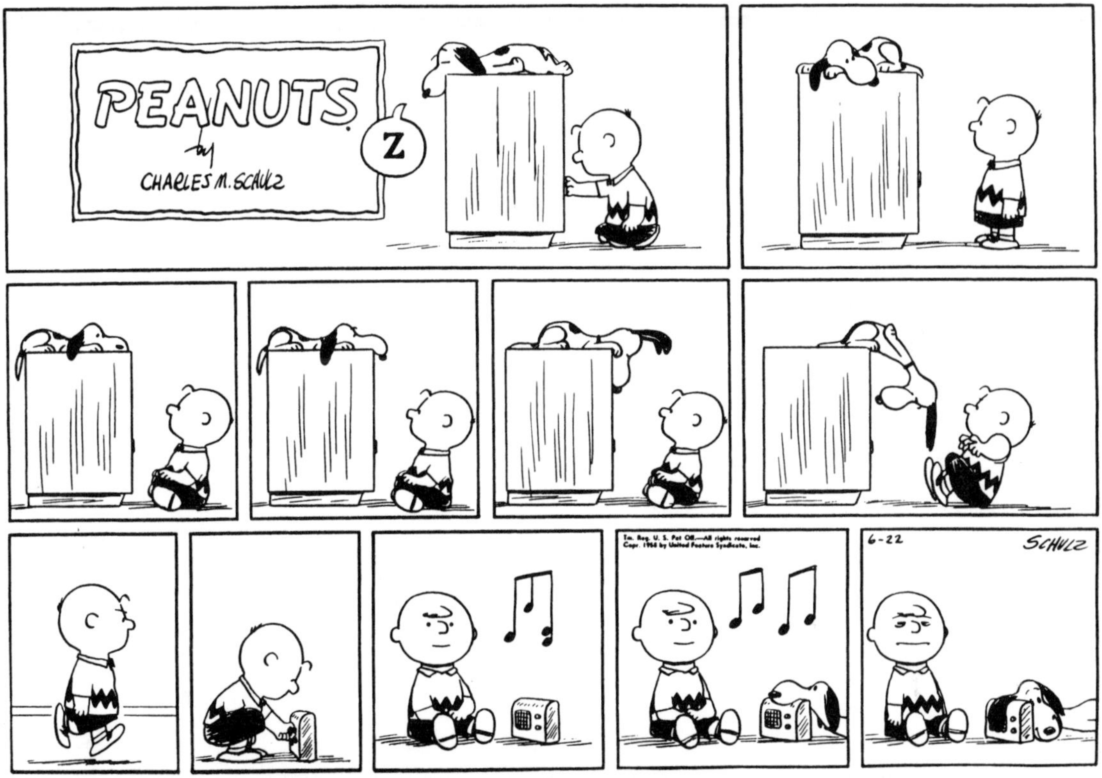
PEANUTS
by
CHARLES M. SCHULZ
Z
Tm. Reg. U. S. Pat Off.—All rights reserved
Copr. 1958 by United Feature Syndicate, Inc.
6-22
SCHULZ

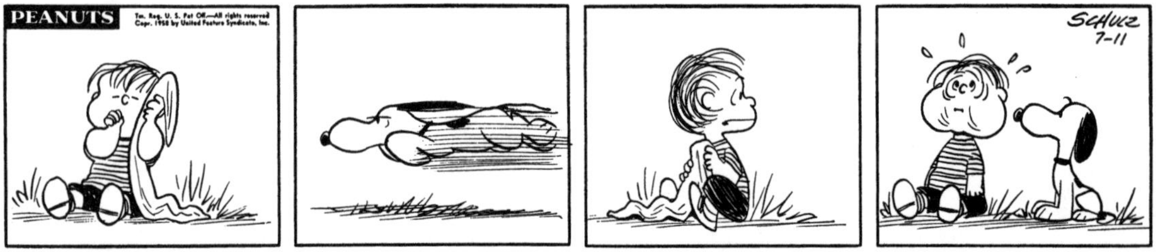
PEANUTS
Tm. Reg. U. S. Pat Off.—All rights reserved
Copr. 1958 by United Feature Syndicate, Inc.
SCHULZ
7-11

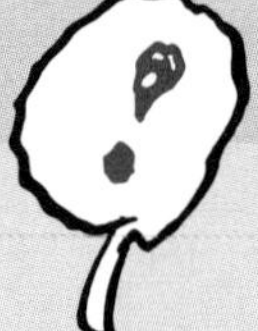
?

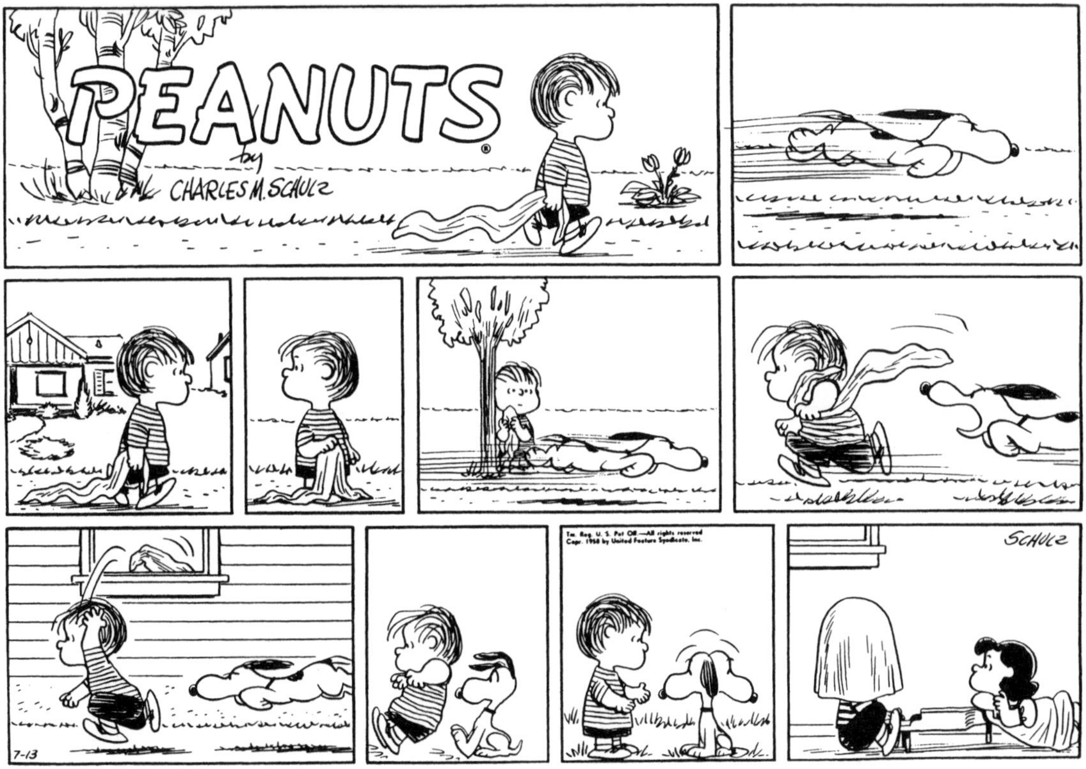
PEANUTS
by
CHARLES M. SCHULZ
7-13
Tm. Reg. U. S. Pat. Off.—All rights reserved
Copr. 1958 by United Feature Syndicate, Inc.
SCHULZ

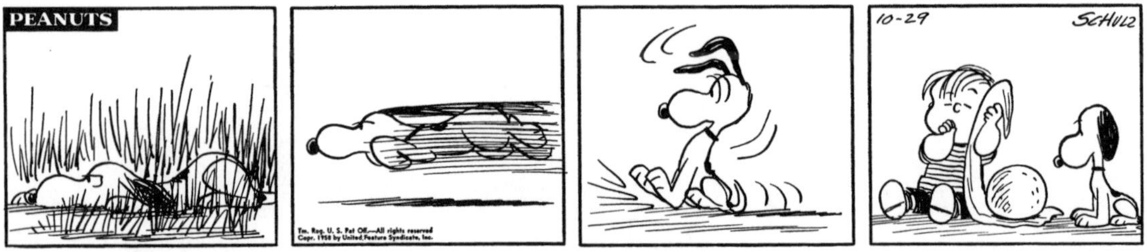
PEANUTS
Tm. Reg. U. S. Pat Off.—All rights reserved
Copr. 1958 by United Feature Syndicate, Inc.
10-29
SCHULZ

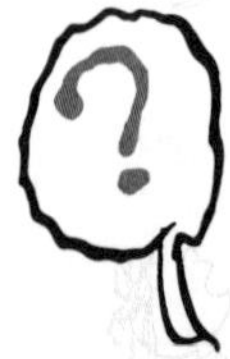
?

PEANUTS
by SCHULZ
Tm. Reg. U. S. Pat Off.—All rights reserved
Copr. 1959 by United Feature Syndicate, Inc.
1-4
SCHULZ

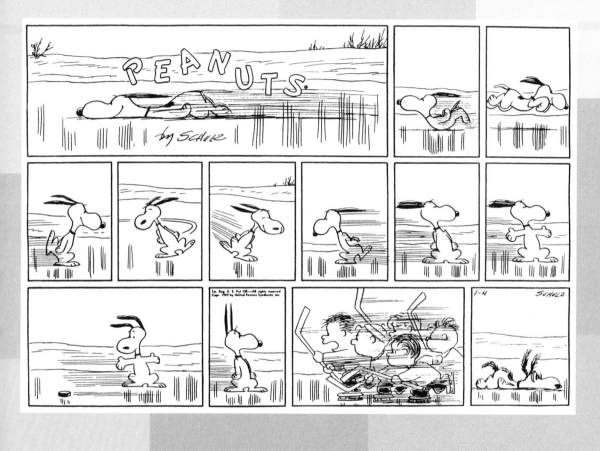

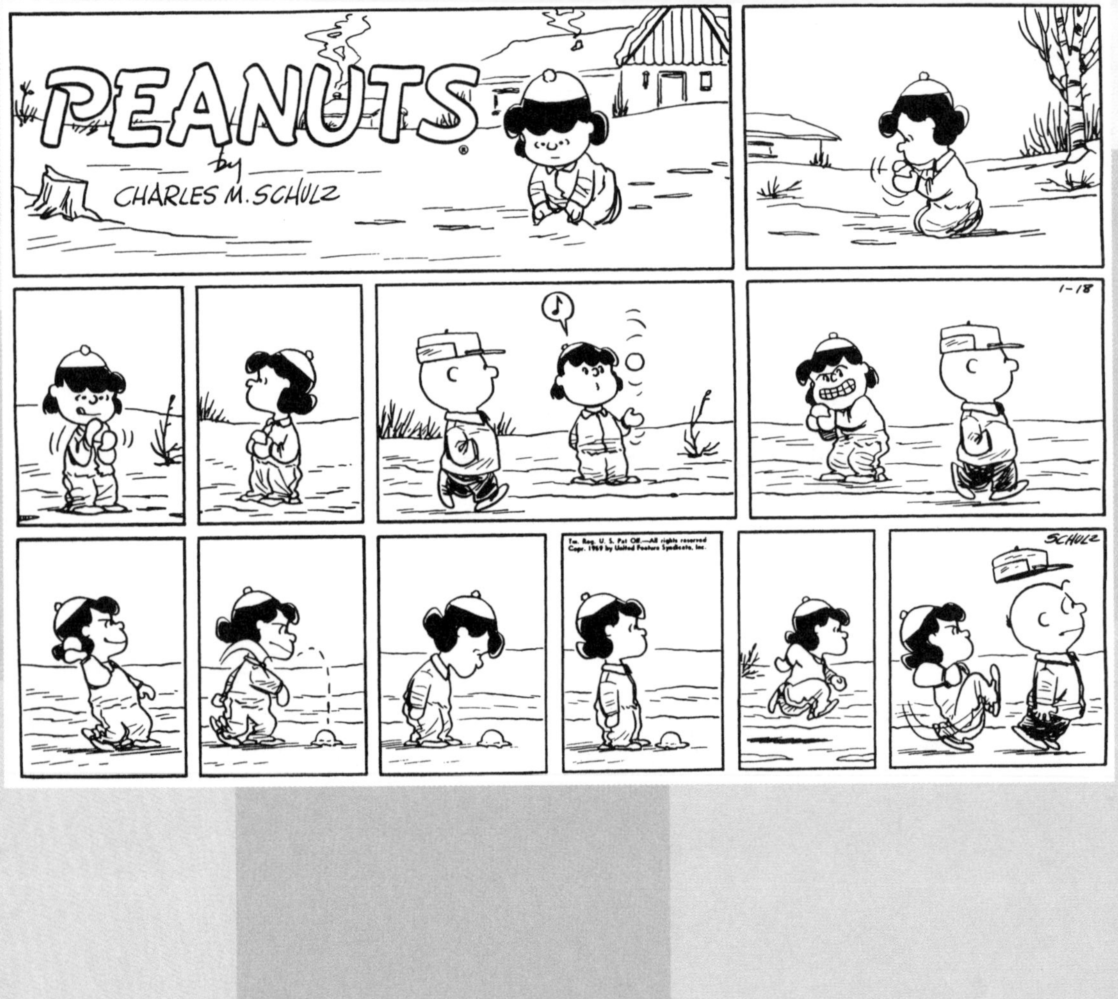
PEANUTS
by
CHARLES M. SCHULZ
1-18
Tm. Reg. U. S. Pat Off.—All rights reserved
SCHULZ

49

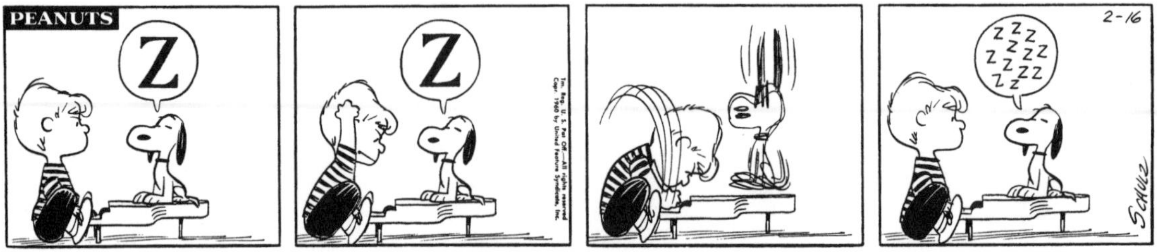
PEANUTS
Z
Z
Tm. Reg. U. S. Pat Off.—All rights reserved
Copr. 1960 by United Feature Syndicate, Inc.
2-16
Z Z Z Z Z Z Z Z Z Z Z
SCHULZ

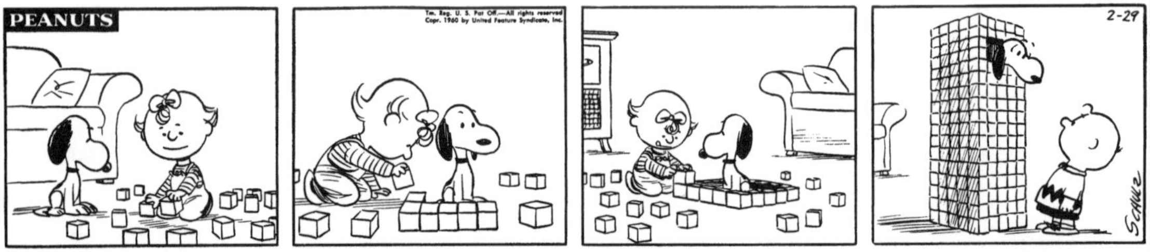
PEANUTS
Tm. Reg. U. S. Pat Off.—All rights reserved
Copr. 1960 by United Feature Syndicate, Inc.
2-29
SCHULZ

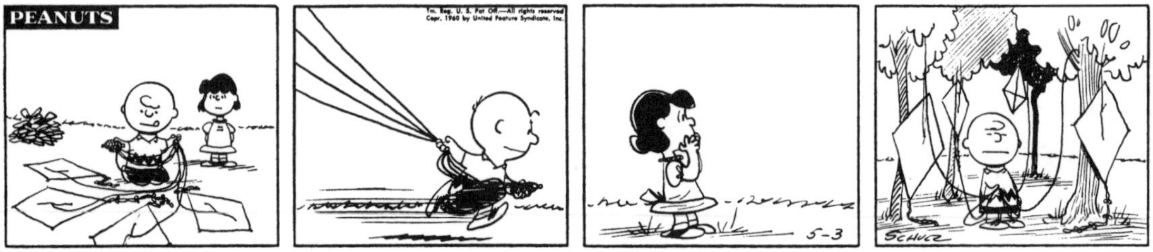
PEANUTS
Tm. Reg. U. S. Pat Off.—All rights reserved
Copr. 1960 by United Feature Syndicate, Inc.
5-3
SCHULZ

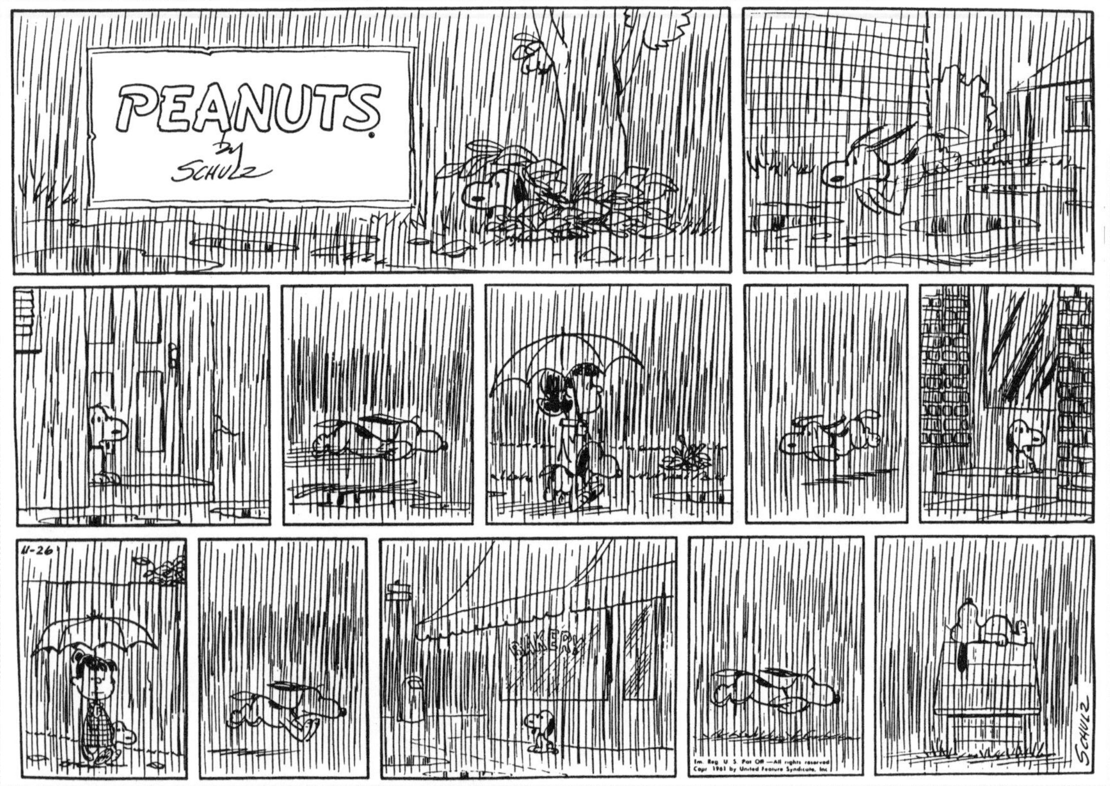

PEANUTS
by
SCHULZ
11-26
BAKERY
Tm. Reg U.S. Pat Off —All rights reserved
Copr 1961 by United Feature Syndicate, Inc
SCHULZ

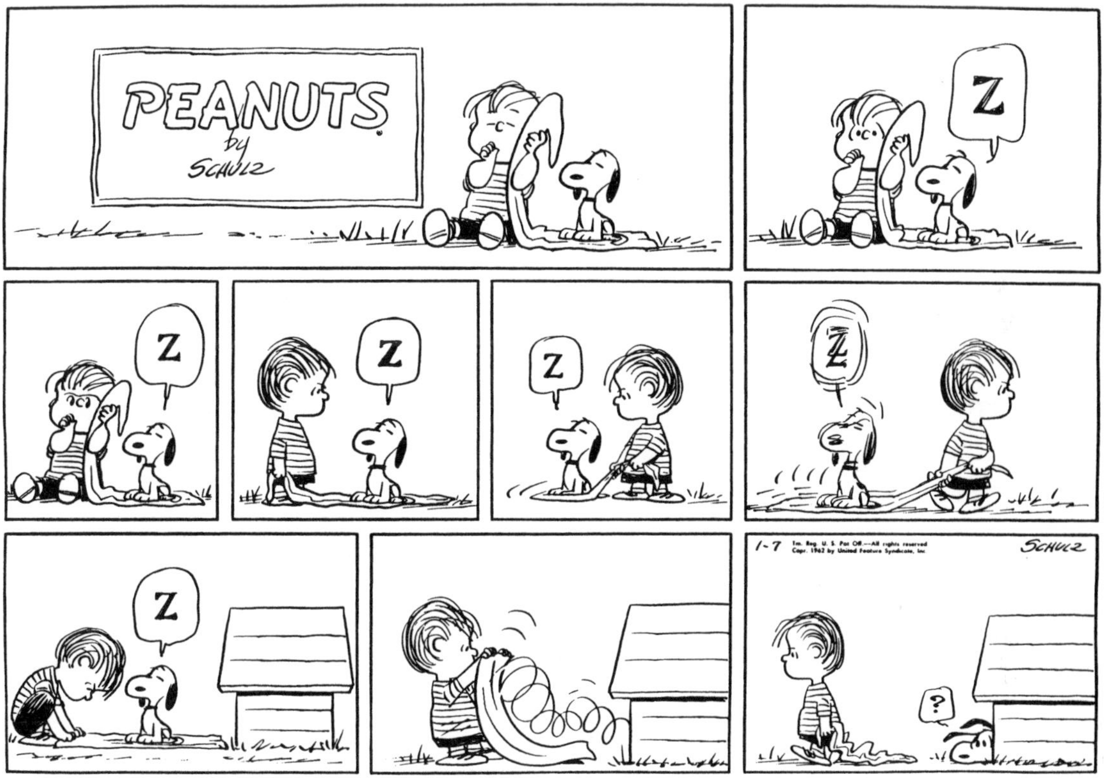
PEANUTS
by
SCHULZ
Z
Z
Z
Z
Z
Z
Z
1-7
Tm. Reg. U. S. Pat. Off.—All rights reserved
Copr. 1962 by United Feature Syndicate, Inc.
SCHULZ
?

PEANUTS
Tm. Reg. U. S. Pat. Off.—All rights reserved
Copr. 1962 by United Feature Syndicate, Inc.
10-5
SCHULZ

PEANUTS
11-13
SCHULZ

PEANUTS
Tm. Reg. U. S. Pat. Off.—All rights reserved
Copr. 1963 by United Feature Syndicate, Inc
3-13
SCHULZ

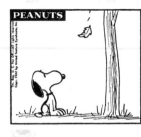

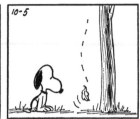

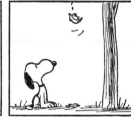

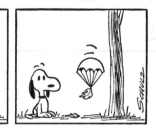

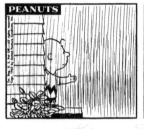

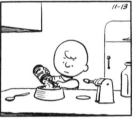

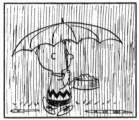

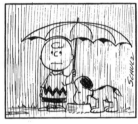

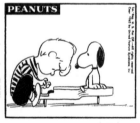

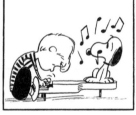

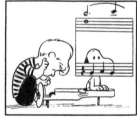

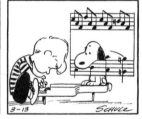

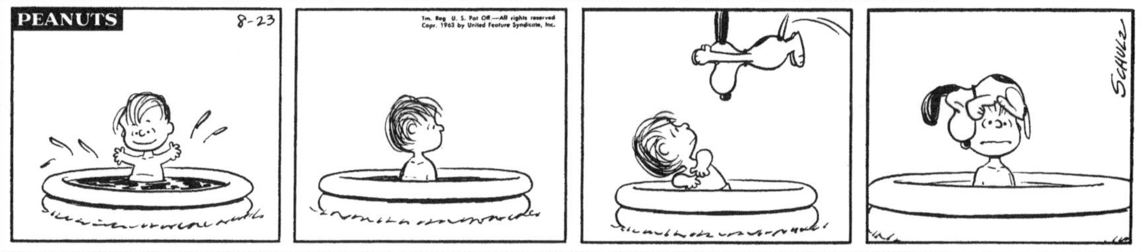
PEANUTS
8-23
Tm. Reg. U. S. Pat. Off.—All rights reserved
Copr. 1963 by United Feature Syndicate, Inc.
SCHULZ

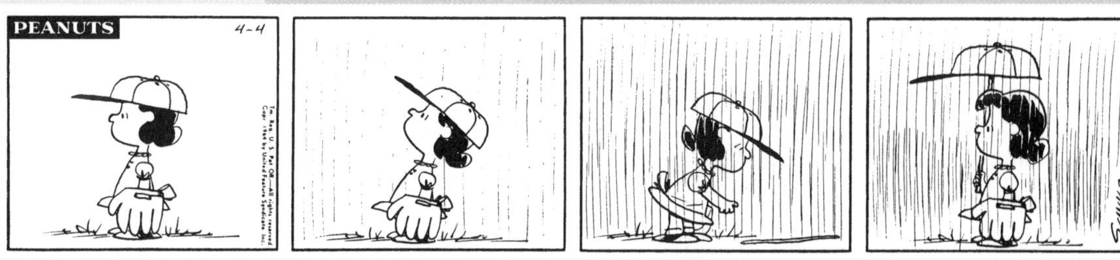
PEANUTS
4-4
Tm. Reg. U. S. Pat. Off.—All rights reserved
Copr. 1964 by United Feature Syndicate, Inc.
SCHULZ

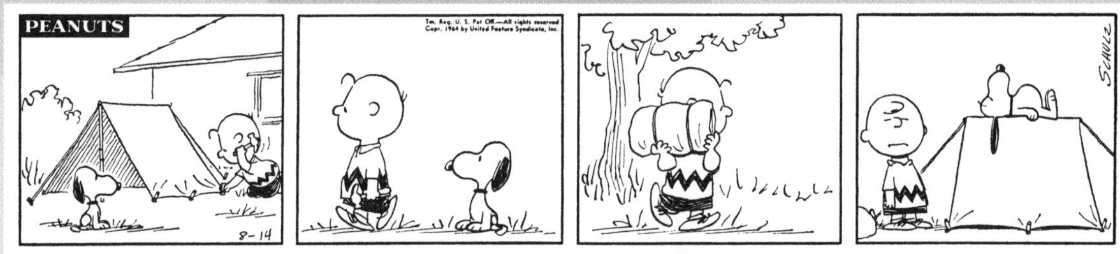
PEANUTS
8-14
Tm. Reg. U. S. Pat. Off.—All rights reserved
Copr. 1964 by United Feature Syndicate, Inc.
SCHULZ

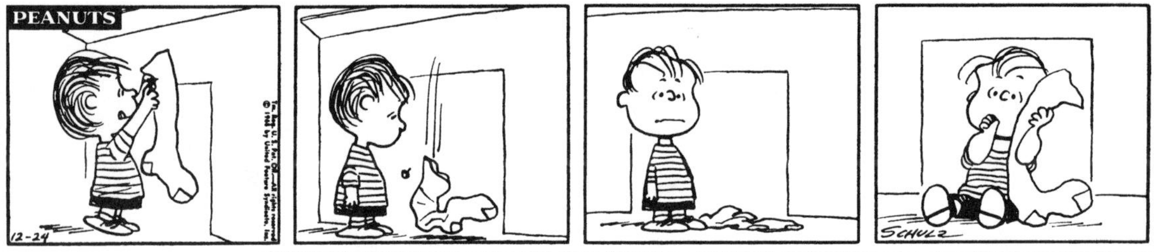

PEANUTS
Tm. Reg. U. S. Pat. Off.—All rights reserved
12-24
SCHULZ

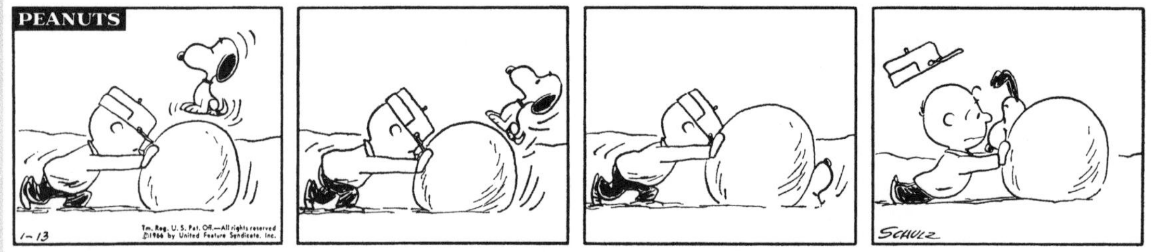

PEANUTS
1-13
Tm. Reg. U. S. Pat. Off.—All rights reserved
©1966 by United Feature Syndicate, Inc.
SCHULZ

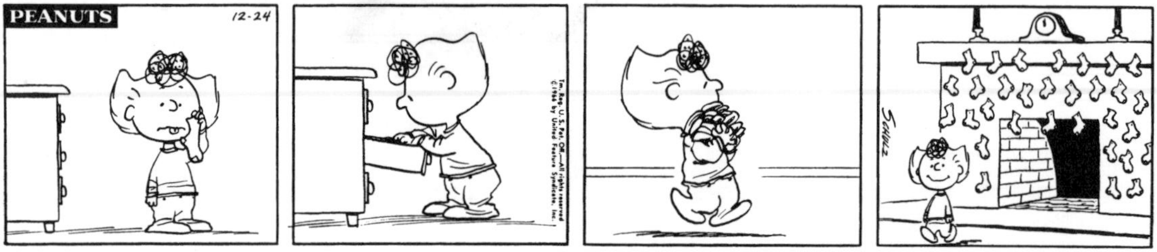
PEANUTS
12-24
SCHULZ

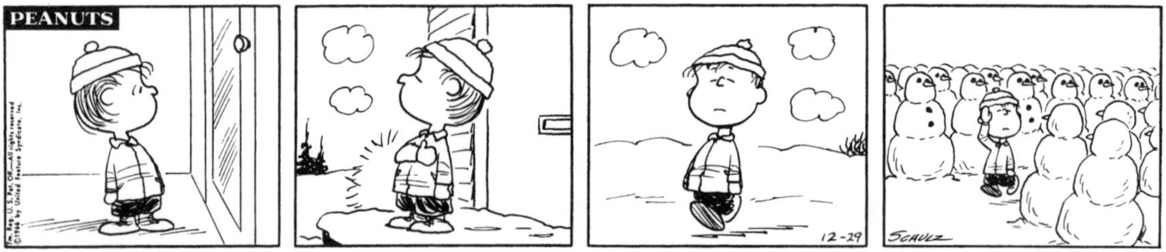
PEANUTS
12-29
SCHULZ

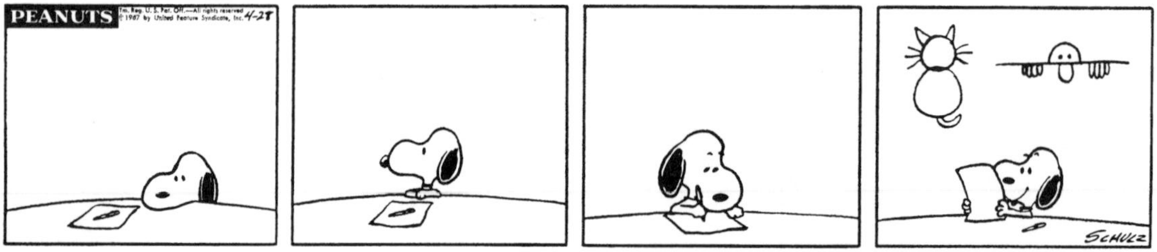
PEANUTS
Tm. Reg. U. S. Pat. Off.—All rights reserved
© 1987 by United Feature Syndicate, Inc.
4-28
SCHULZ

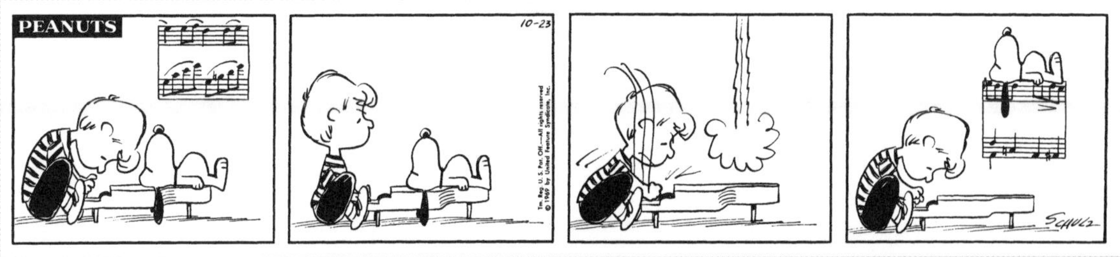
PEANUTS
10-23
Tm. Reg. U. S. Pat. Off.—All rights reserved © 1969 by United Feature Syndicate, Inc.
SCHULZ

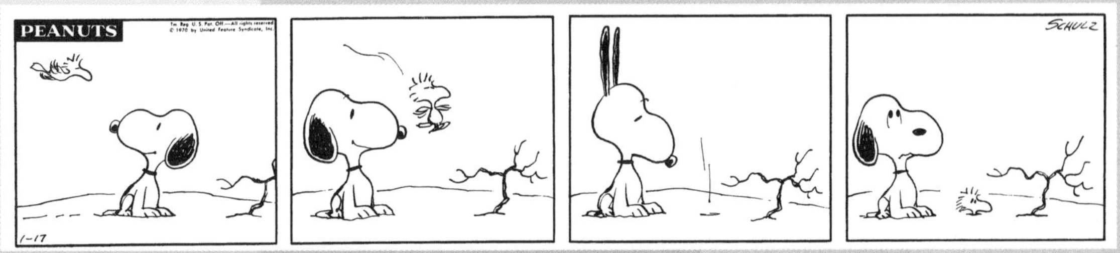
PEANUTS
Tm. Reg. U. S. Pat. Off.—All rights reserved © 1970 by United Feature Syndicate, Inc.
1-17
SCHULZ

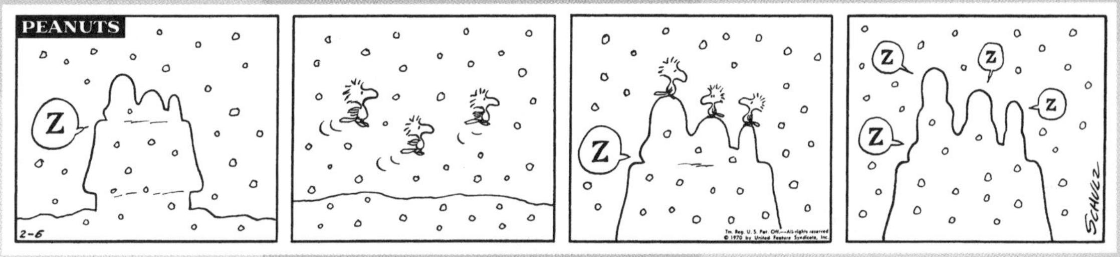
PEANUTS
Z
2-6
Z
Tm. Reg. U. S. Pat. Off.—All rights reserved © 1970 by United Feature Syndicate, Inc.
Z
Z
Z
Z
SCHULZ

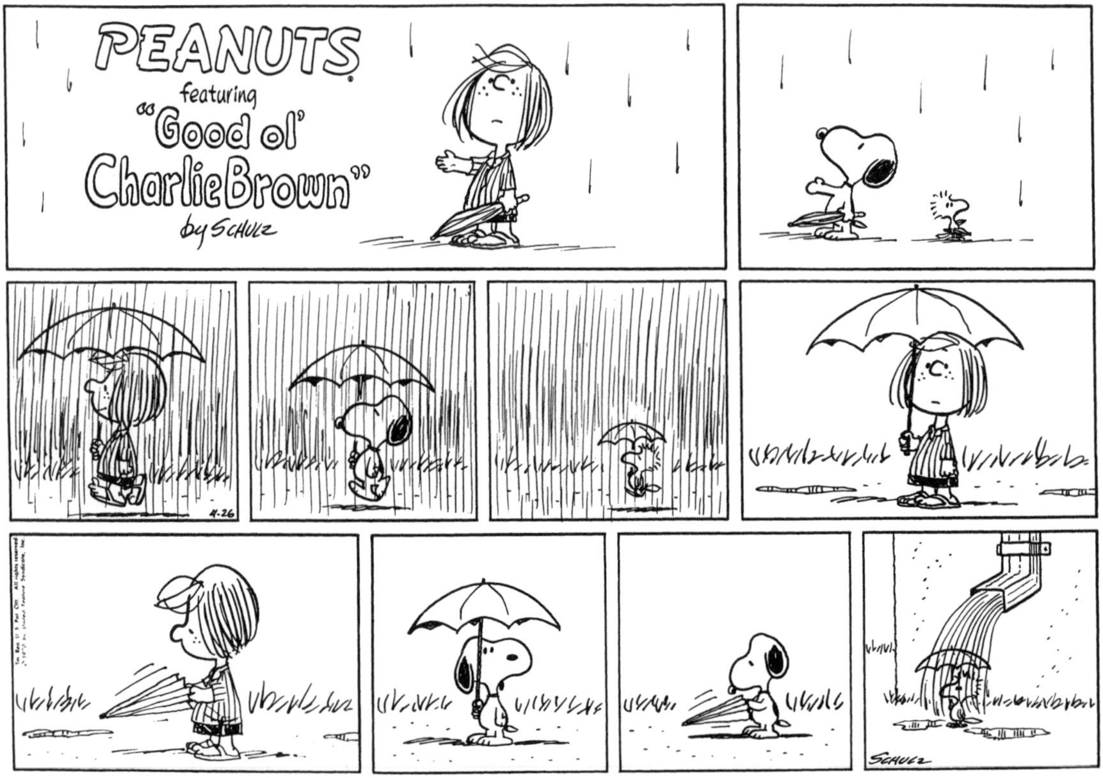
PEANUTS
featuring
"Good ol'
CharlieBrown"
by SCHULZ
4-26
SCHULZ

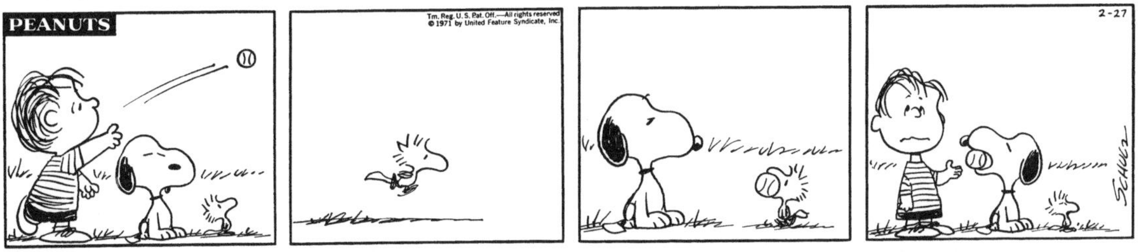
PEANUTS
Tm. Reg. U. S. Pat. Off.—All rights reserved
© 1971 by United Feature Syndicate, Inc.
2-27
SCHULZ

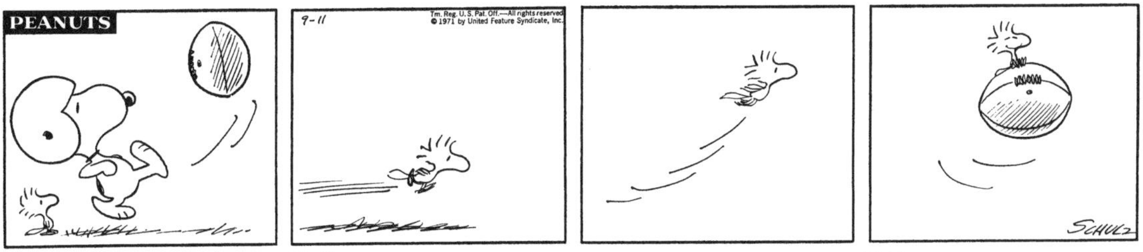
PEANUTS
9-11
Tm. Reg. U. S. Pat. Off.—All rights reserved
© 1971 by United Feature Syndicate, Inc.
SCHULZ

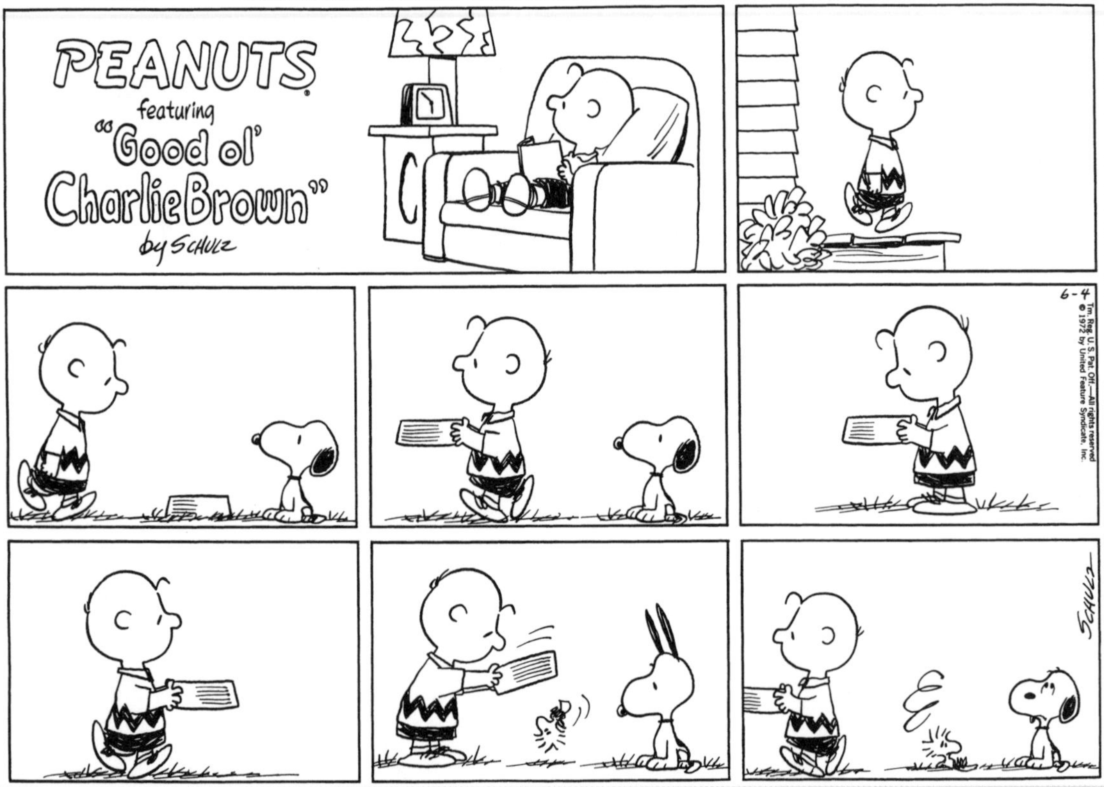
PEANUTS
featuring
"Good ol' CharlieBrown"
by SCHULZ
6-4
Tm. Reg. U.S. Pat. Off.—All rights reserved
© 1972 by United Feature Syndicate, Inc.
SCHULZ

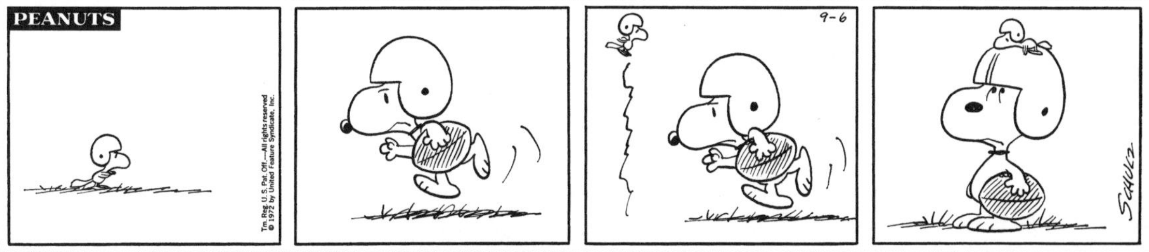
PEANUTS
Tm. Reg. U.S. Pat. Off.—All rights reserved
© 1972 by United Feature Syndicate, Inc.
9-6
SCHULZ

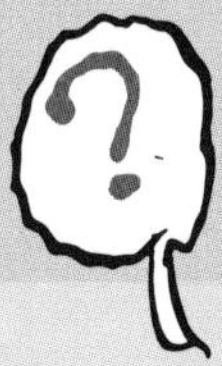
?

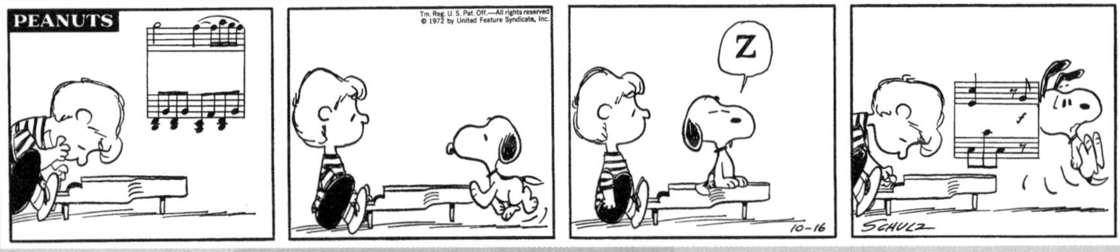
PEANUTS
Tm. Reg. U. S. Pat. Off.—All rights reserved
© 1972 by United Feature Syndicate, Inc.
Z
10-16
SCHULZ

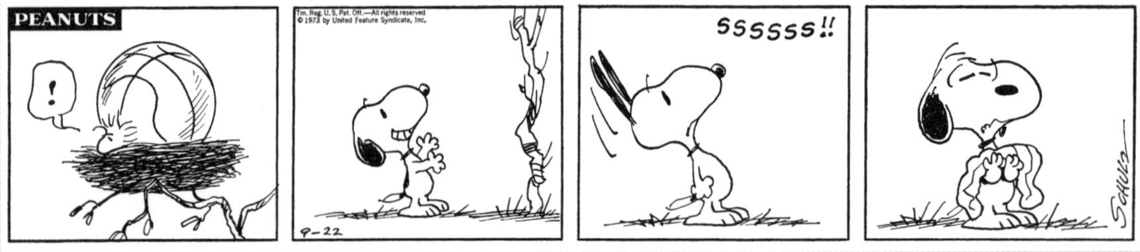
PEANUTS
!
Tm. Reg. U. S. Pat. Off.—All rights reserved
© 1973 by United Feature Syndicate, Inc.
9-22
SSSSSS!!
SCHULZ

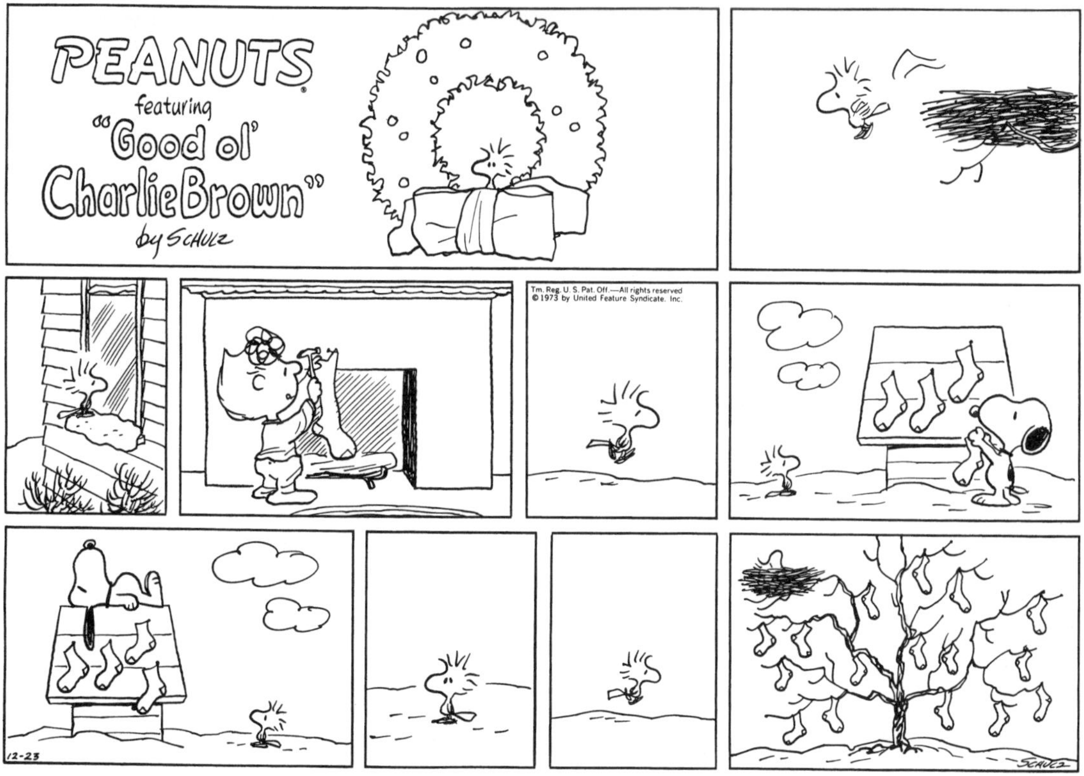
PEANUTS
featuring
"Good ol' Charlie Brown"
by SCHULZ
Tm. Reg. U. S. Pat. Off.—All rights reserved
© 1973 by United Feature Syndicate, Inc.
12-23
SCHULZ

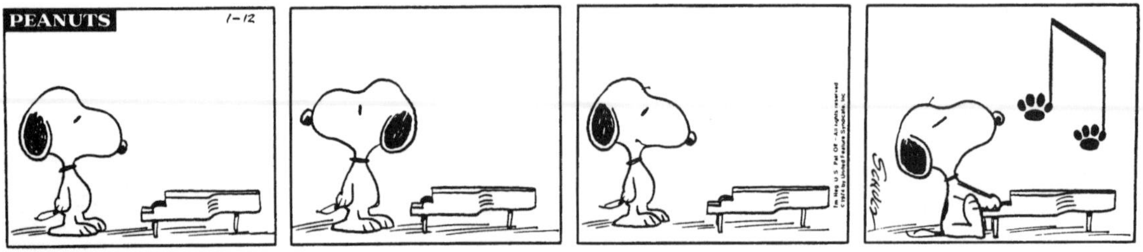
PEANUTS
1-12
SCHULZ

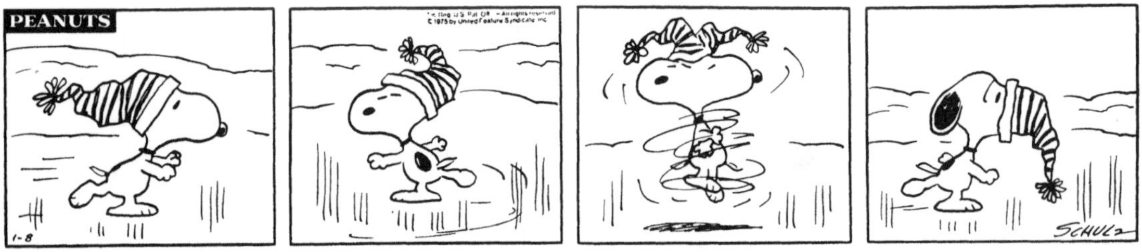
PEANUTS
1-8
SCHULZ

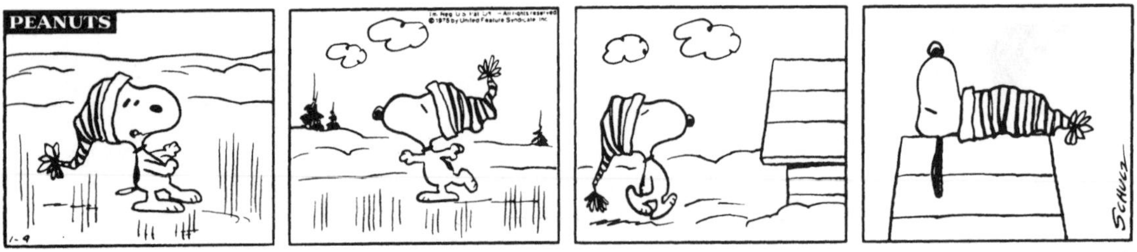
PEANUTS
1-9
SCHULZ

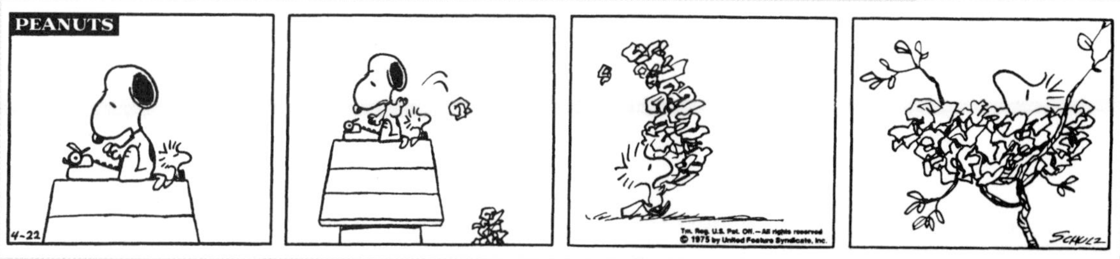
PEANUTS
4-22
Tm. Reg. U.S. Pat. Off.—All rights reserved
© 1975 by United Feature Syndicate, Inc.
SCHULZ

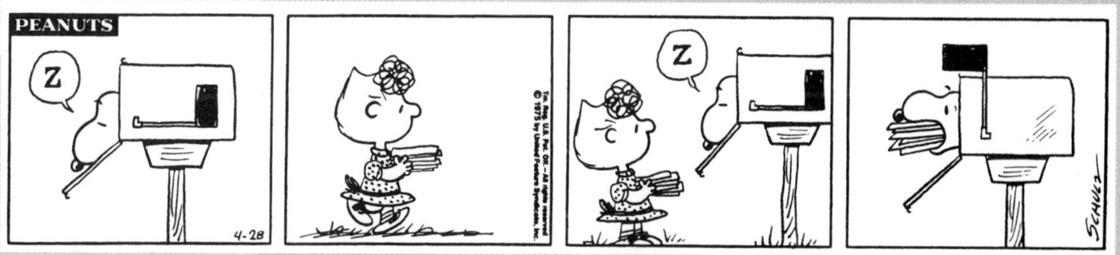
PEANUTS
Z
4-28
Tm. Reg. U.S. Pat. Off.—All rights reserved
© 1975 by United Feature Syndicate, Inc.
Z
SCHULZ

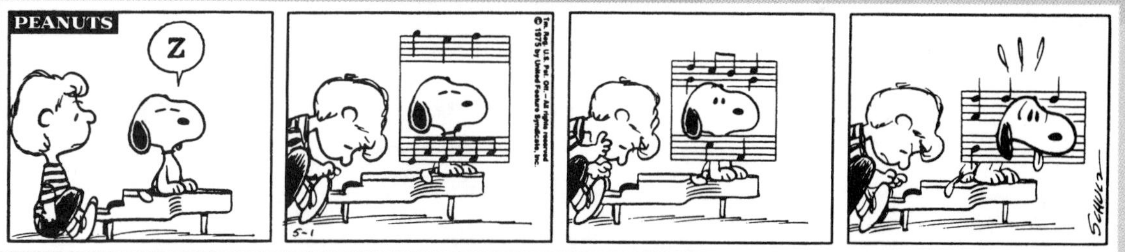
PEANUTS
Z
Tm. Reg. U.S. Pat. Off.—All rights reserved
© 1975 by United Feature Syndicate, Inc.
5-1
SCHULZ

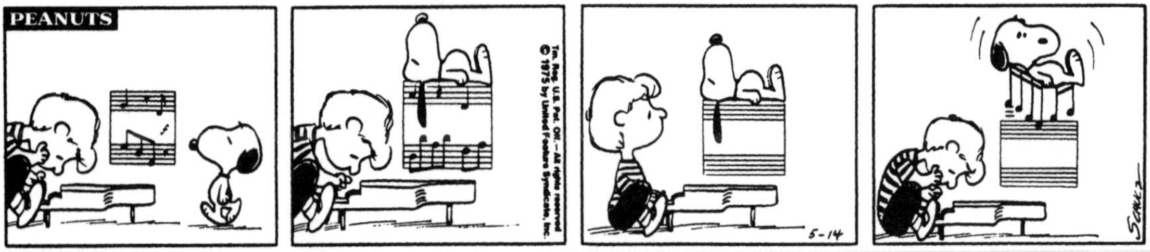
PEANUTS
Tm. Reg. U.S. Pat. Off.—All rights reserved
© 1975 by United Feature Syndicate, Inc.
5-14
SCHULZ

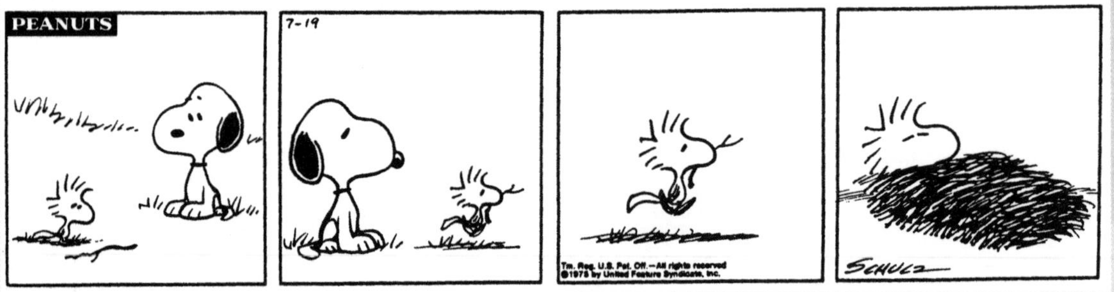
PEANUTS
7-19
Tm. Reg. U.S. Pat. Off.—All rights reserved
©1975 by United Feature Syndicate, Inc.
SCHULZ

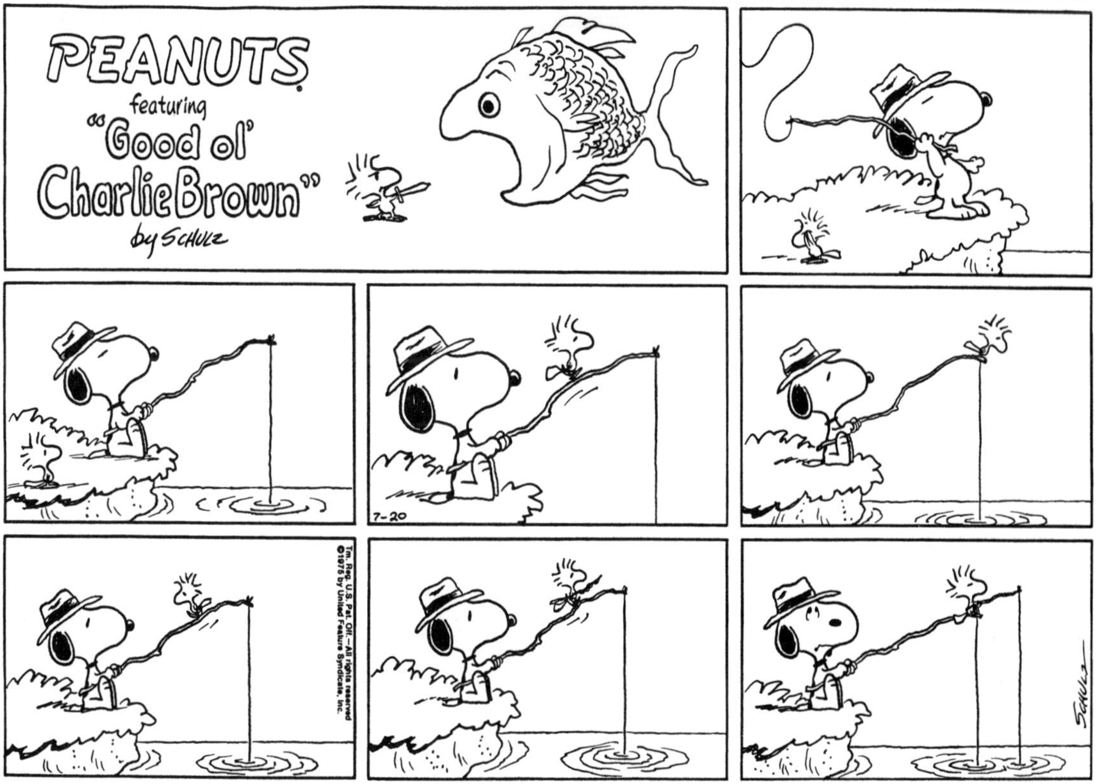

PEANUTS
featuring
"Good ol' Charlie Brown"
by SCHULZ
7-20
Tm. Reg. U.S. Pat. Off.—All rights reserved
©1975 by United Feature Syndicate, Inc.
SCHULZ

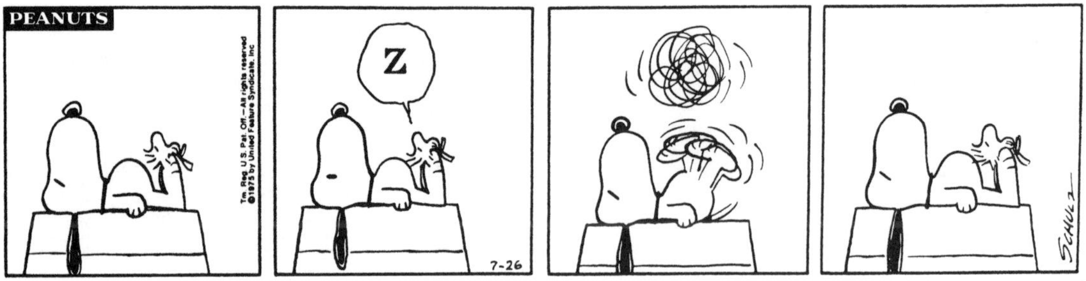
PEANUTS
Tm. Reg. U.S. Pat. Off.—All rights reserved
©1975 by United Feature Syndicate, Inc
Z
7-26
SCHULZ

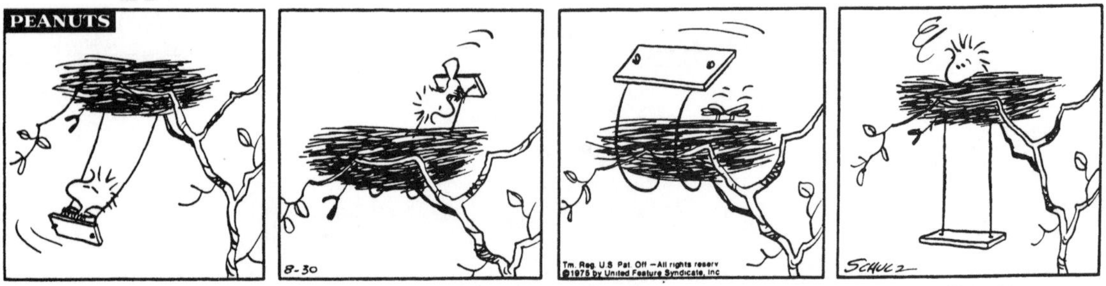
PEANUTS
8-30
Tm. Reg. U.S. Pat. Off.—All rights reserv
©1975 by United Feature Syndicate, Inc
SCHULZ

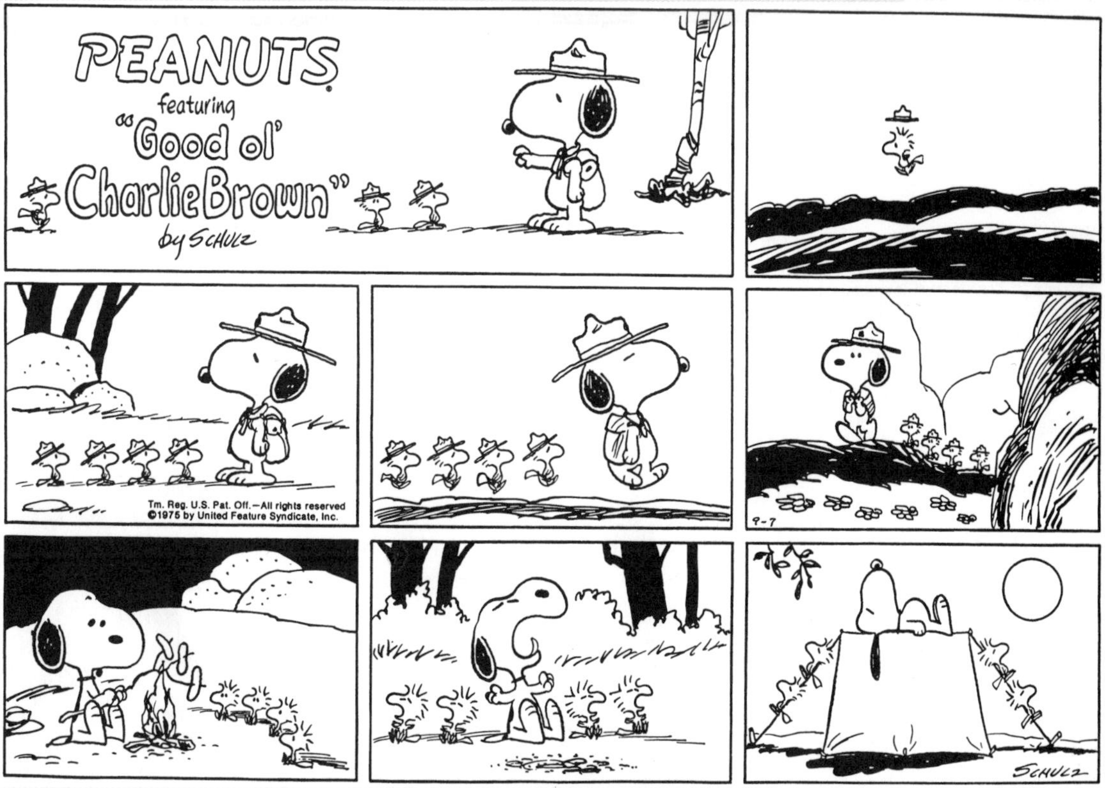
PEANUTS
featuring
"Good ol' CharlieBrown"
by SCHULZ
Tm. Reg. U.S. Pat. Off.—All rights reserved
©1975 by United Feature Syndicate, Inc.
9-7
SCHULZ

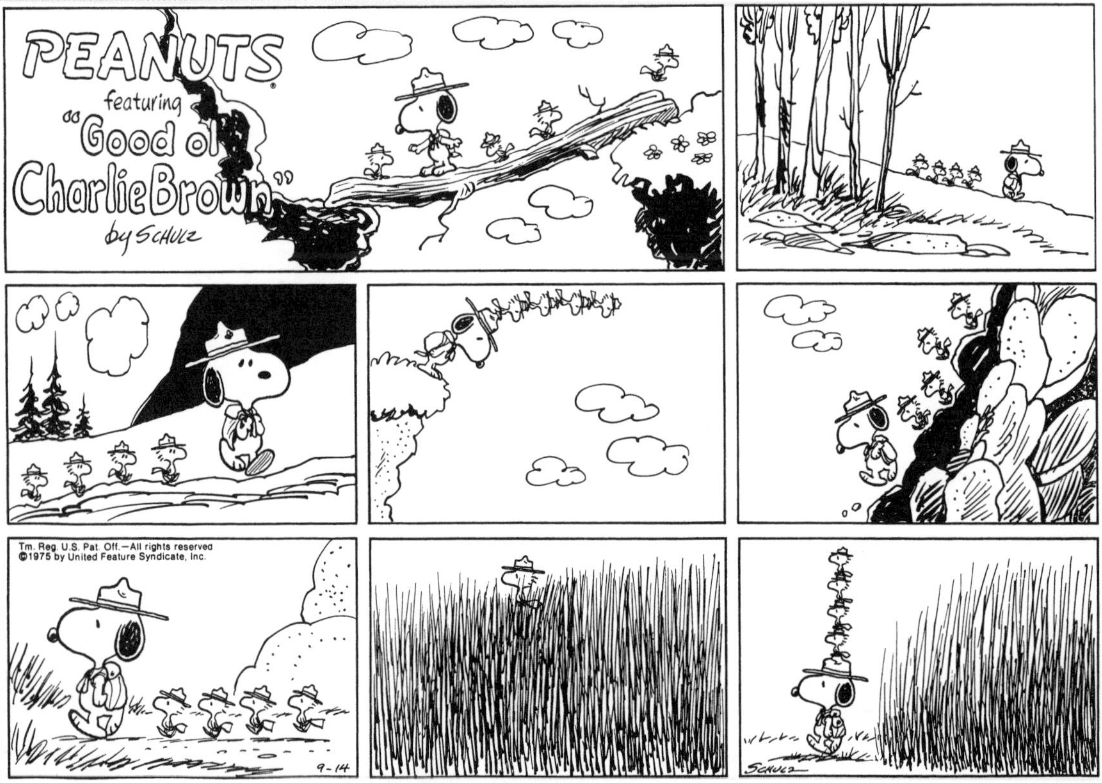
PEANUTS
featuring
"Good ol' Charlie Brown"
by SCHULZ
Tm. Reg. U.S. Pat. Off.—All rights reserved
©1975 by United Feature Syndicate, Inc.
9-14
SCHULZ

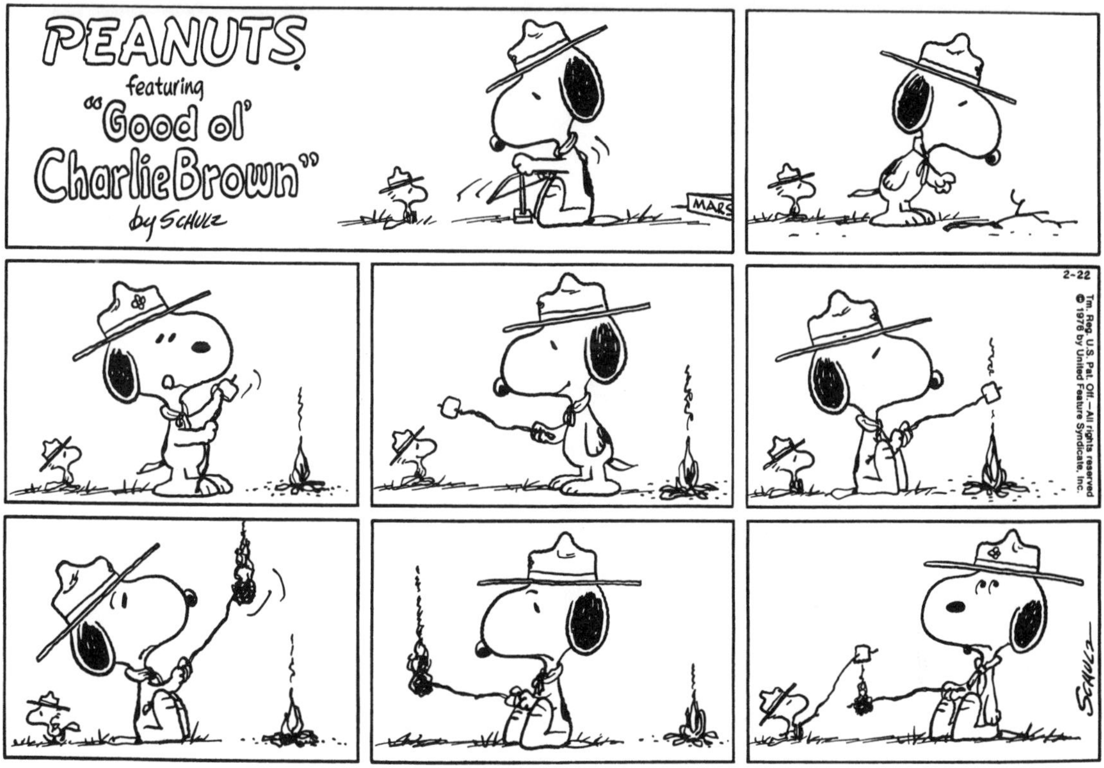
PEANUTS
featuring
"Good ol' Charlie Brown"
by SCHULZ
2-22
Tm. Reg. U.S. Pat. Off.—All rights reserved
© 1976 by United Feature Syndicate, Inc.
SCHULZ

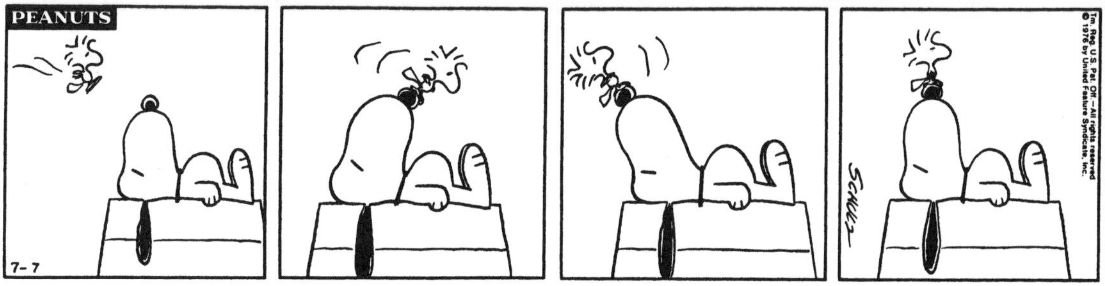
PEANUTS
7-7
SCHULZ
Tm. Reg. U.S. Pat. Off.—All rights reserved
© 1976 by United Feature Syndicate, Inc.

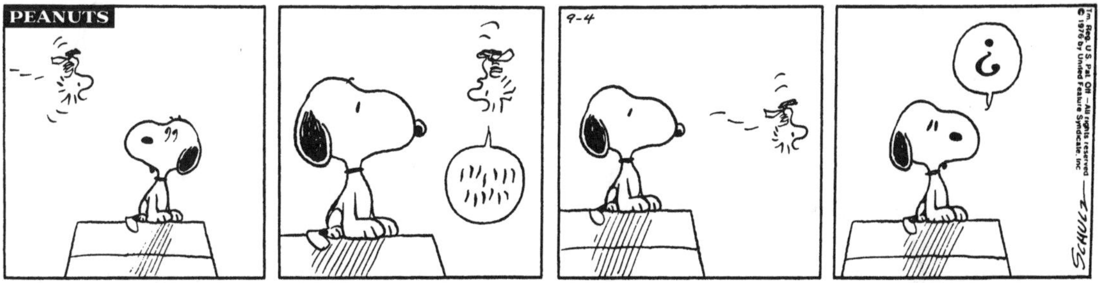
PEANUTS
9-4
¿
SCHULZ
Tm. Reg. U.S. Pat. Off.—All rights reserved
© 1976 by United Feature Syndicate, Inc.

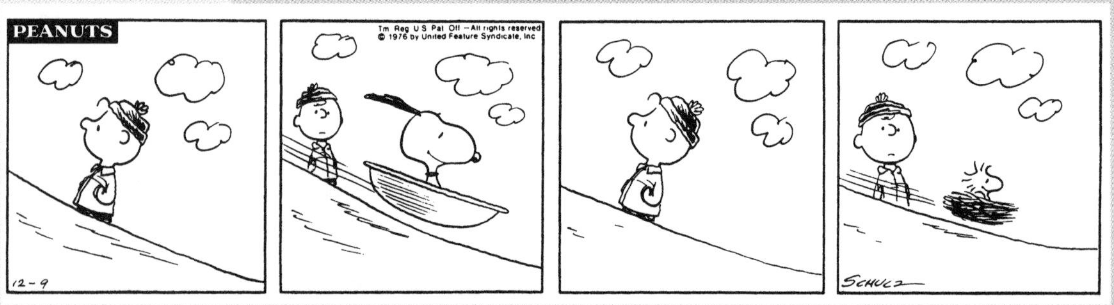
PEANUTS
Tm Reg U S Pat Off — All rights reserved
© 1976 by United Feature Syndicate, Inc
12-9
SCHULZ

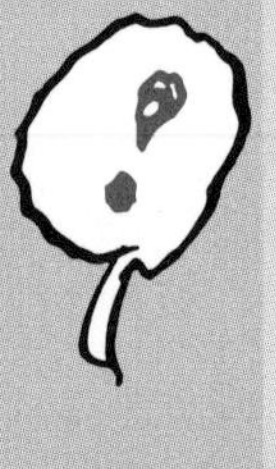

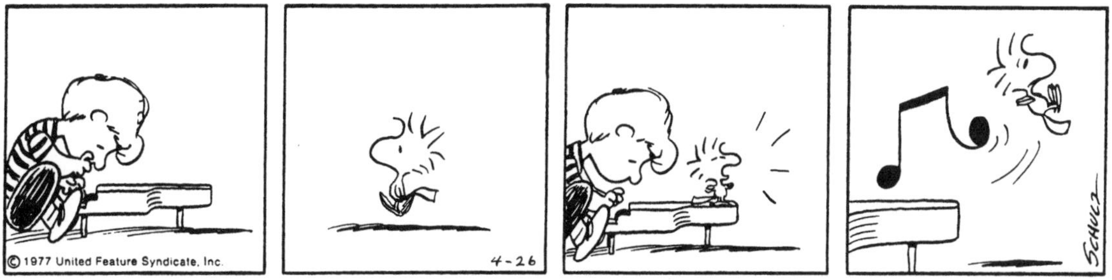
© 1977 United Feature Syndicate, Inc.
4-26
SCHULZ

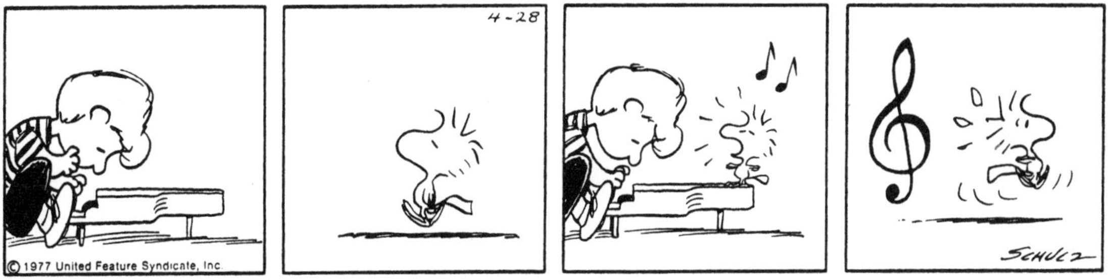
© 1977 United Feature Syndicate, Inc.
4-28
SCHULZ

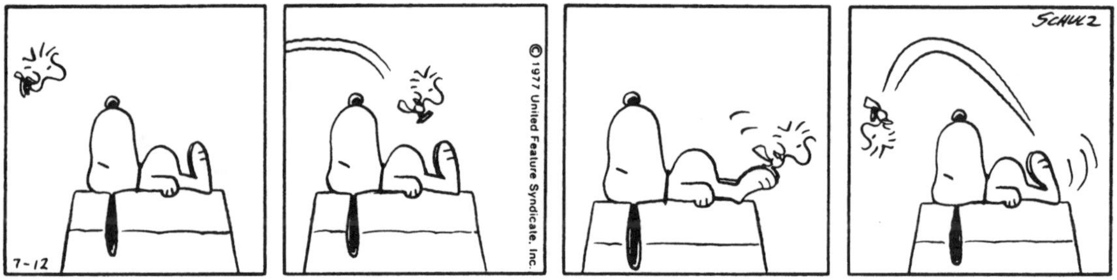
7-12
© 1977 United Feature Syndicate, Inc.
SCHULZ

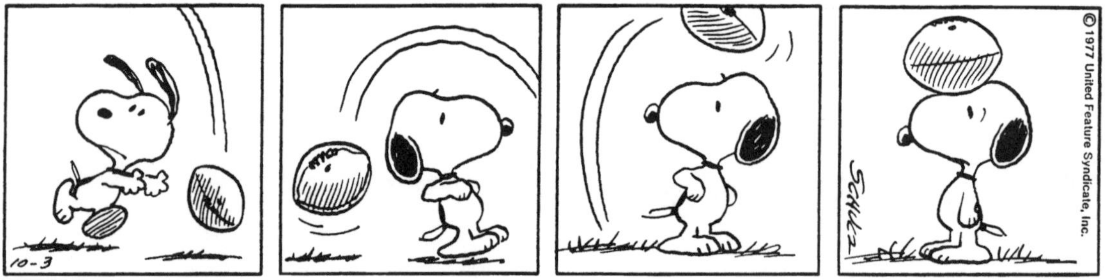
10-3
SCHULZ
© 1977 United Feature Syndicate, Inc.

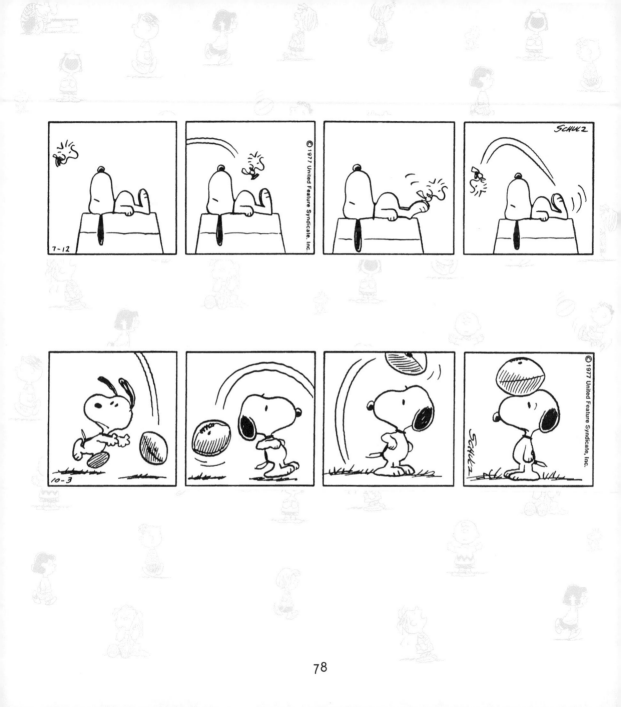

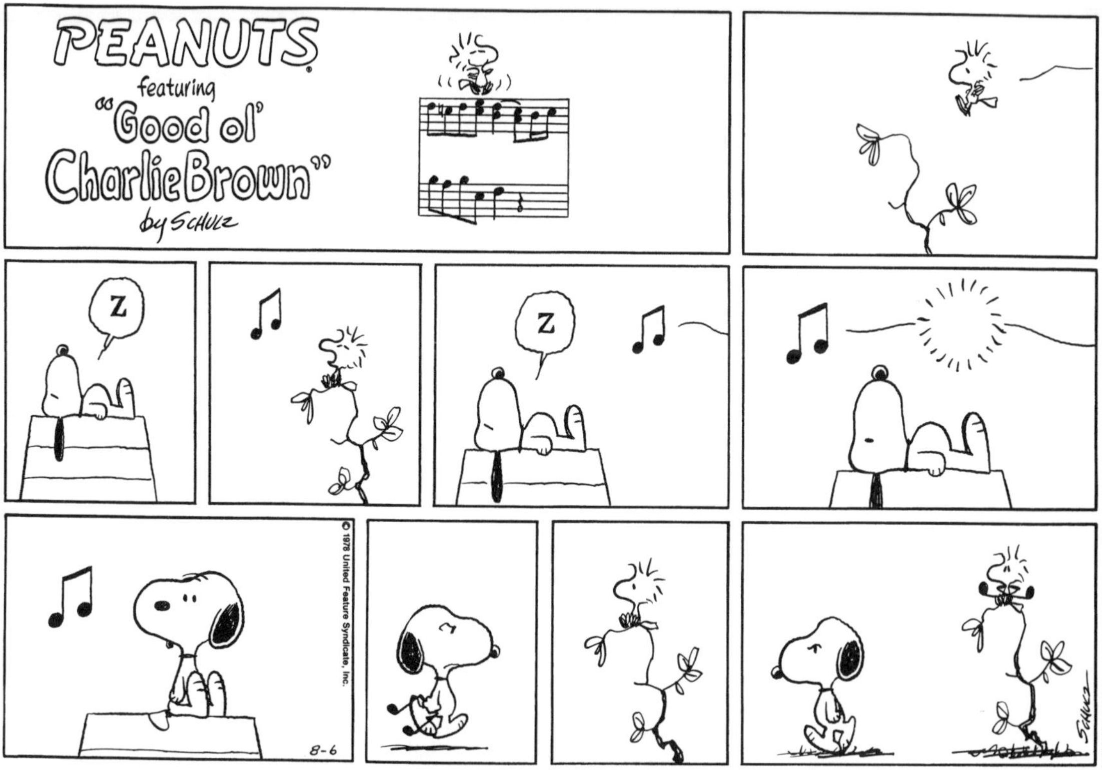
PEANUTS
featuring
"Good ol' Charlie Brown"
by SCHULZ
Z
Z
© 1978 United Feature Syndicate, Inc.
8-6
SCHULZ

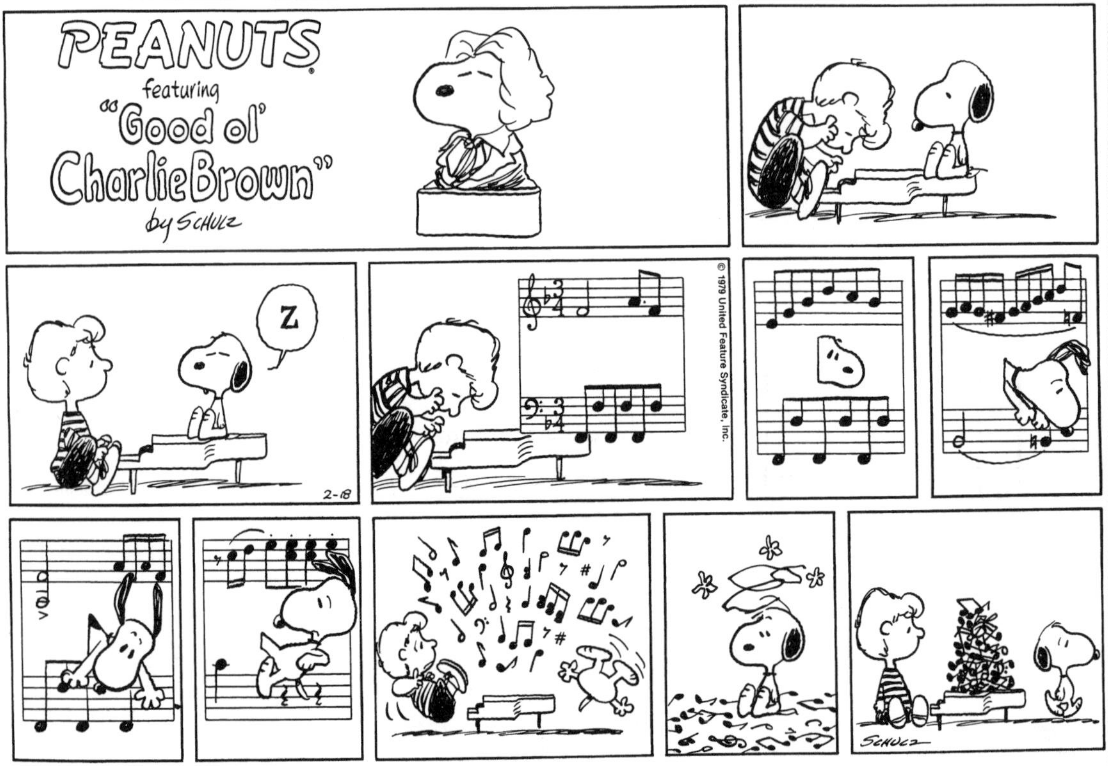
PEANUTS
featuring
"Good ol' CharlieBrown"
by SCHULZ
Z
2-18
© 1979 United Feature Syndicate, Inc.
SCHULZ

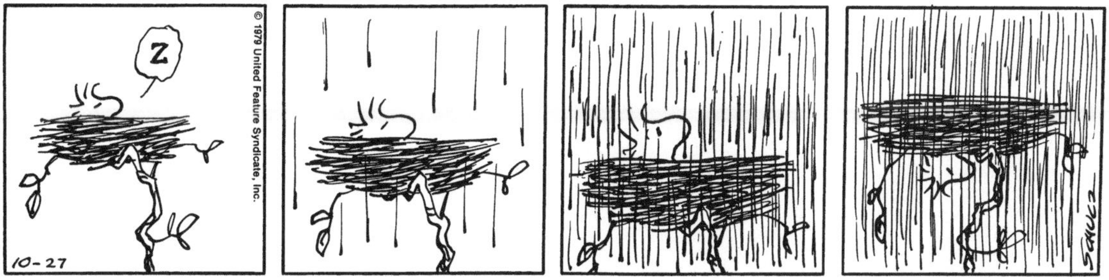
Z
© 1979 United Feature Syndicate, Inc.
10-27
SCHULZ

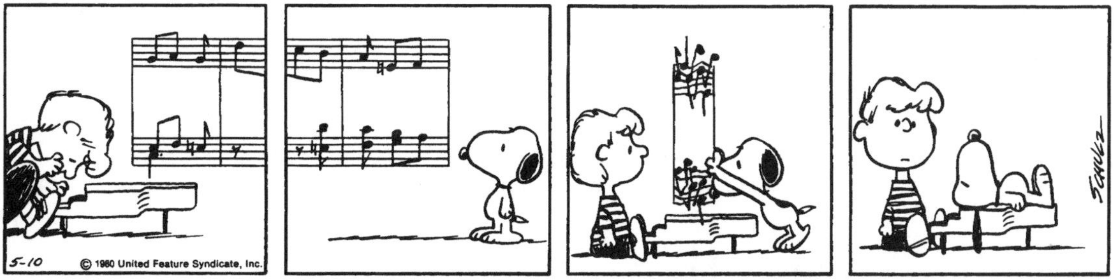
5-10
© 1980 United Feature Syndicate, Inc.
SCHULZ

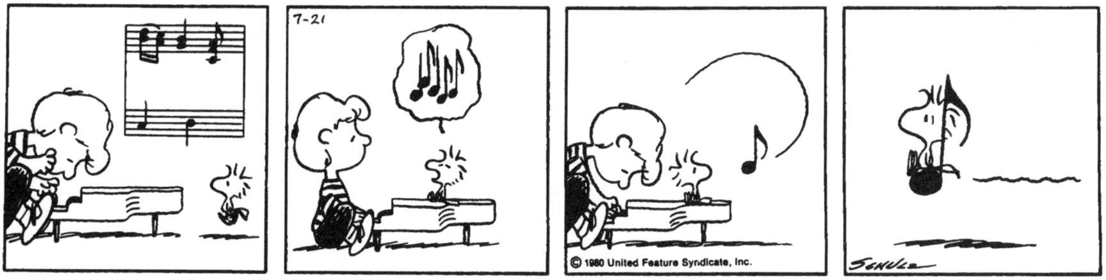
7-21
© 1980 United Feature Syndicate, Inc.
SCHULZ

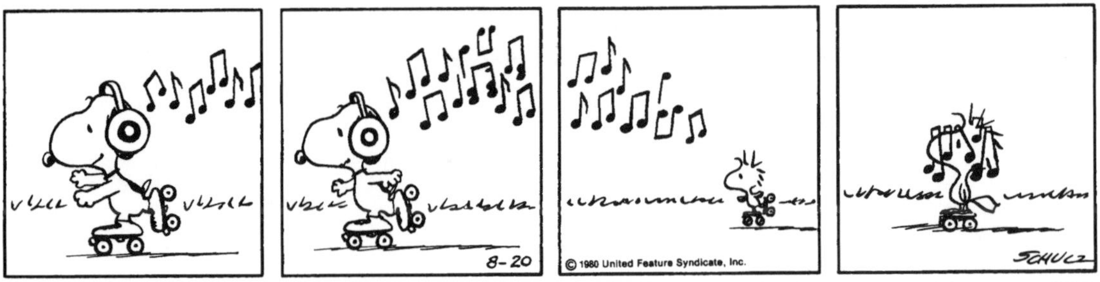
8-20
© 1980 United Feature Syndicate, Inc.
SCHULZ

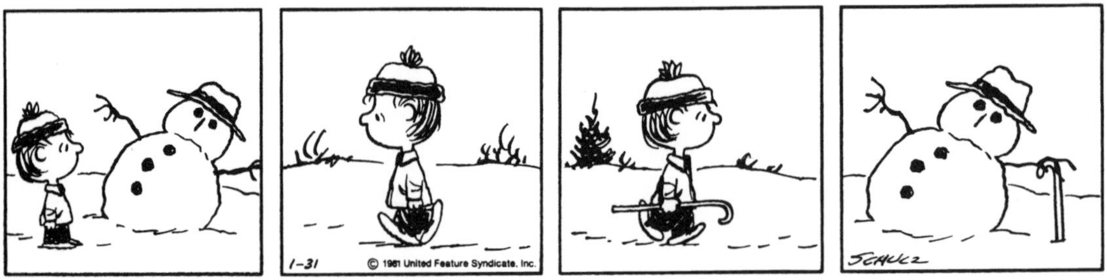
1-31
© 1981 United Feature Syndicate, Inc.
SCHULZ

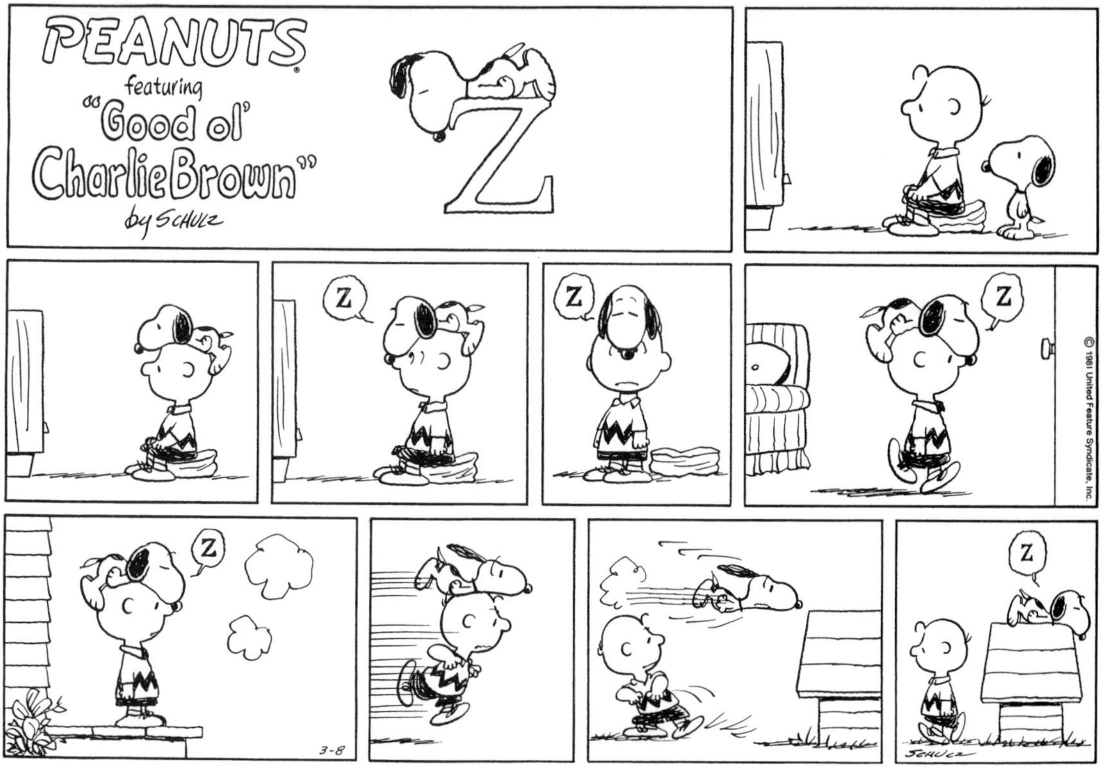
PEANUTS
featuring "Good ol' CharlieBrown"
by SCHULZ
Z
Z
Z
Z
Z
3-8
Z
SCHULZ
© 1981 United Feature Syndicate, Inc.

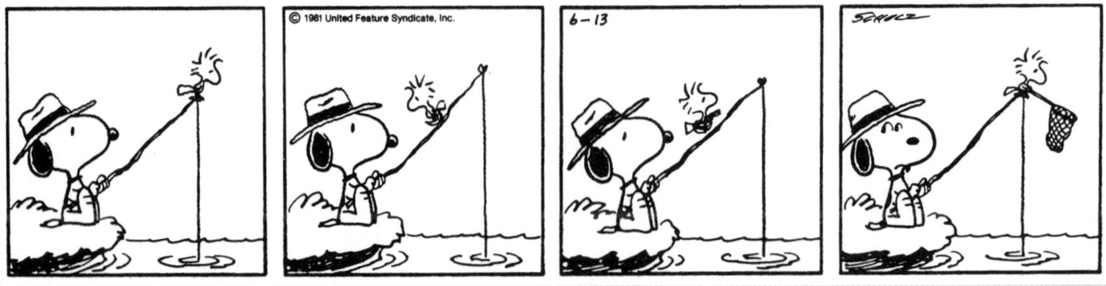
© 1981 United Feature Syndicate, Inc.
6-13
SCHULZ

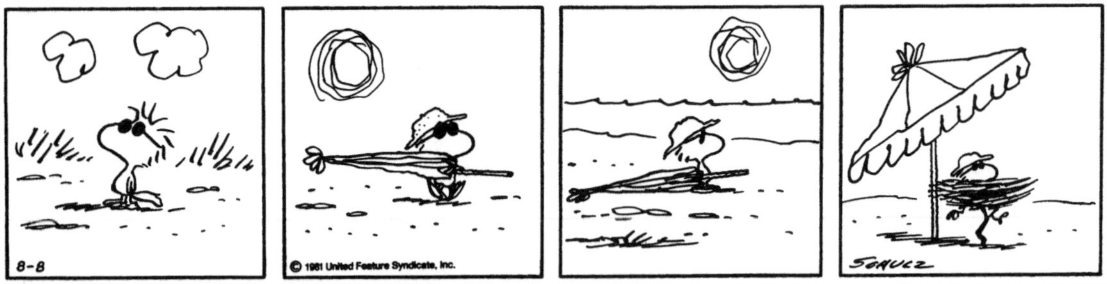
8-8
© 1981 United Feature Syndicate, Inc.
SCHULZ

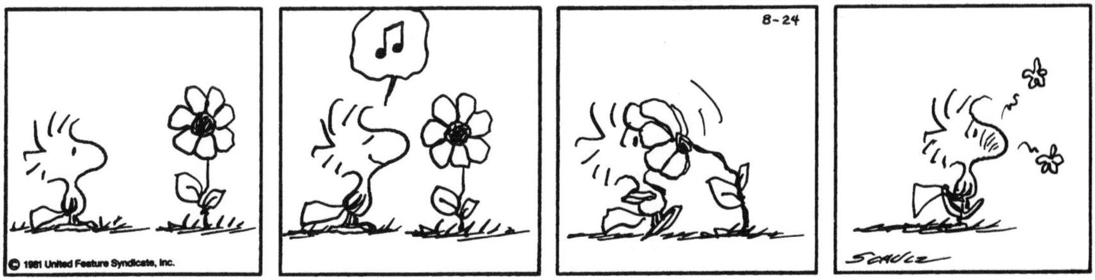
8-24
© 1981 United Feature Syndicate, Inc.
SCHULZ

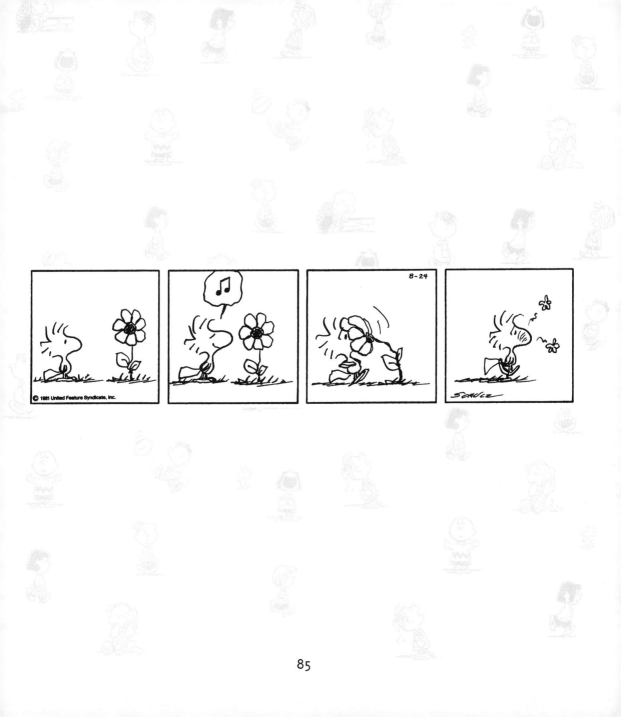

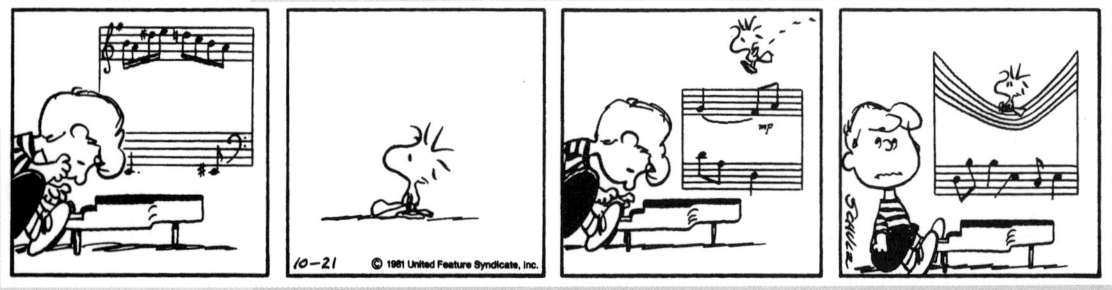
mp
10-21
© 1981 United Feature Syndicate, Inc.
SCHULZ

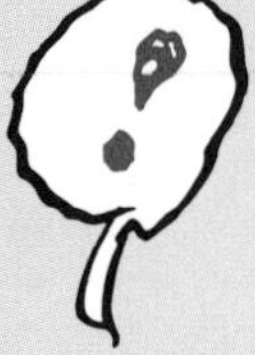

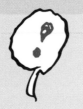

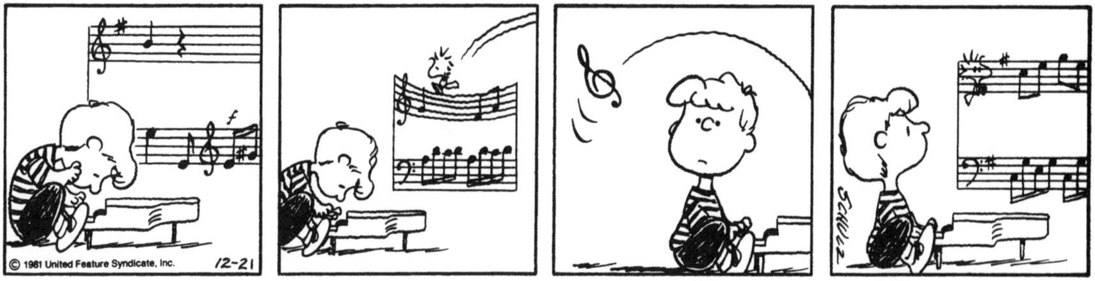
© 1981 United Feature Syndicate, Inc.
12-21
SCHULZ

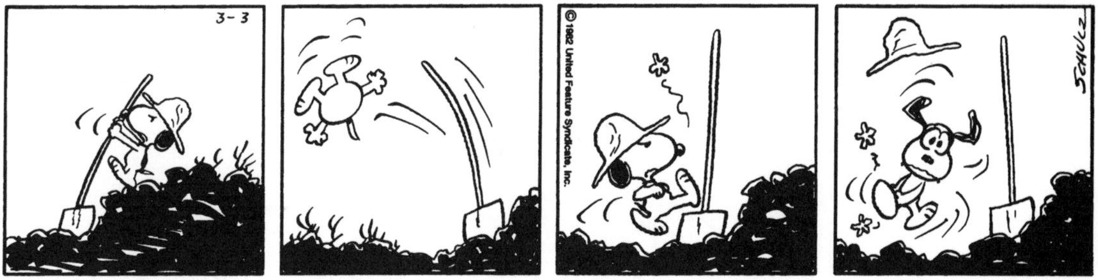
3-3
© 1982 United Feature Syndicate, Inc.
SCHULZ

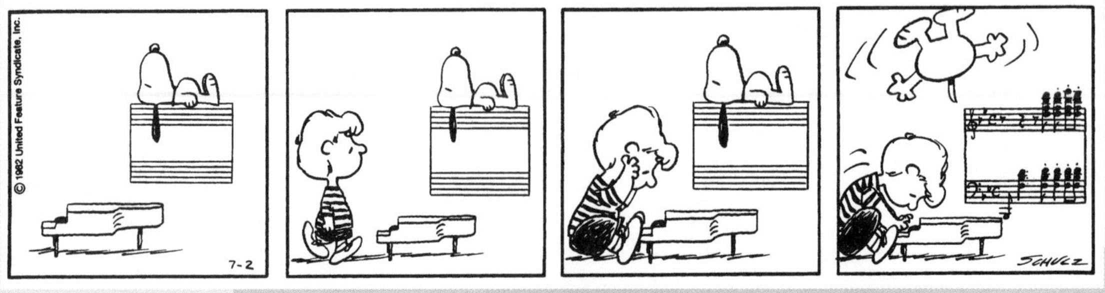
© 1982 United Feature Syndicate, Inc.
7-2
SCHULZ

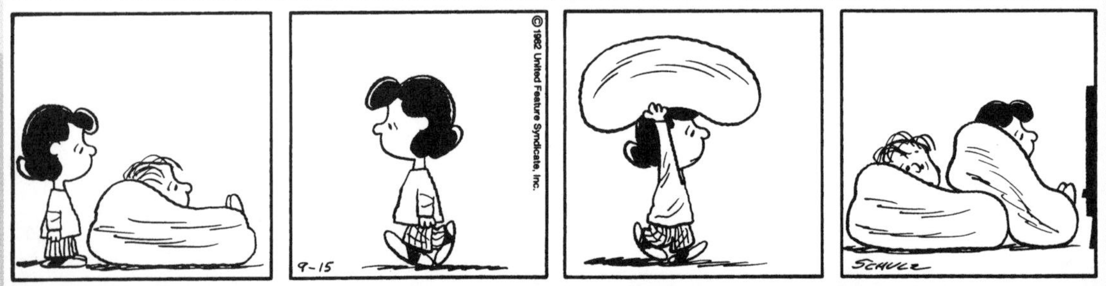
© 1982 United Feature Syndicate, Inc.
9-15
SCHULZ

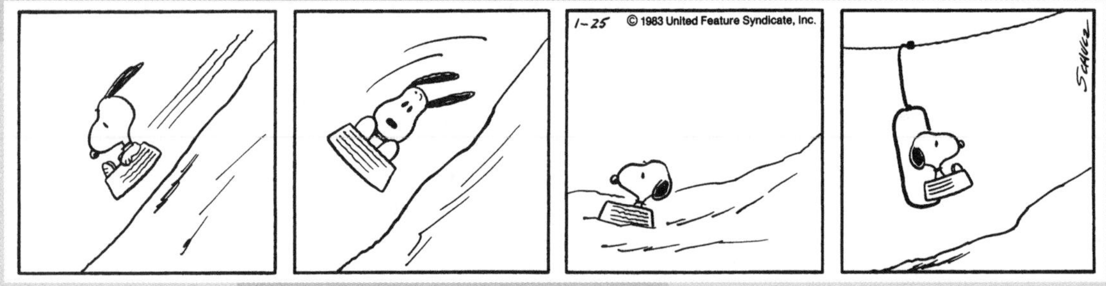
1-25
© 1983 United Feature Syndicate, Inc.
SCHULZ

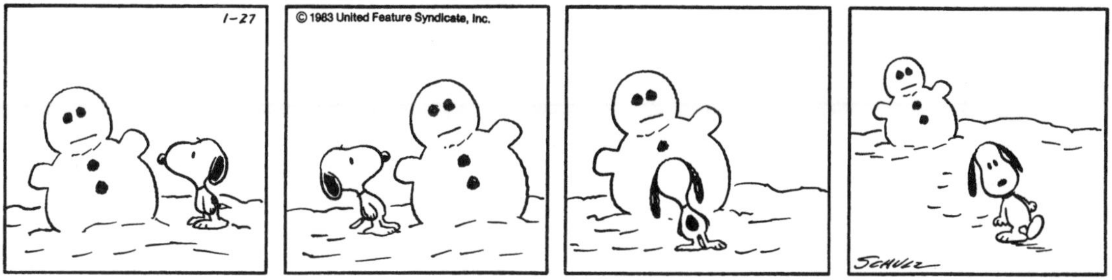
1-27
© 1983 United Feature Syndicate, Inc.
SCHULZ

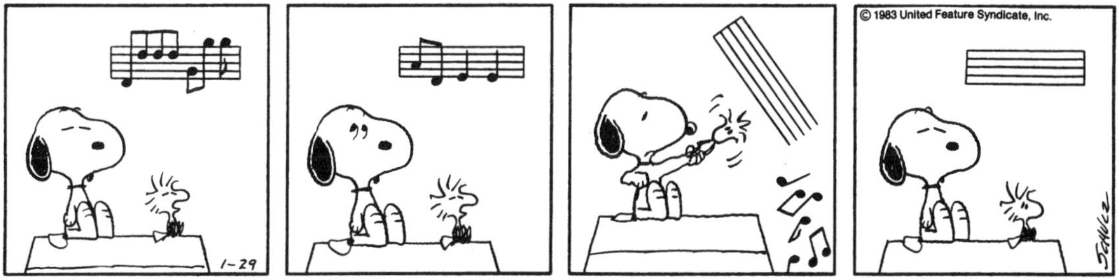
1-29
© 1983 United Feature Syndicate, Inc.
SCHULZ

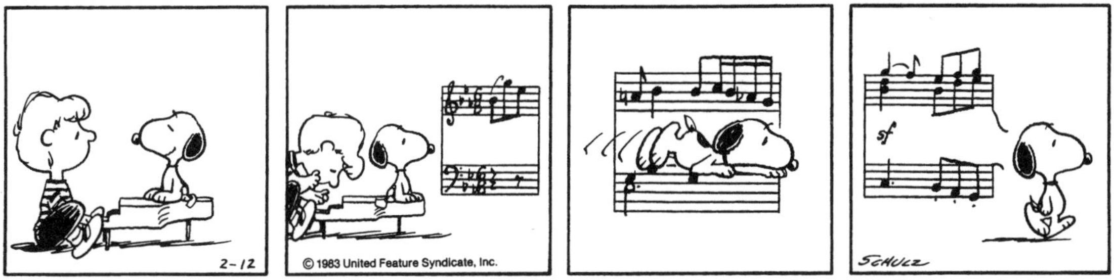
2-12
© 1983 United Feature Syndicate, Inc.
sf
SCHULZ

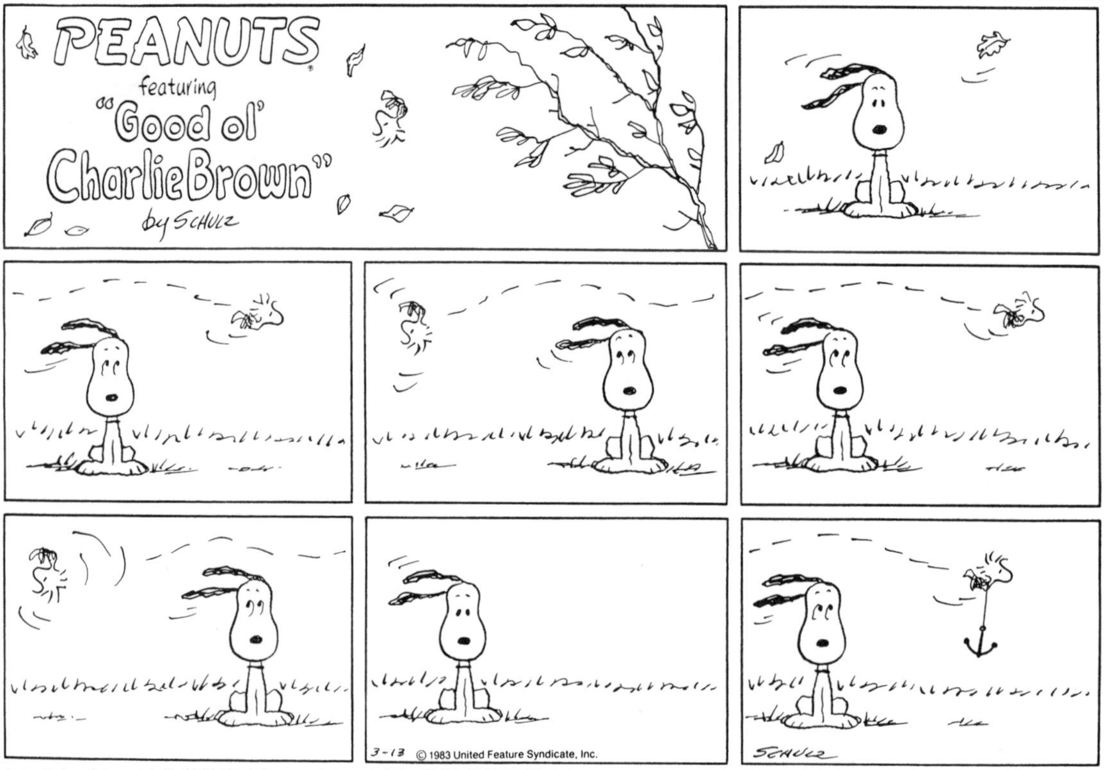
PEANUTS
featuring
"Good ol' Charlie Brown"
by SCHULZ
3-13 © 1983 United Feature Syndicate, Inc.
SCHULZ

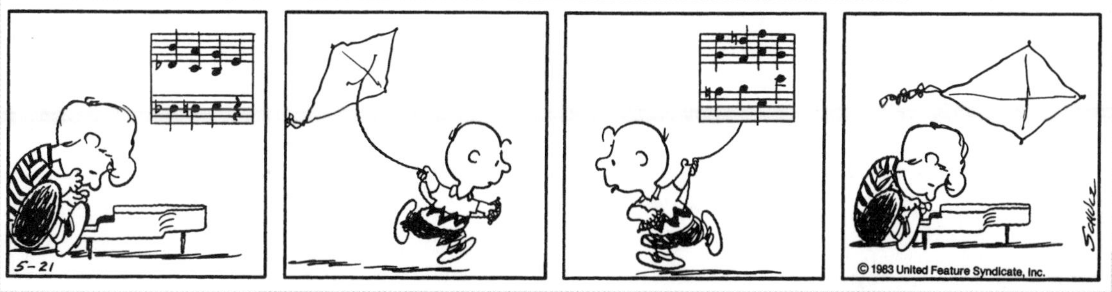
5-21
© 1983 United Feature Syndicate, Inc.

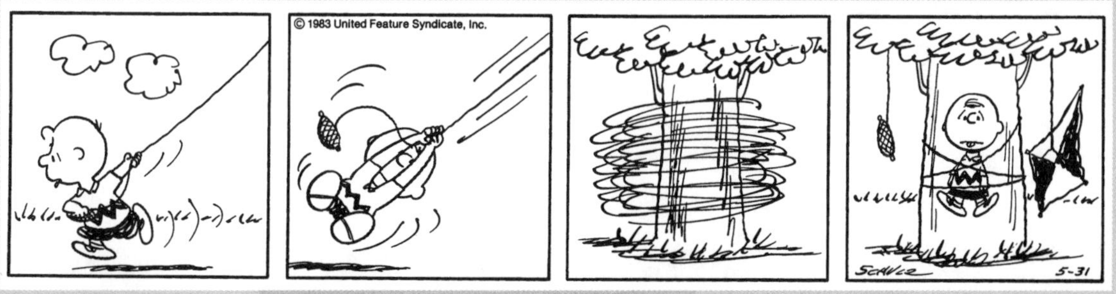
© 1983 United Feature Syndicate, Inc.
5-31

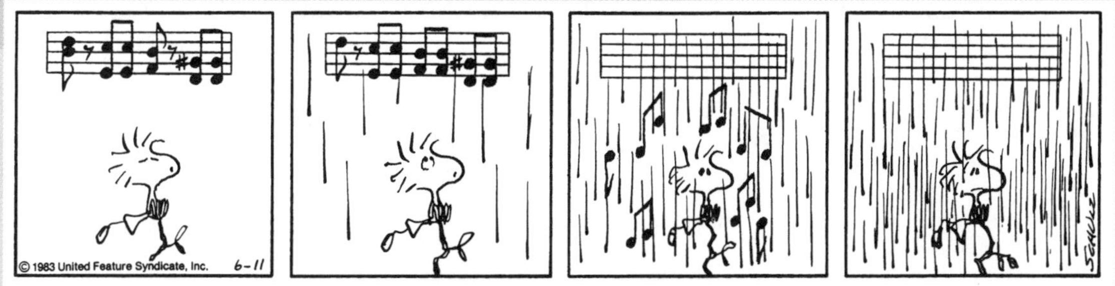
© 1983 United Feature Syndicate, Inc.
6-11

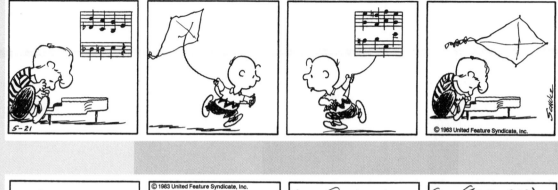

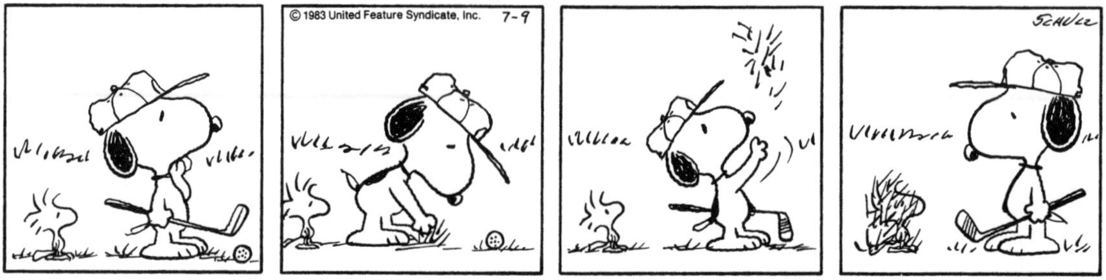
© 1983 United Feature Syndicate, Inc.
7-9
SCHULZ

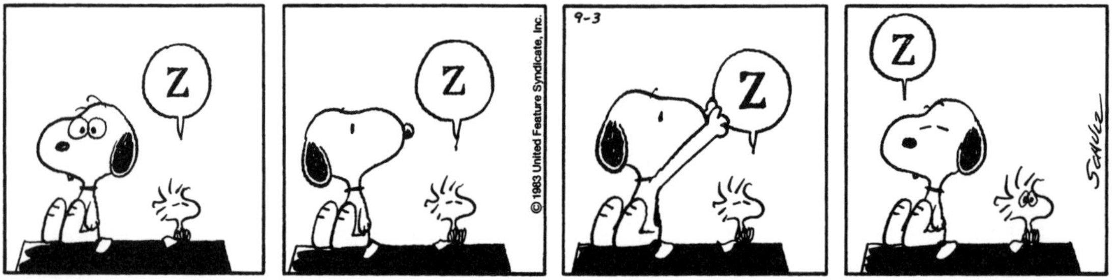
Z
Z
© 1983 United Feature Syndicate, Inc.
9-3
Z
Z
SCHULZ

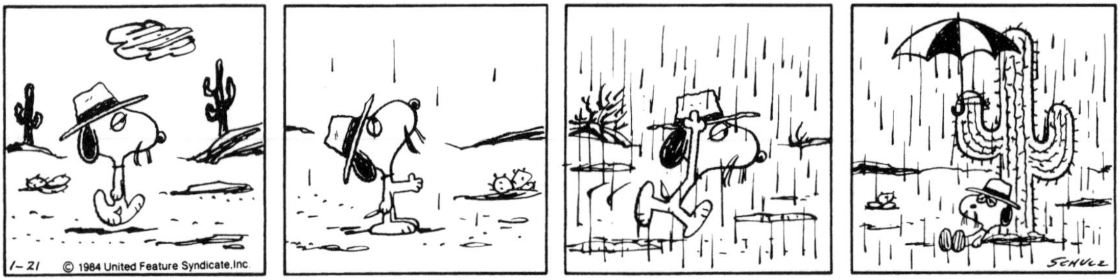
1-21
© 1984 United Feature Syndicate,Inc.
SCHULZ

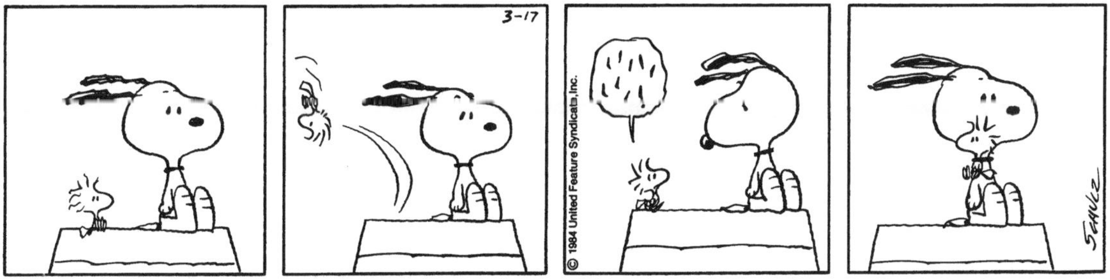
3-17
© 1984 United Feature Syndicate,Inc.
SCHULZ

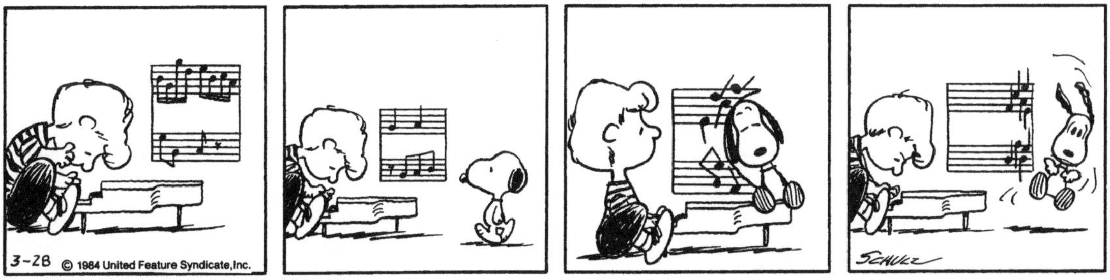
3-28
© 1984 United Feature Syndicate,Inc.
SCHULZ

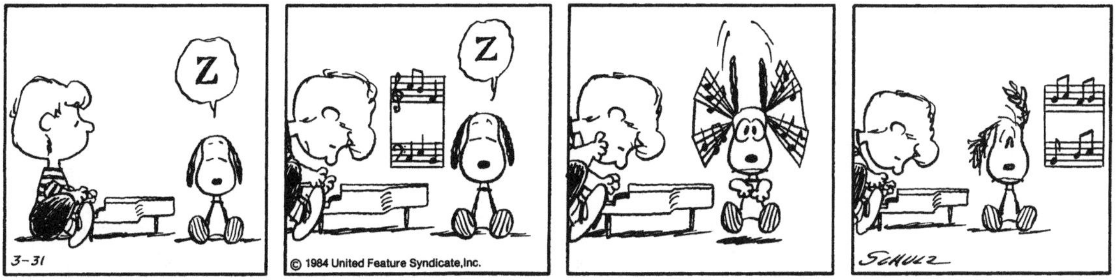
Z
3-31
Z
© 1984 United Feature Syndicate,Inc.
SCHULZ

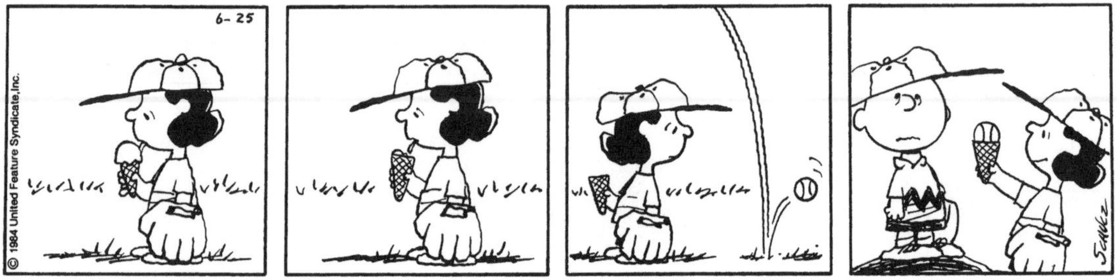
6-25
© 1984 United Feature Syndicate,Inc.
SCHULZ

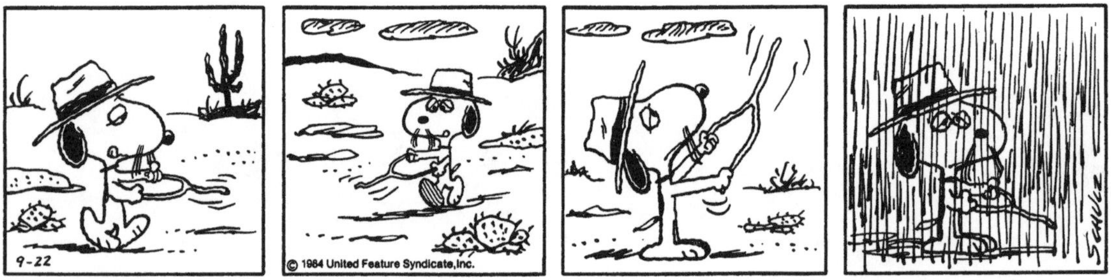
9-22
© 1984 United Feature Syndicate,Inc.
SCHULZ

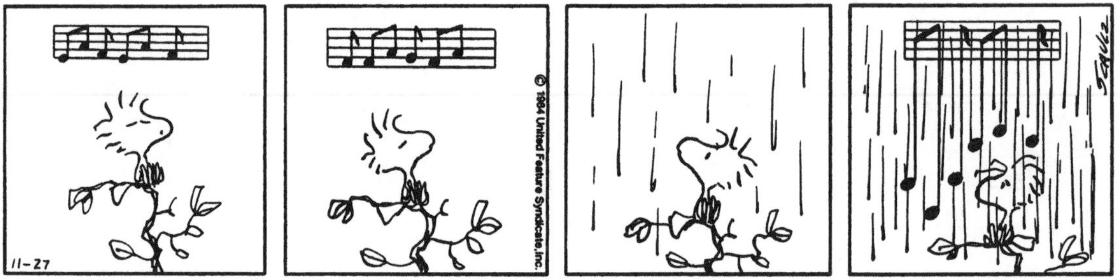
11-27
© 1984 United Feature Syndicate,Inc.
SCHULZ

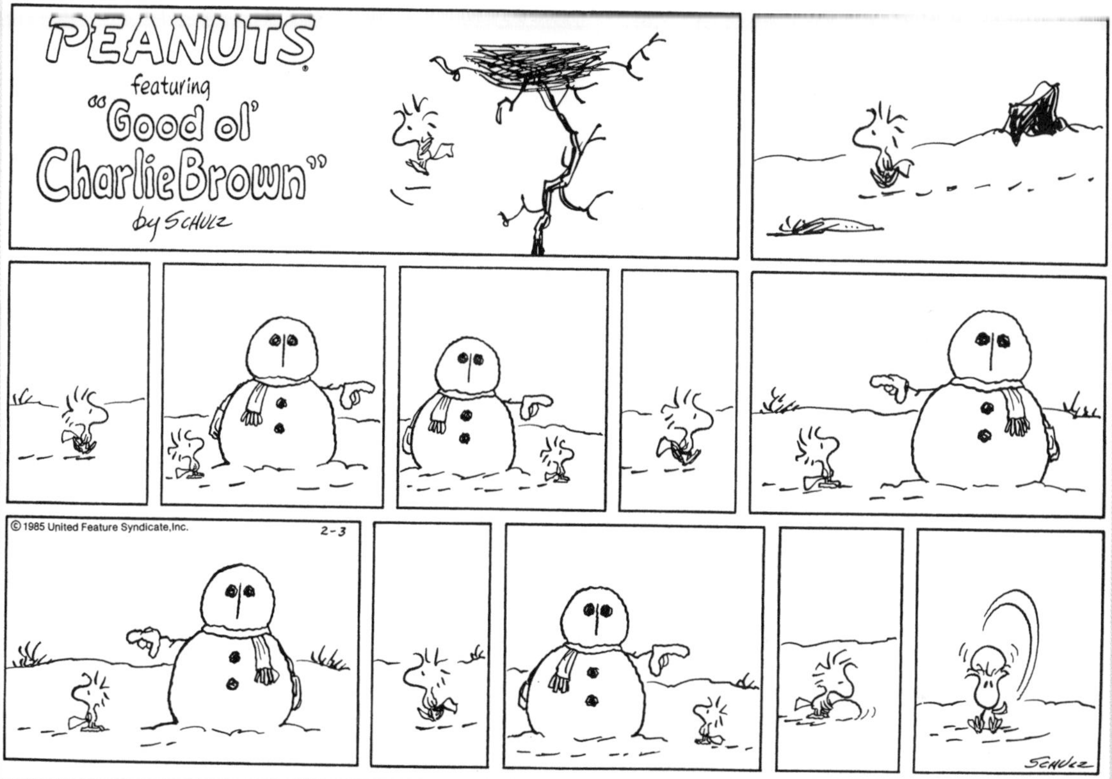
PEANUTS
featuring
"Good ol' CharlieBrown"
by SCHULZ
© 1985 United Feature Syndicate,Inc.
2-3
SCHULZ

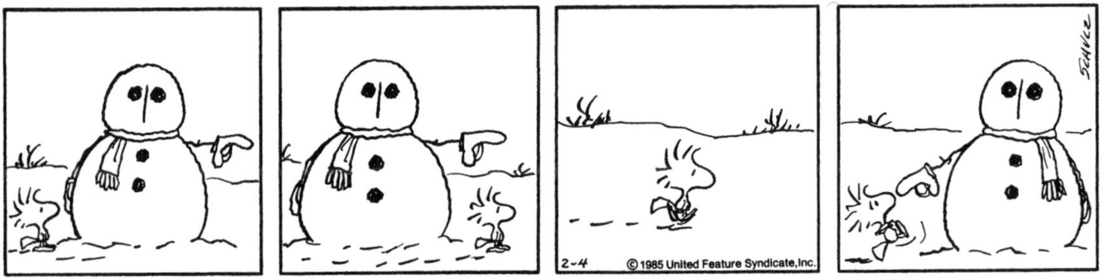
SCHULZ
2-4
© 1985 United Feature Syndicate, Inc.

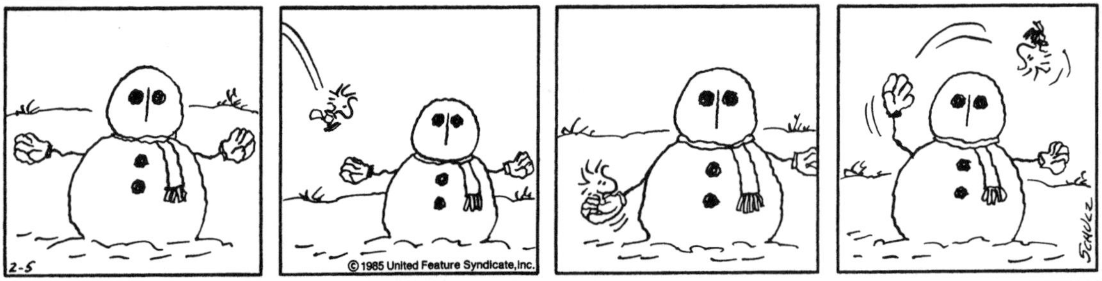
2-5
© 1985 United Feature Syndicate, Inc.
SCHULZ

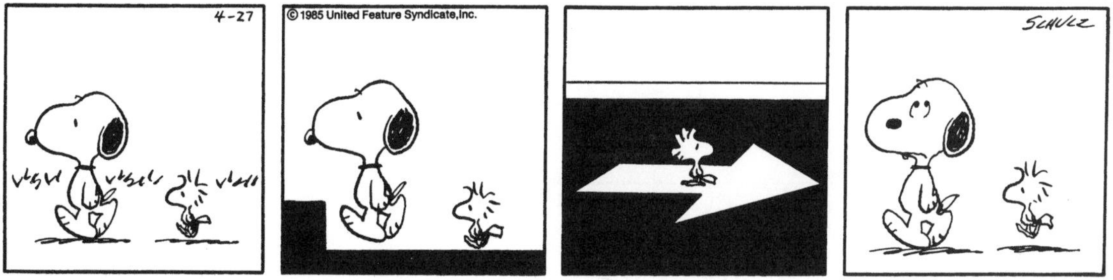
4-27
© 1985 United Feature Syndicate, Inc.
SCHULZ

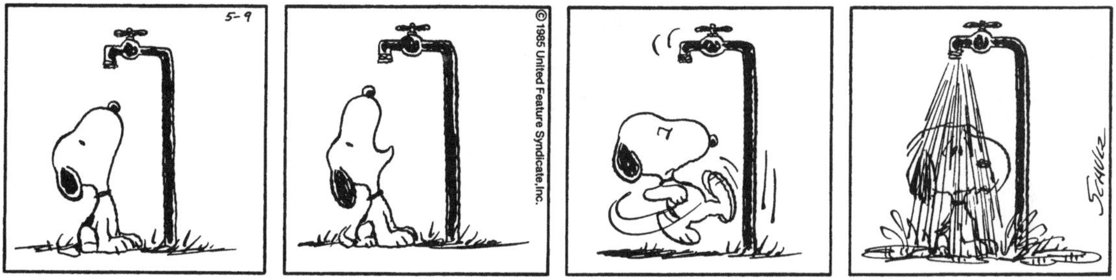
5-9
© 1985 United Feature Syndicate, Inc.
SCHULZ

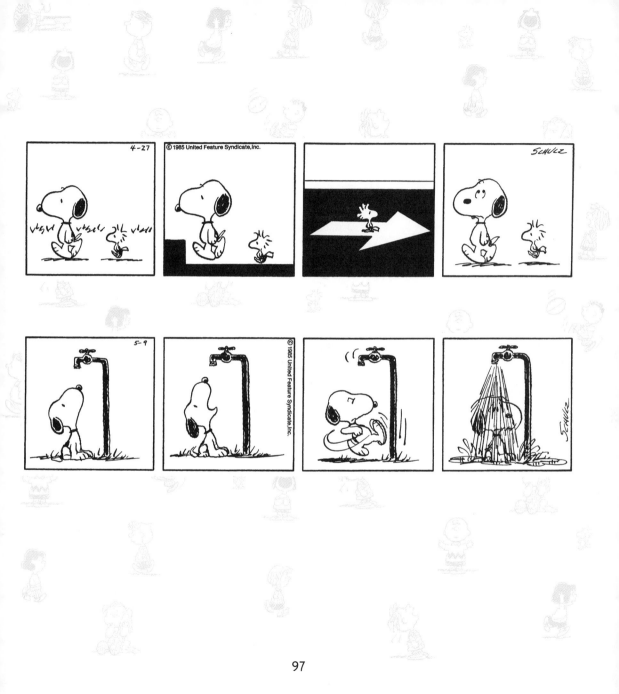

3-10
© 1986 United Feature Syndicate, Inc.
SCHULZ

4-12
© 1986 United Feature Syndicate, Inc.
SCHULZ

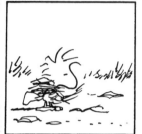

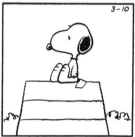

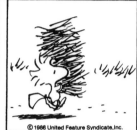

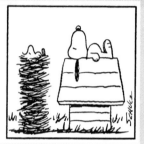

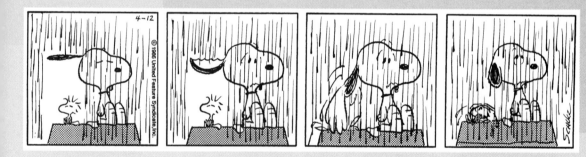

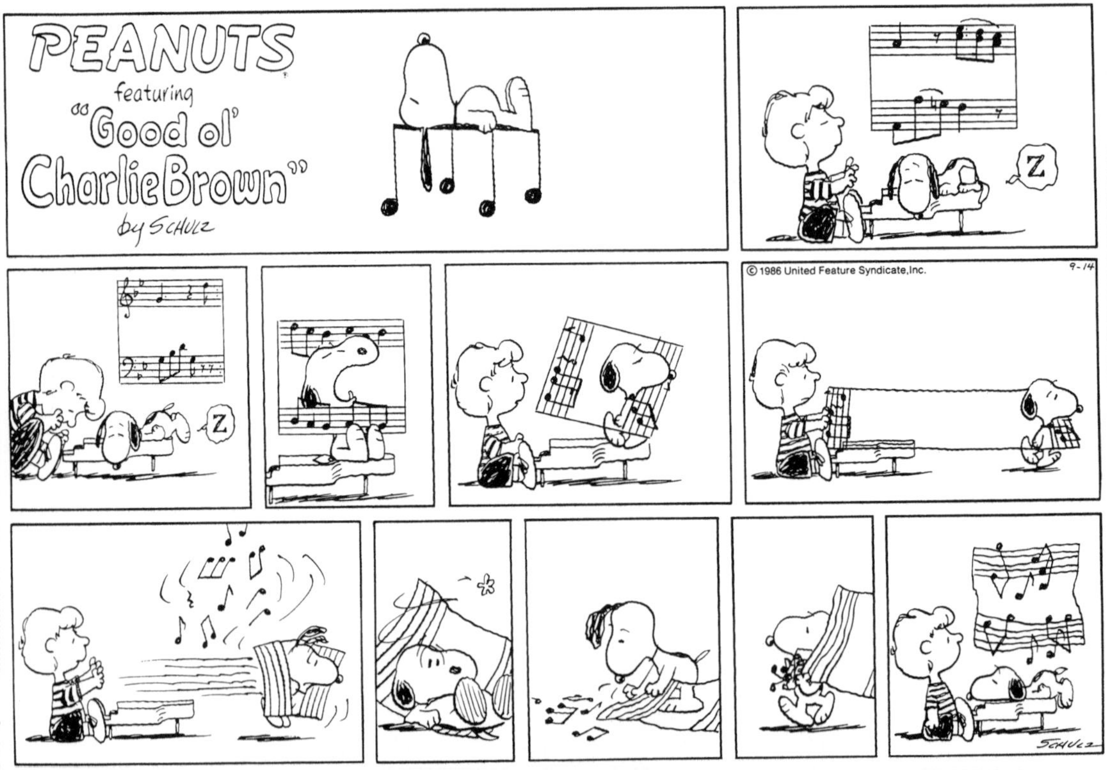
PEANUTS
featuring
"Good ol' Charlie Brown"
by SCHULZ
Z
Z
© 1986 United Feature Syndicate, Inc.
9-14
SCHULZ

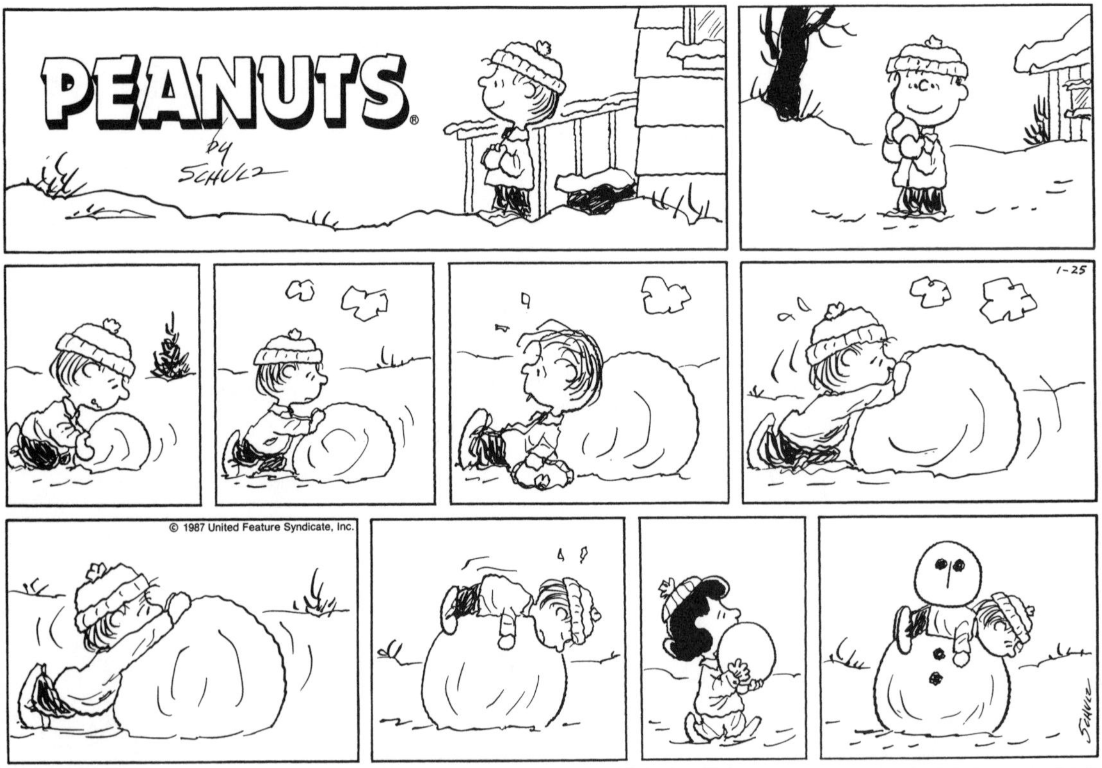
PEANUTS®
by SCHULZ
1-25
© 1987 United Feature Syndicate, Inc.
SCHULZ

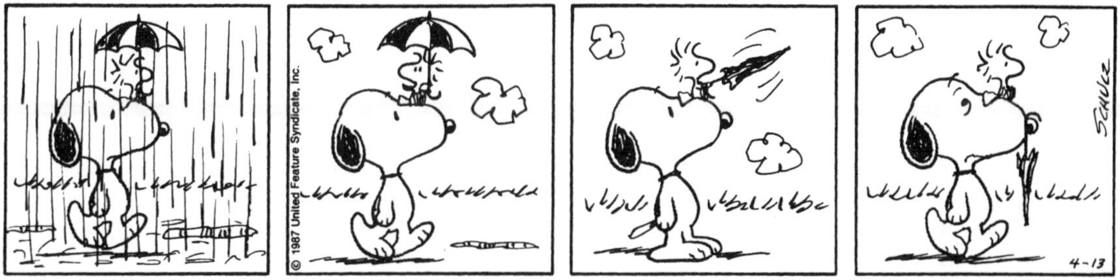
© 1987 United Feature Syndicate, Inc.
4-13

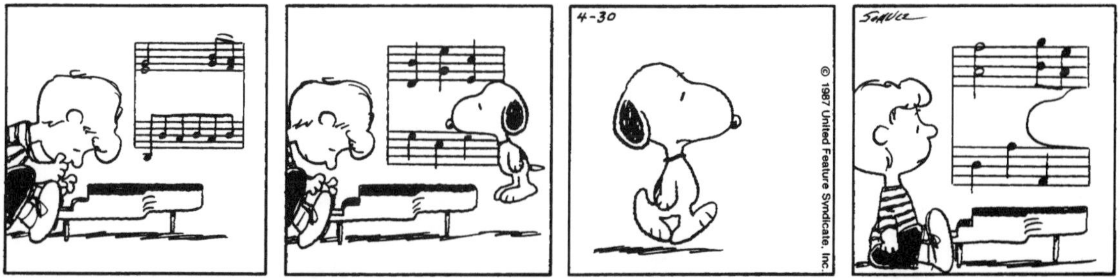
4-30
© 1987 United Feature Syndicate, Inc.

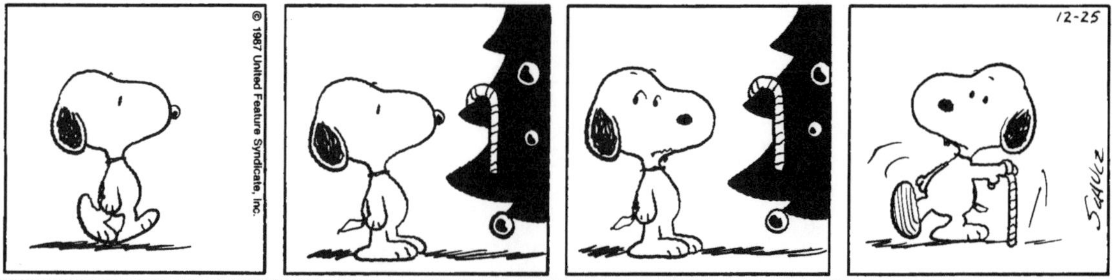
© 1987 United Feature Syndicate, Inc.
12-25

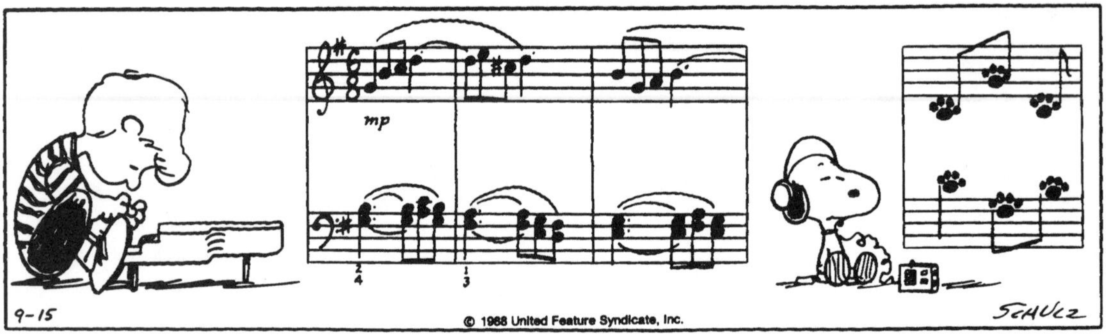
9-15
mp
© 1988 United Feature Syndicate, Inc.
SCHULZ

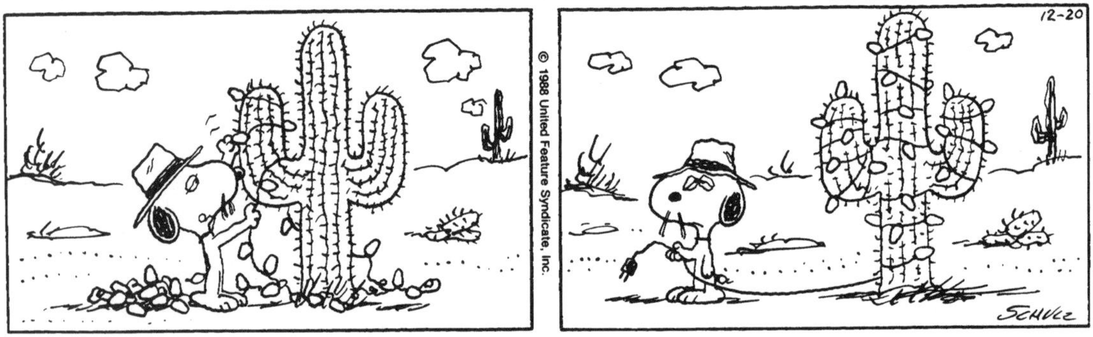
© 1988 United Feature Syndicate, Inc.
12-20
SCHULZ

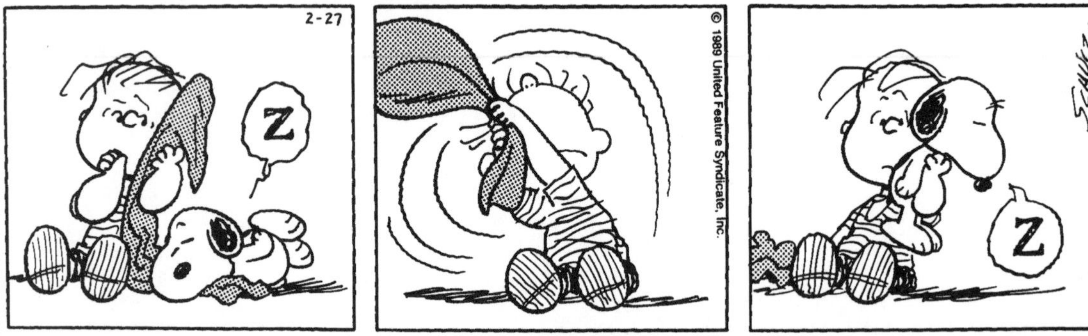
2-27
Z
© 1989 United Feature Syndicate, Inc.
SCHULZ
Z

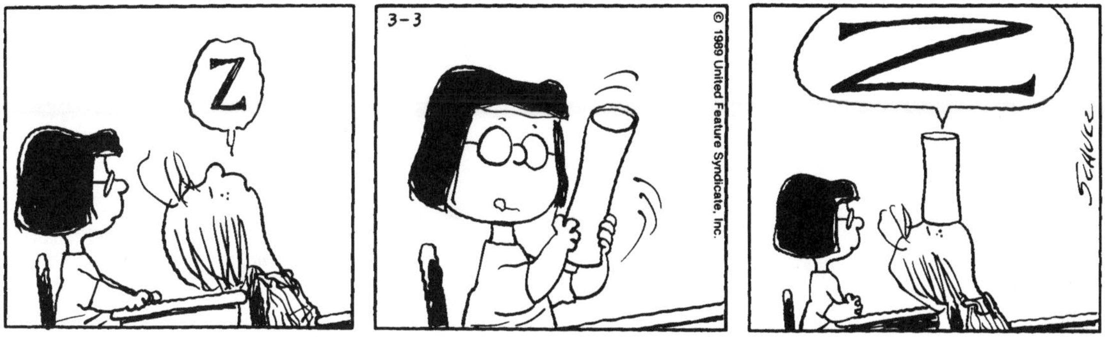
Z
3-3
© 1989 United Feature Syndicate, Inc.
Z
SCHULZ

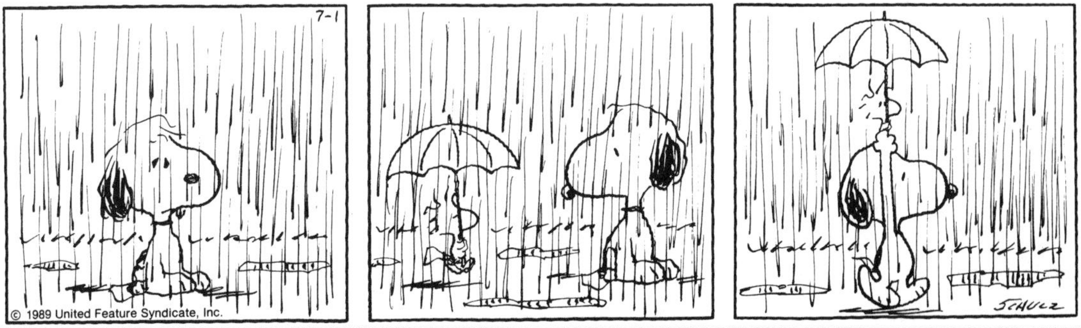
7-1
© 1989 United Feature Syndicate, Inc.
SCHULZ

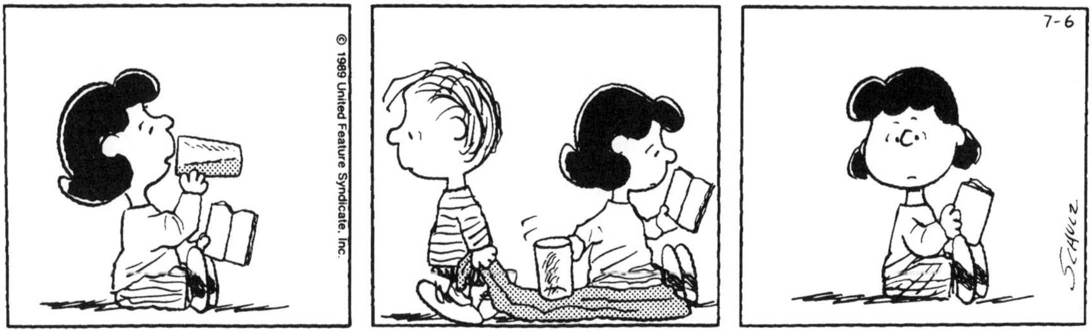
© 1989 United Feature Syndicate, Inc.
7-6
SCHULZ

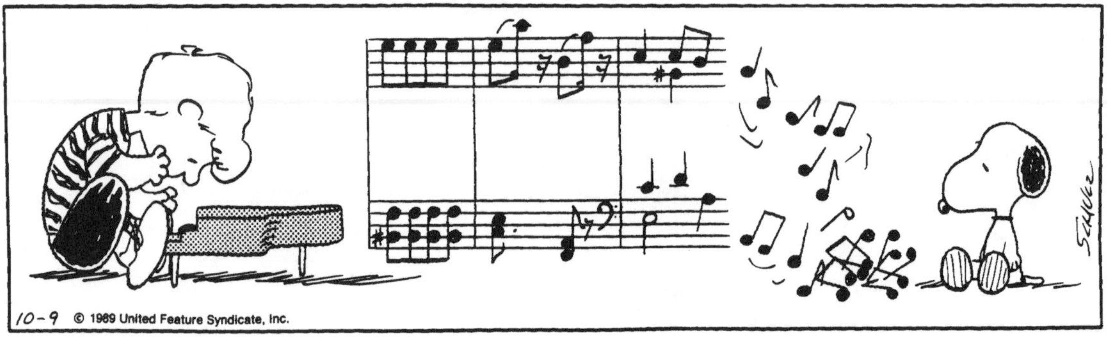
SCHULZ
10-9 © 1989 United Feature Syndicate, Inc.

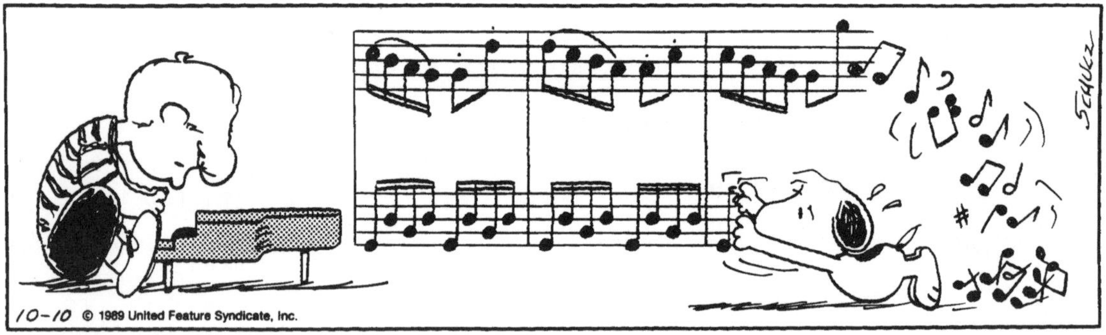
SCHULZ
10-10 © 1989 United Feature Syndicate, Inc.

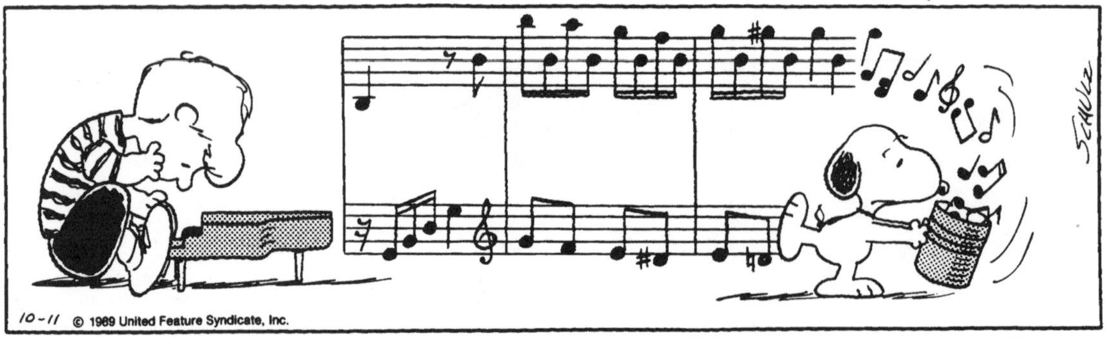
SCHULZ
10-11 © 1989 United Feature Syndicate, Inc.

10-12 © 1989 United Feature Syndicate, Inc.

© 1989 United Feature Syndicate, Inc.

10-13

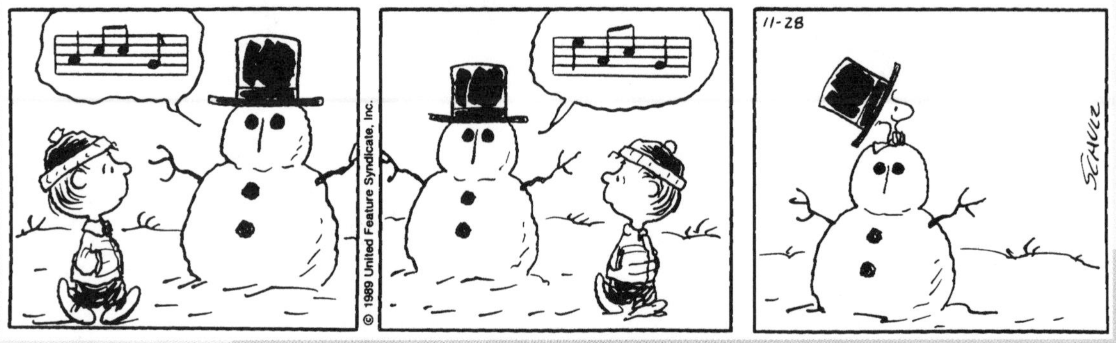
© 1989 United Feature Syndicate, Inc.
11-28
SCHULZ

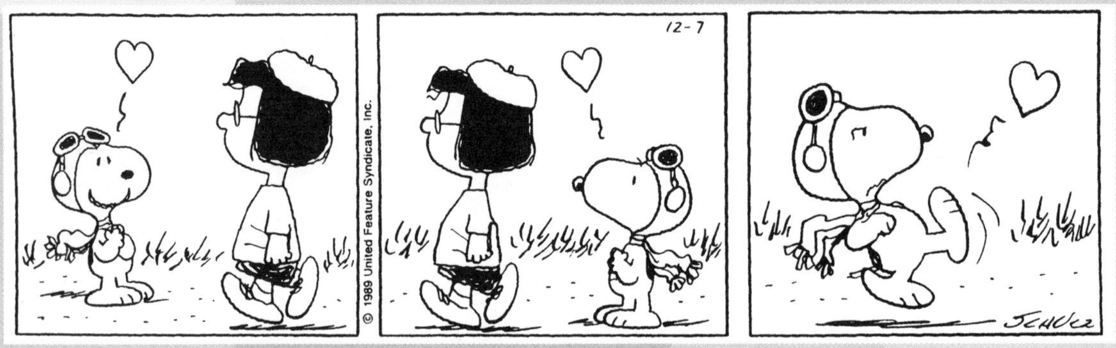
© 1989 United Feature Syndicate, Inc.
12-7
SCHULZ

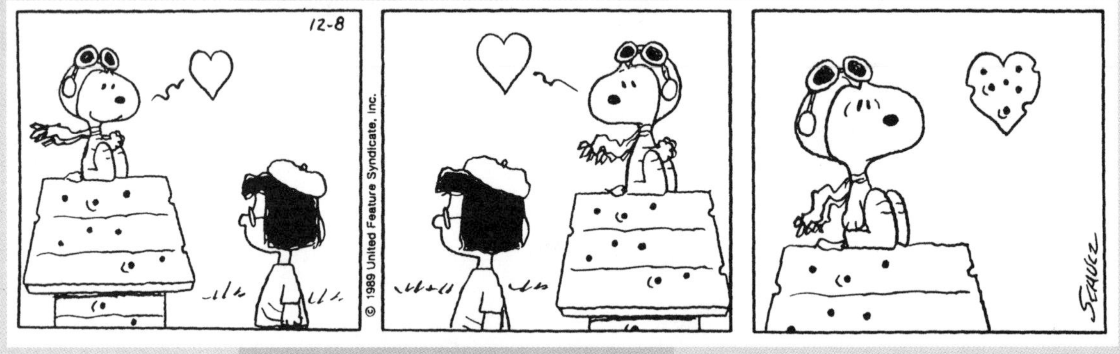
12-8
© 1989 United Feature Syndicate, Inc.
SCHULZ

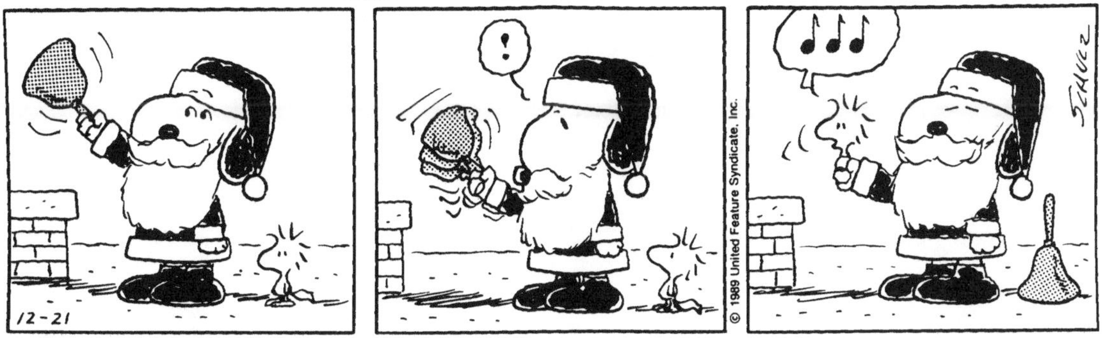
12-21
!
© 1989 United Feature Syndicate, Inc.
SCHULZ

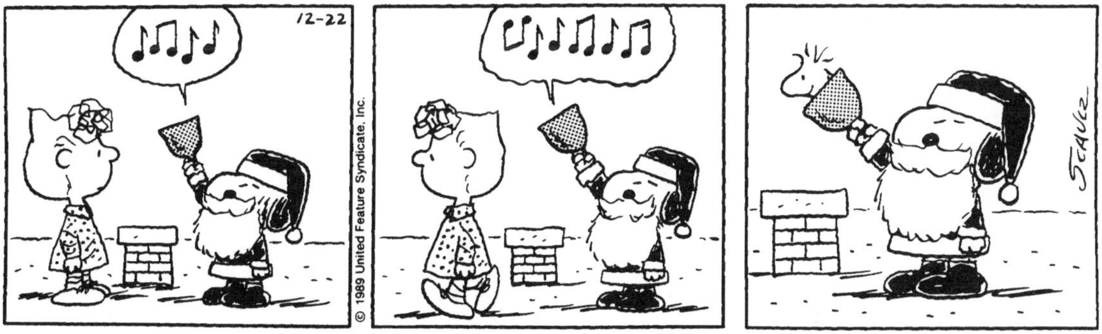
12-22
© 1989 United Feature Syndicate, Inc.
SCHULZ

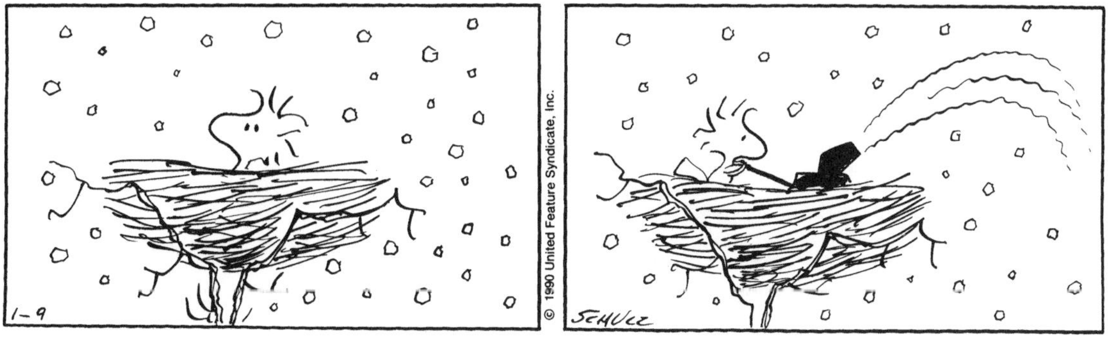
1-9
© 1990 United Feature Syndicate, Inc.
SCHULZ

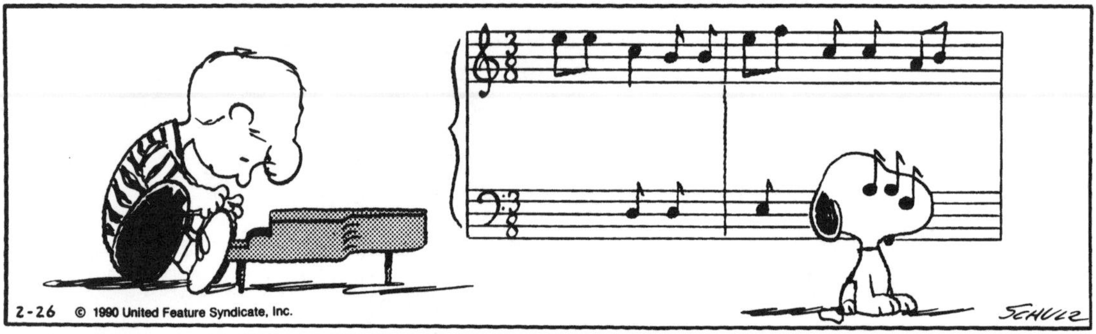
2-26
© 1990 United Feature Syndicate, Inc.
SCHULZ

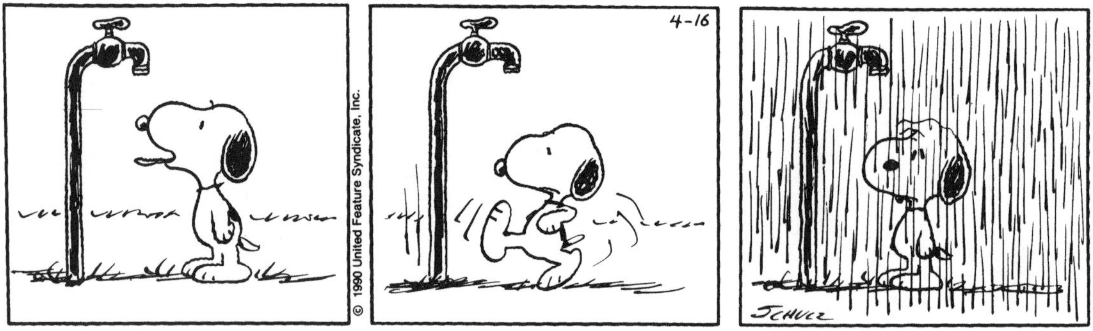
4-16
© 1990 United Feature Syndicate, Inc.
SCHULZ

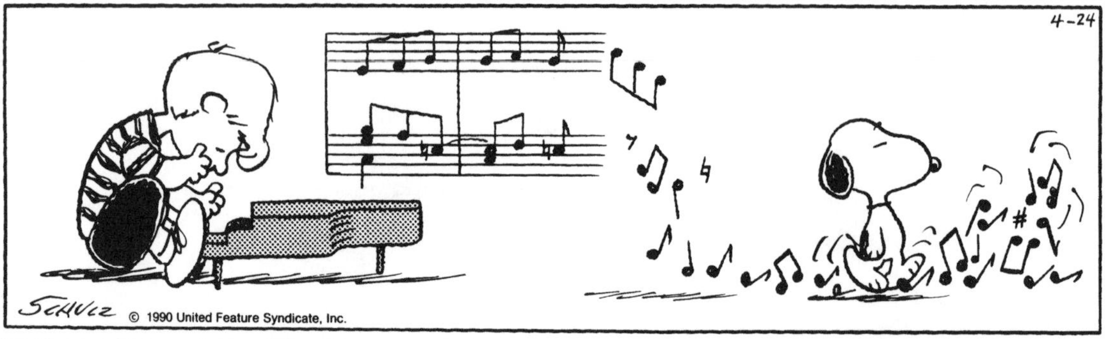
4-24
SCHULZ
© 1990 United Feature Syndicate, Inc.

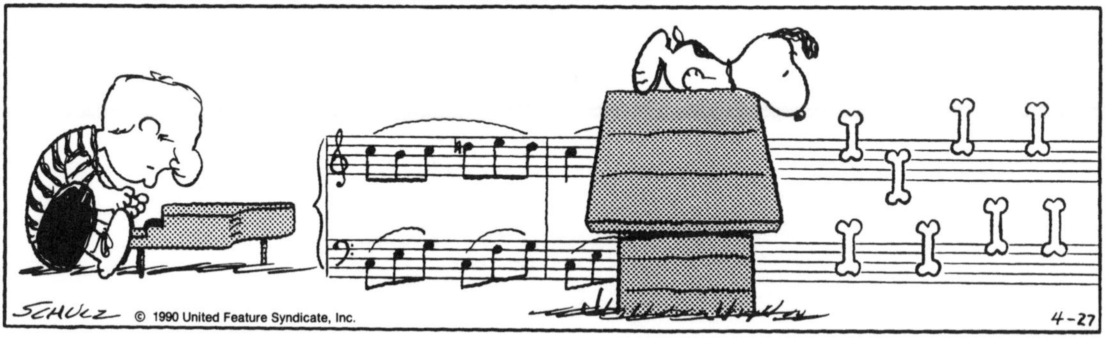
SCHULZ
© 1990 United Feature Syndicate, Inc.
4-27

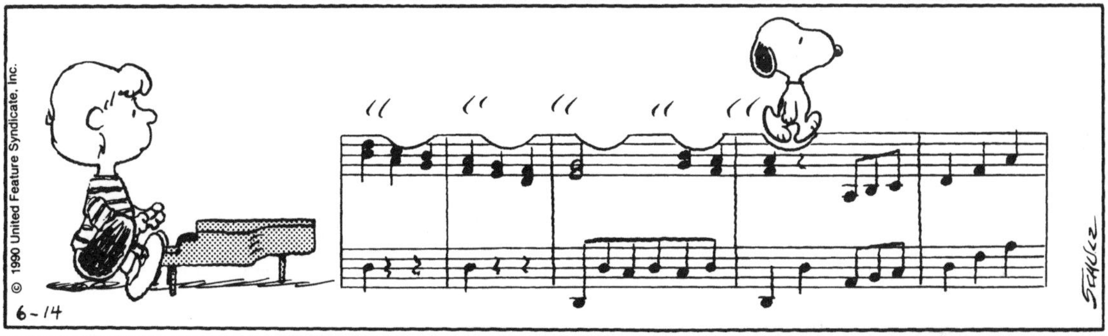
© 1990 United Feature Syndicate, Inc.
6-14
SCHULZ

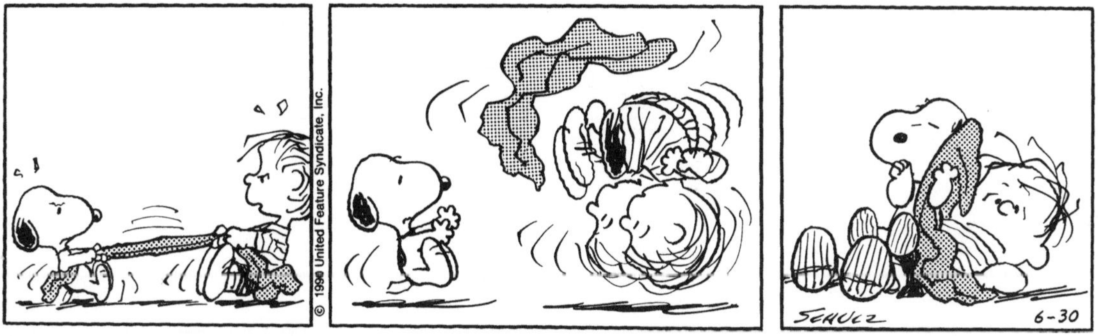
© 1990 United Feature Syndicate, Inc.
SCHULZ
6-30

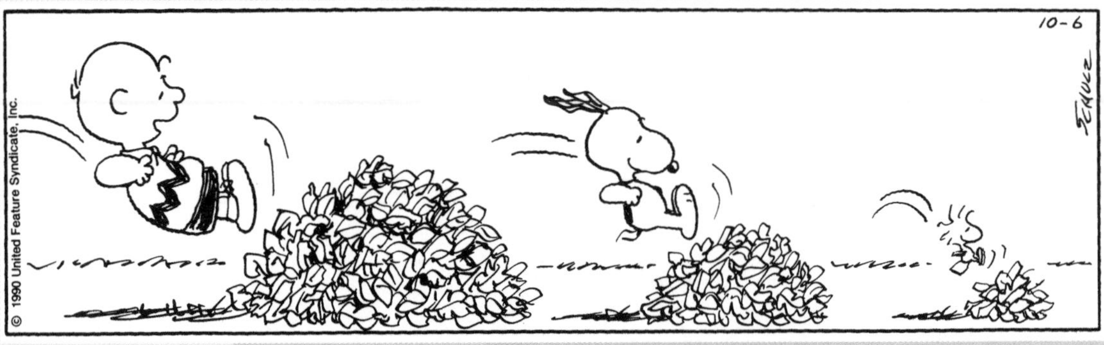
© 1990 United Feature Syndicate, Inc.
10-6
SCHULZ

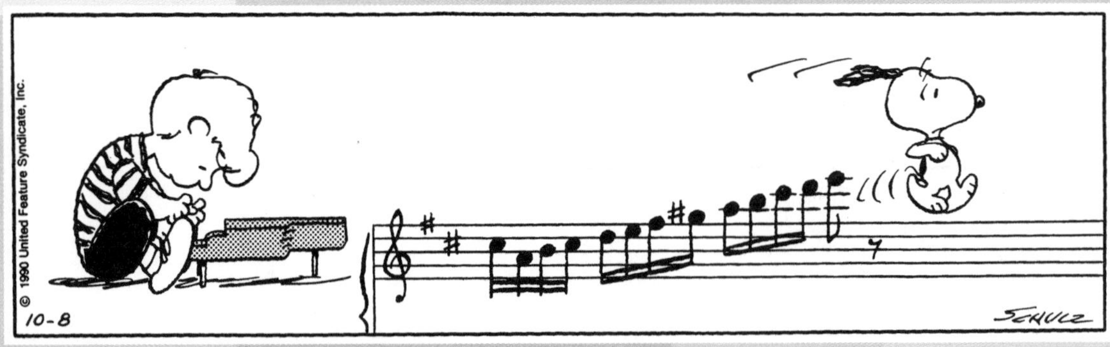
© 1990 United Feature Syndicate, Inc.
10-8
SCHULZ

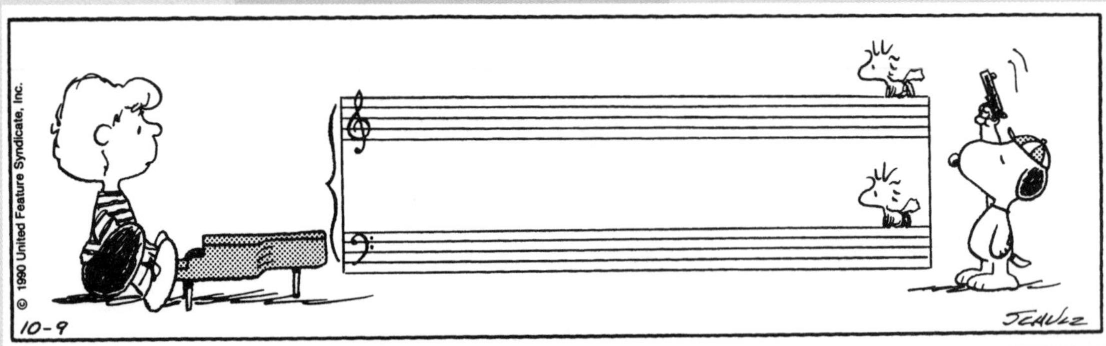
© 1990 United Feature Syndicate, Inc.
10-9
SCHULZ

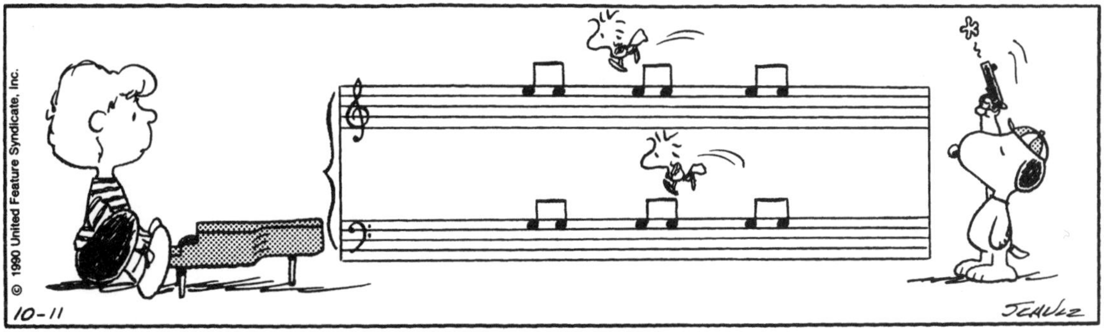
© 1990 United Feature Syndicate, Inc.
10-11
SCHULZ

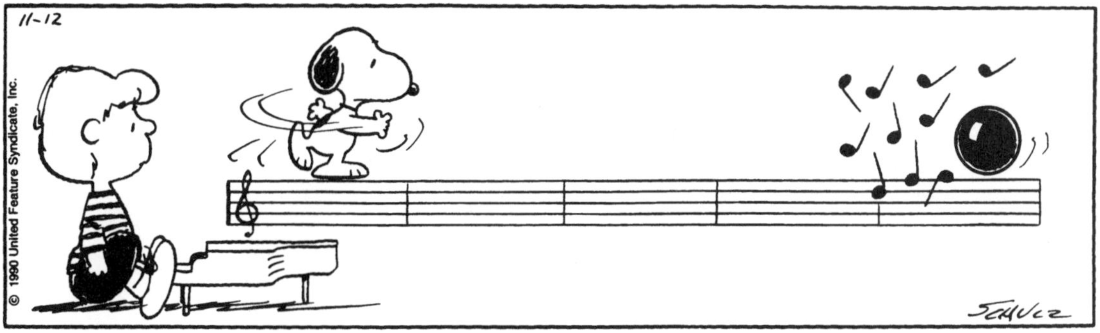
11-12
© 1990 United Feature Syndicate, Inc.
SCHULZ

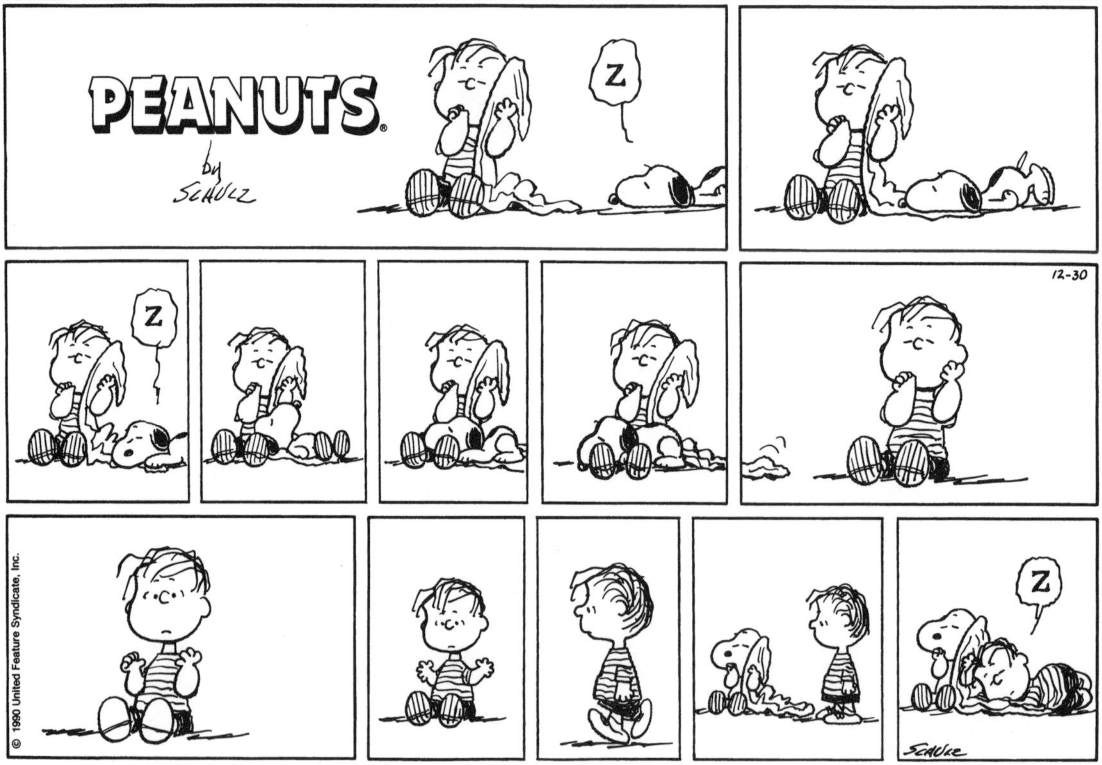
PEANUTS
by SCHULZ
Z
Z
12-30
Z
SCHULZ

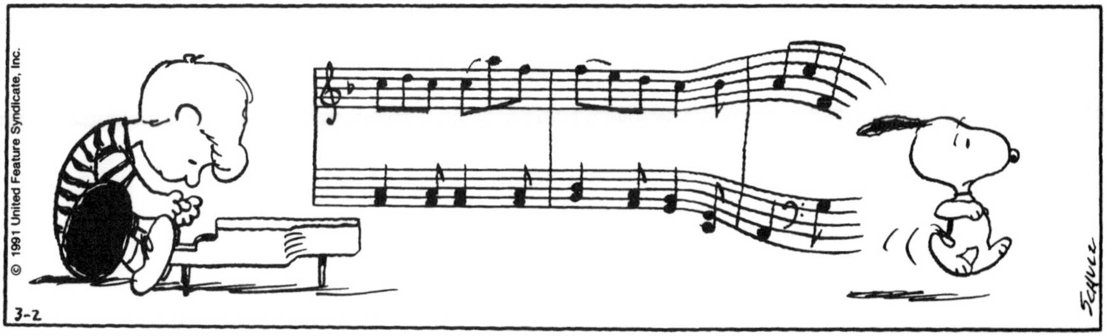
© 1991 United Feature Syndicate, Inc.
3-2
SCHULZ

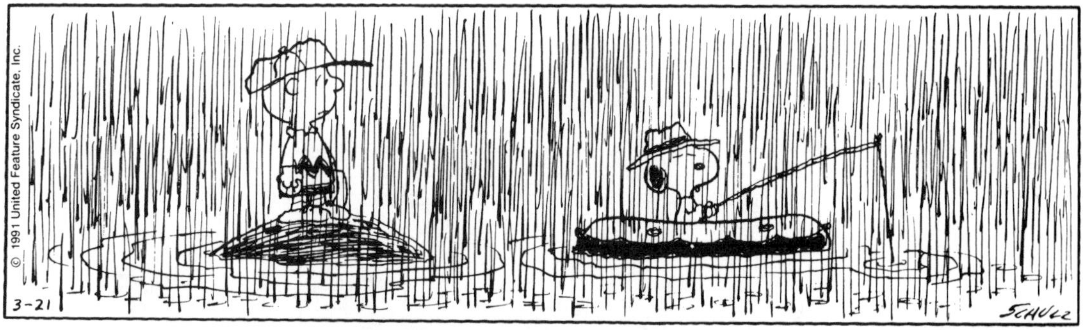
© 1991 United Feature Syndicate, Inc.
3-21
SCHULZ

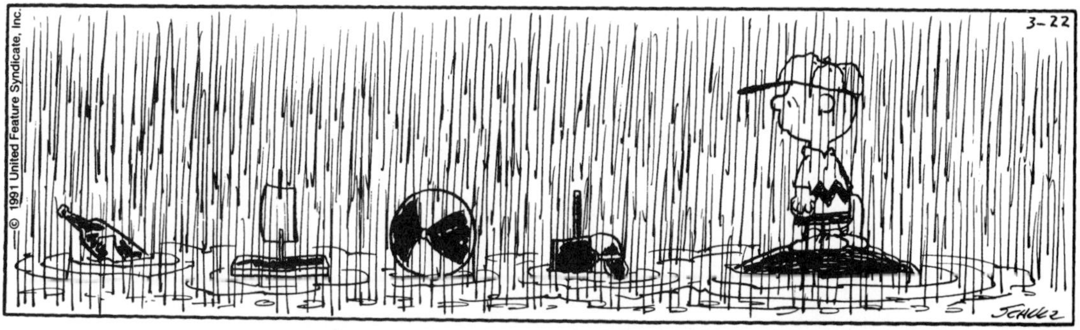
© 1991 United Feature Syndicate, Inc.
3-22
SCHULZ

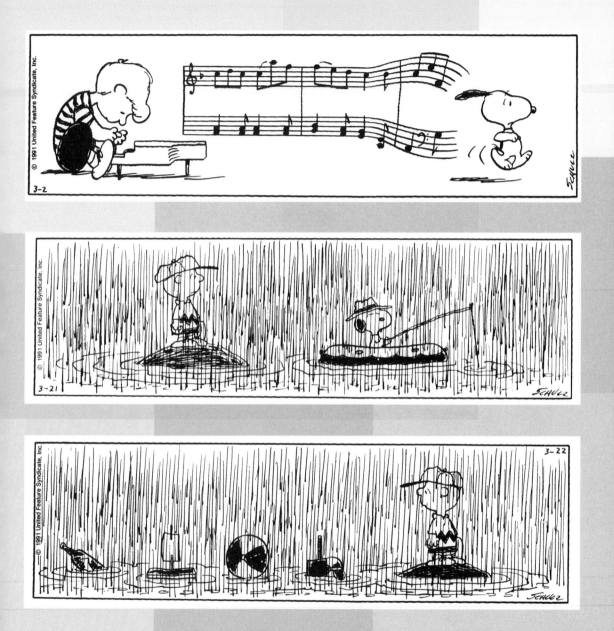

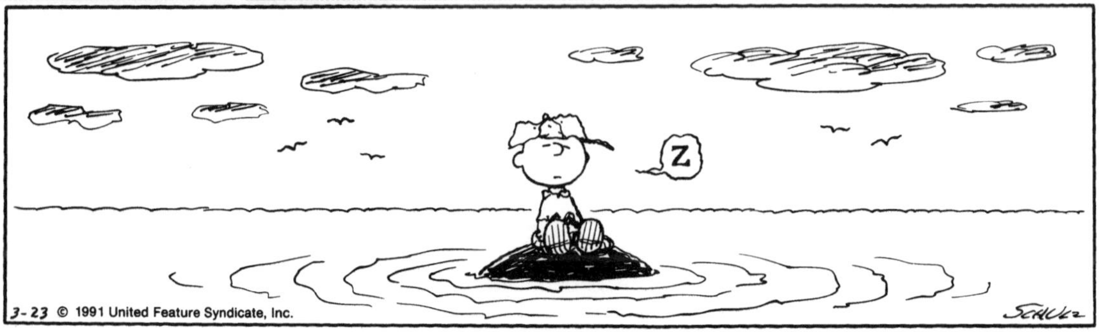
Z
3-23 © 1991 United Feature Syndicate, Inc.
SCHULZ

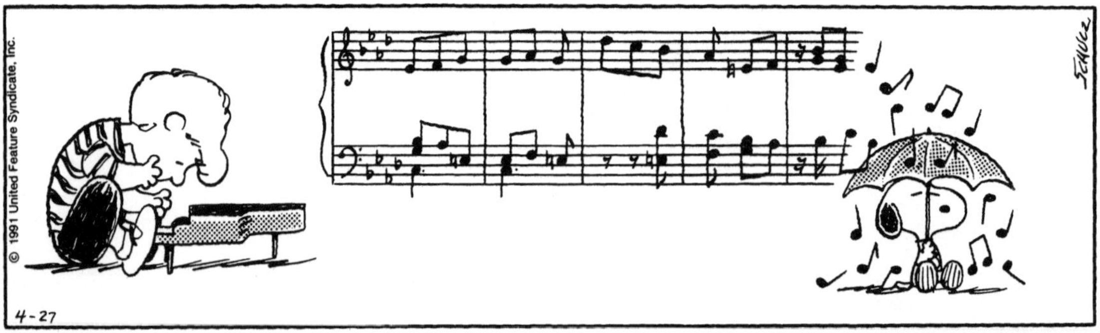
© 1991 United Feature Syndicate, Inc.
SCHULZ
4-27

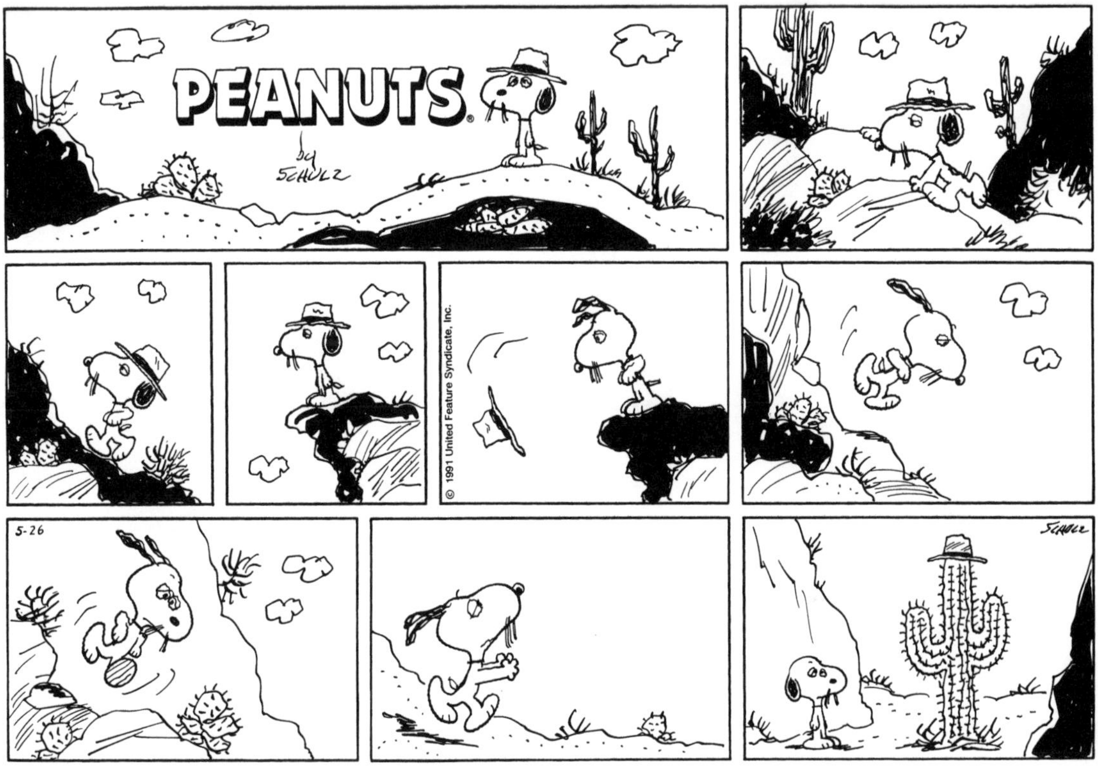
PEANUTS
by SCHULZ
© 1991 United Feature Syndicate, Inc.
5-26
SCHULZ

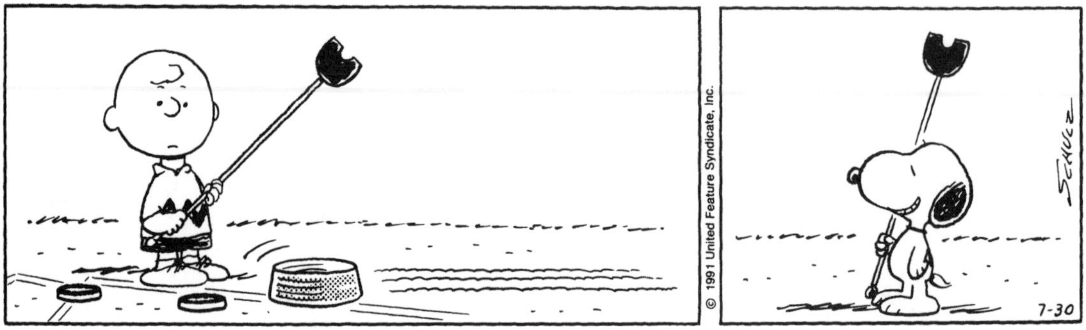
© 1991 United Feature Syndicate, Inc.
SCHULZ
7-30

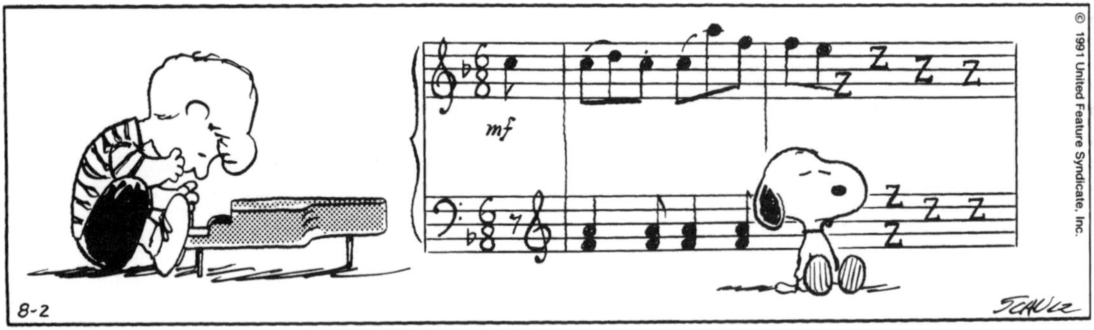
mf
Z Z Z Z
Z Z Z
Z
8-2
© 1991 United Feature Syndicate, Inc.
SCHULZ

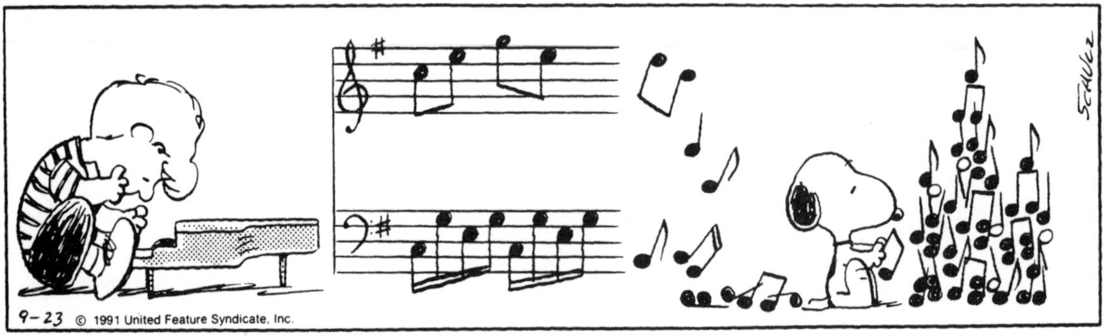
SCHULZ
9-23 © 1991 United Feature Syndicate, Inc.

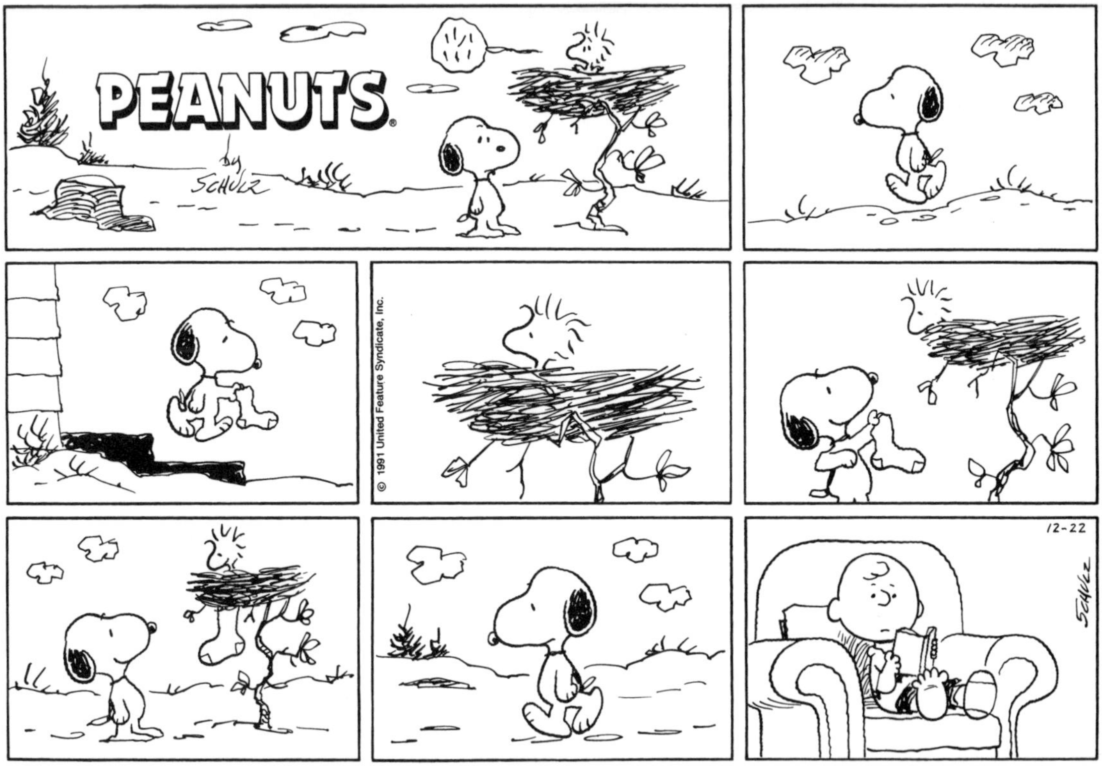
PEANUTS
by SCHULZ
© 1991 United Feature Syndicate, Inc.
12-22
SCHULZ

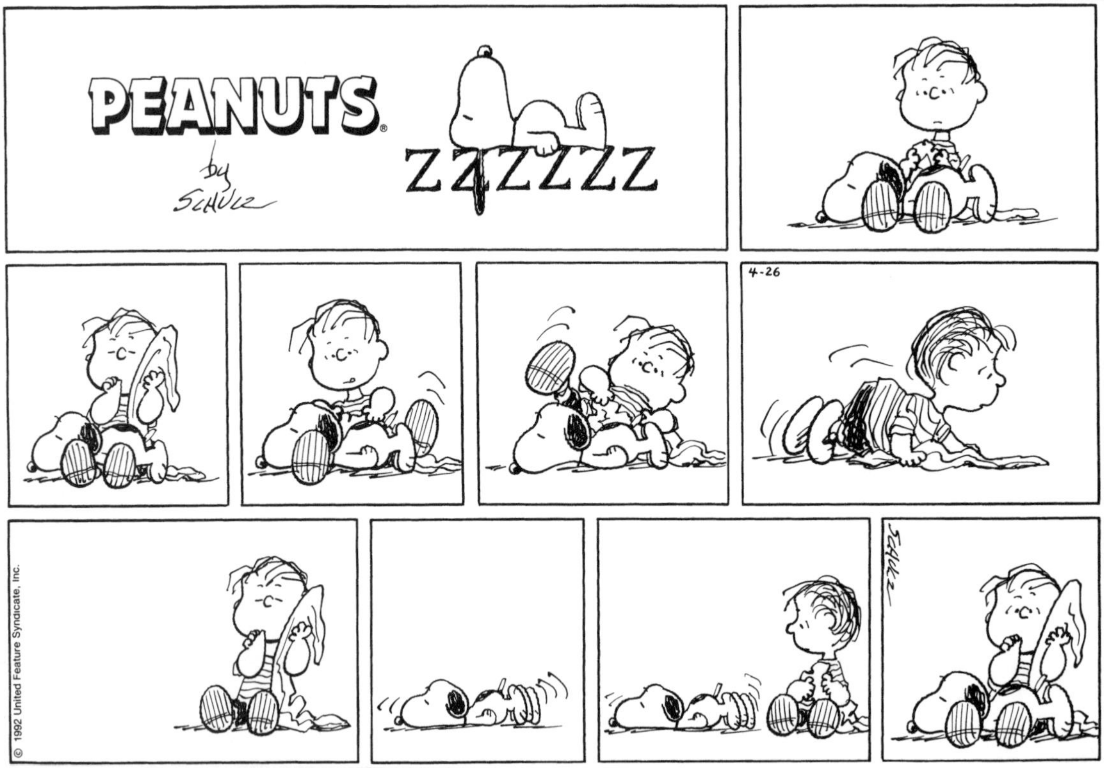

PEANUTS
by SCHULZ
ZZZZZZ
4-26
SCHULZ

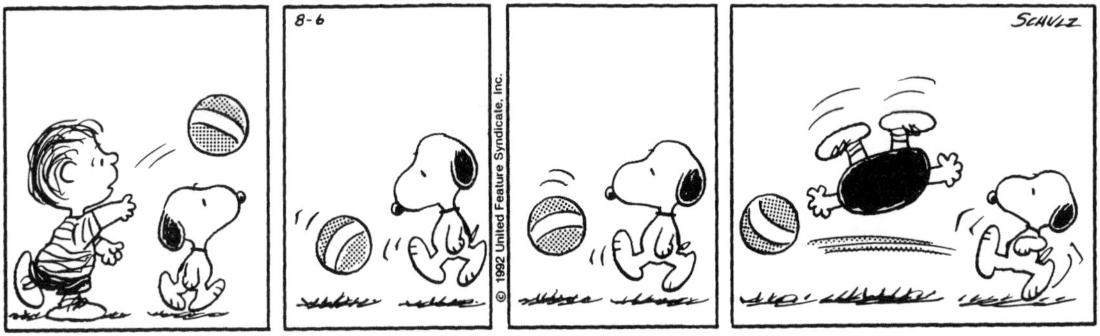
8-6
© 1992 United Feature Syndicate, Inc.
SCHULZ

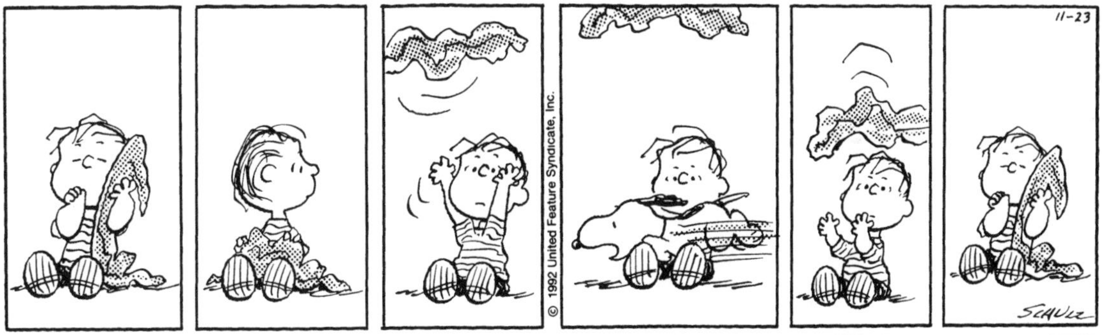
© 1992 United Feature Syndicate, Inc.
11-23
SCHULZ

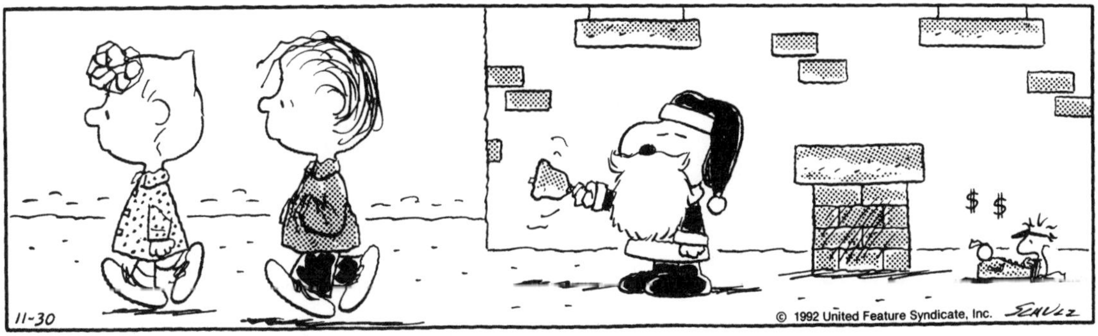
$ $
11-30
© 1992 United Feature Syndicate, Inc.
SCHULZ

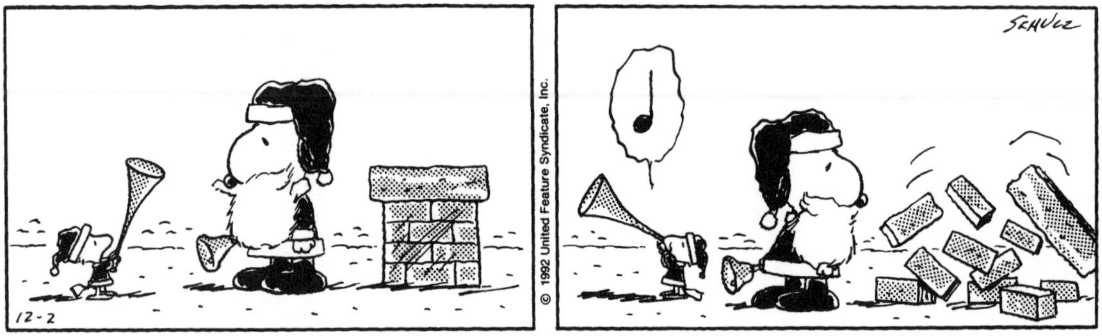
12-2
© 1992 United Feature Syndicate, Inc.
SCHULZ

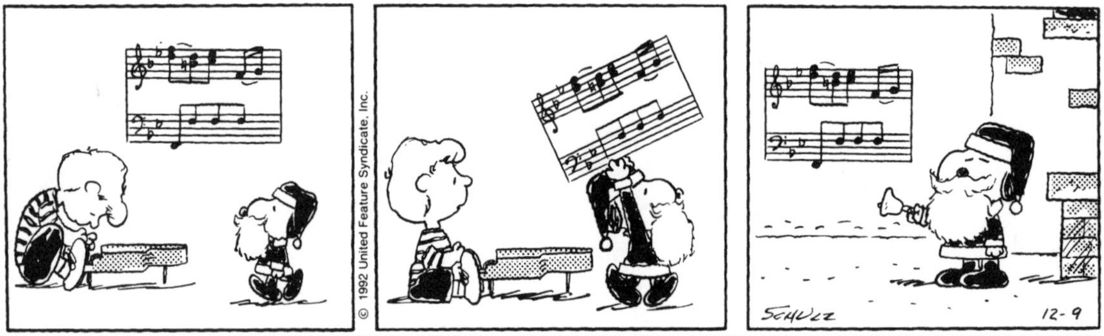
© 1992 United Feature Syndicate, Inc.
SCHULZ
12-9

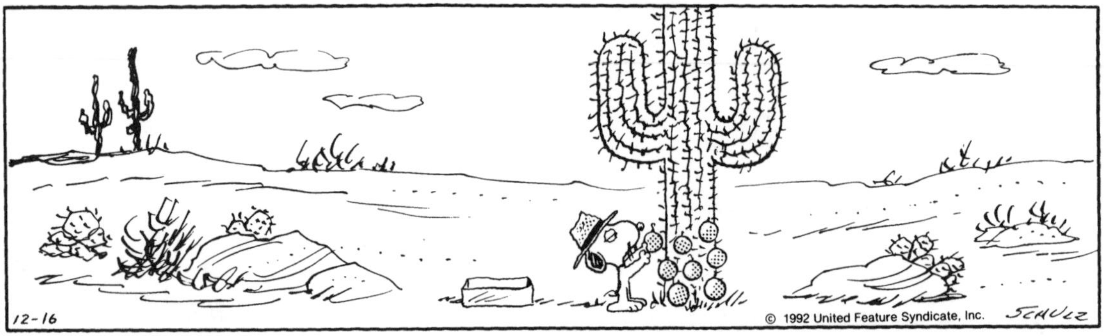
12-16
© 1992 United Feature Syndicate, Inc.
SCHULZ

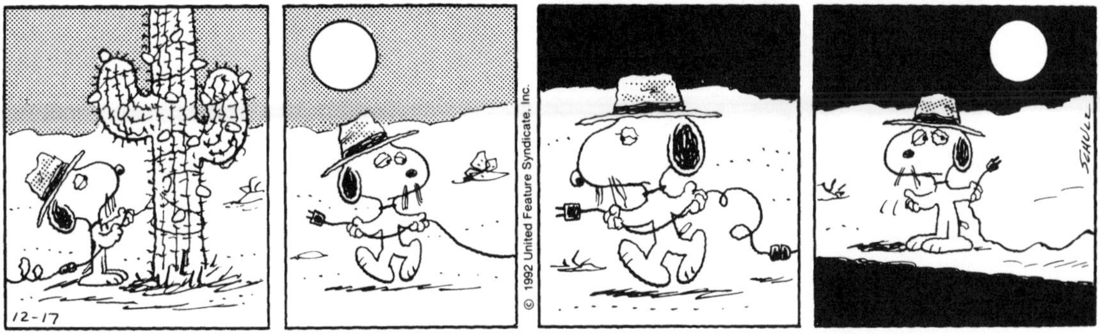
12-17
© 1992 United Feature Syndicate, Inc.
SCHULZ

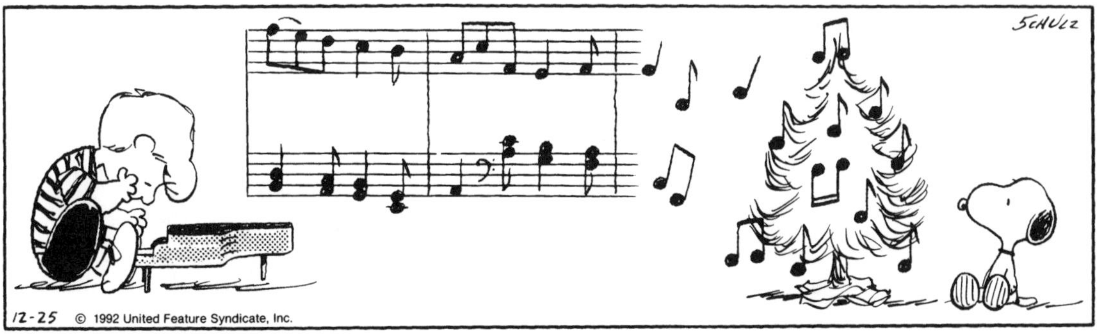
SCHULZ
12-25 © 1992 United Feature Syndicate, Inc.

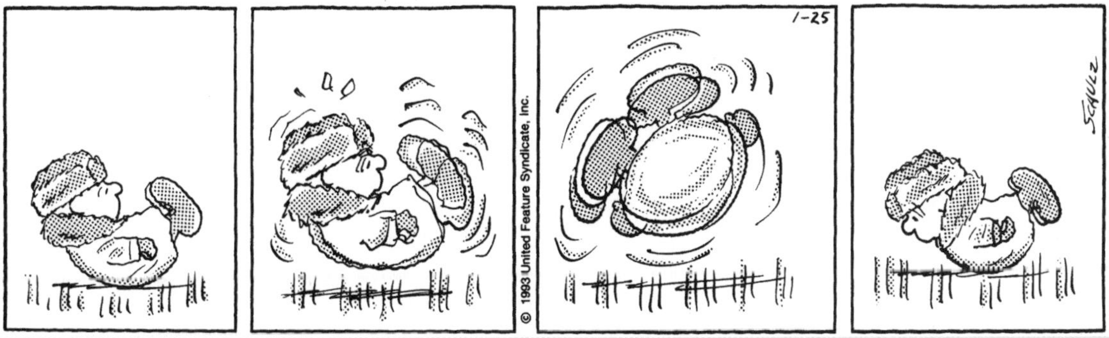
© 1993 United Feature Syndicate, Inc.
1-25
SCHULZ

© 1993 United Feature Syndicate, Inc.
2-27
SCHULZ

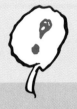

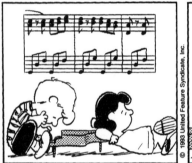

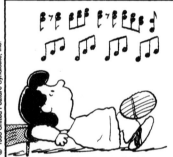

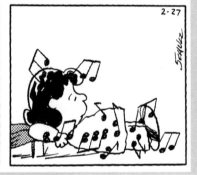

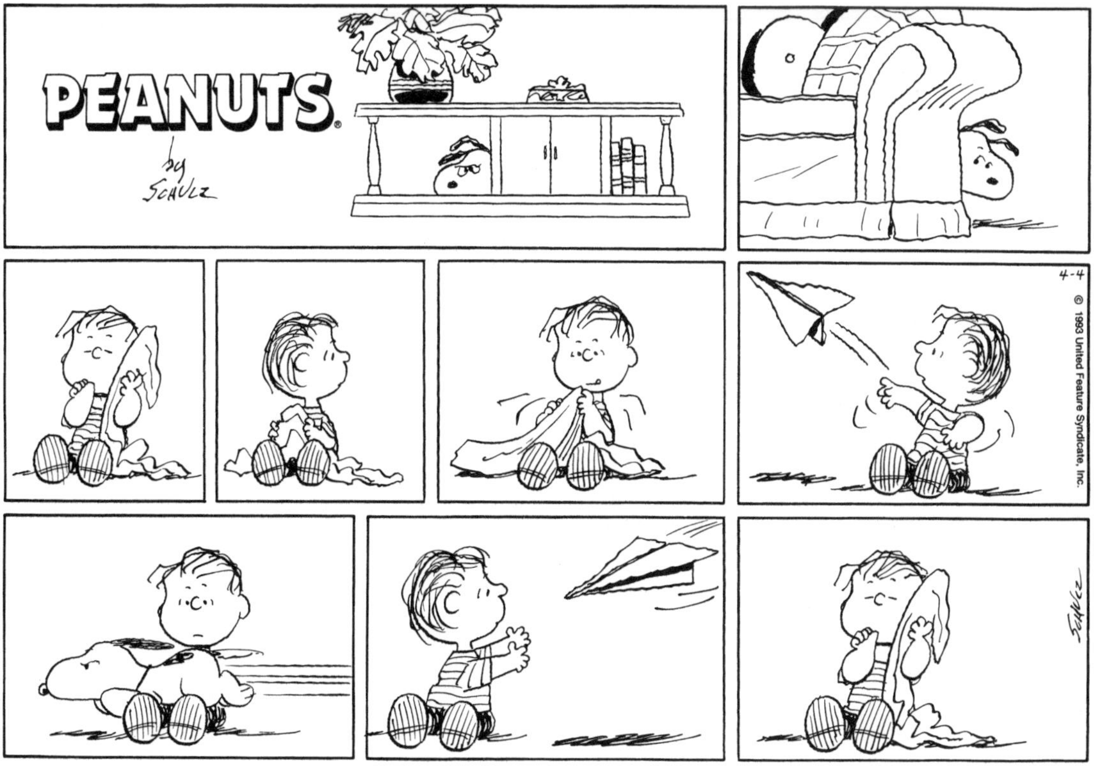
PEANUTS
by SCHULZ
4-4
© 1993 United Feature Syndicate, Inc.
SCHULZ

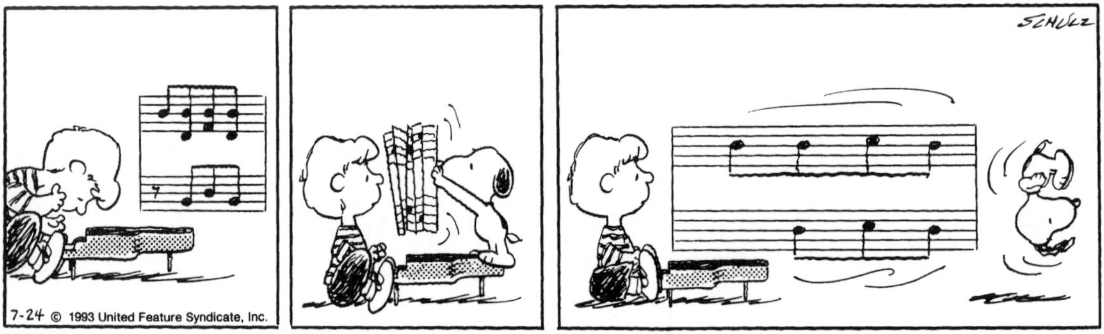
SCHULZ
7-24 © 1993 United Feature Syndicate, Inc.

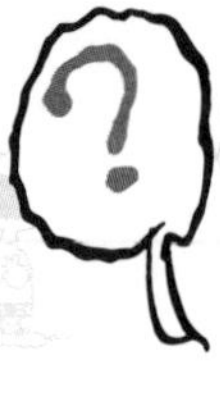
?

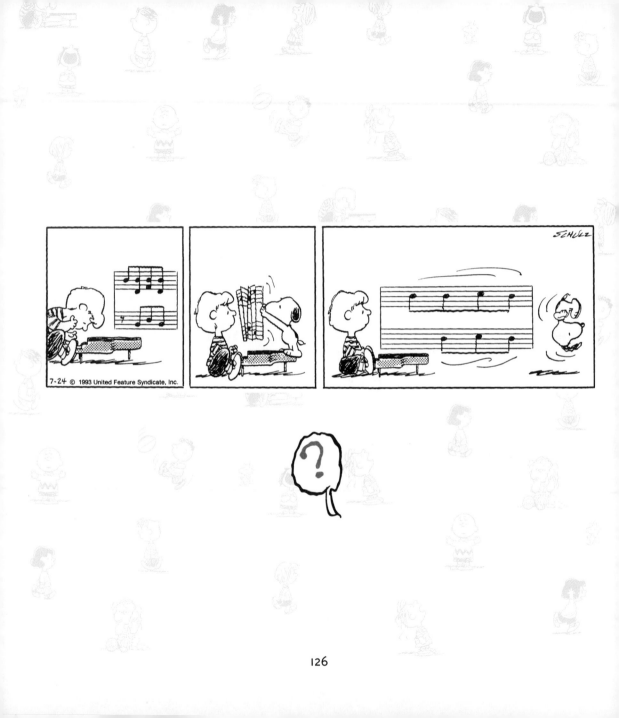

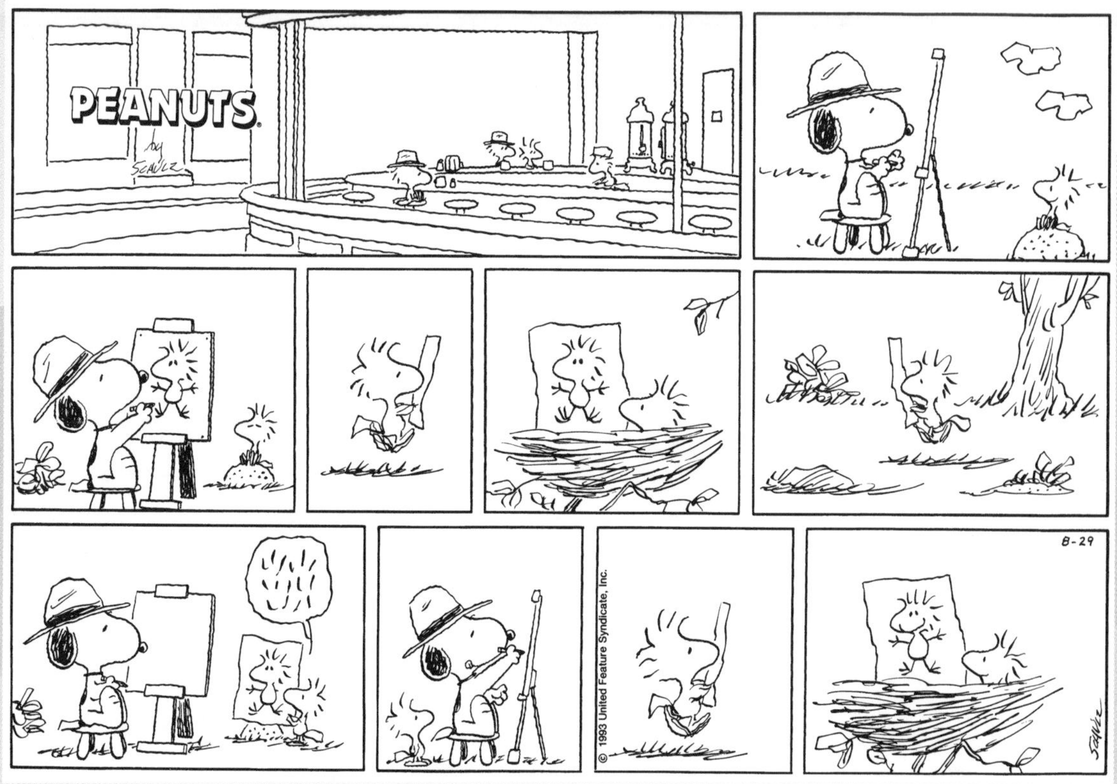
PEANUTS
by SCHULZ
8-29
© 1993 United Feature Syndicate, Inc.
SCHULZ

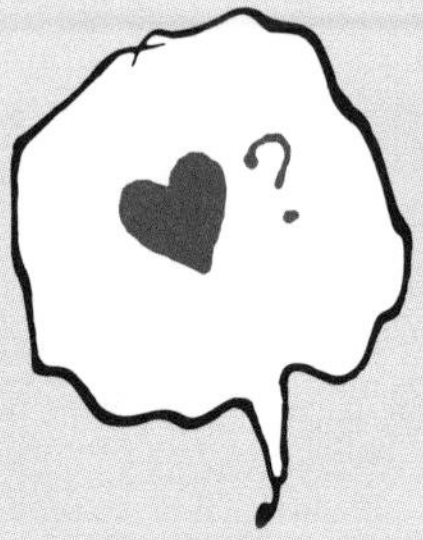
?

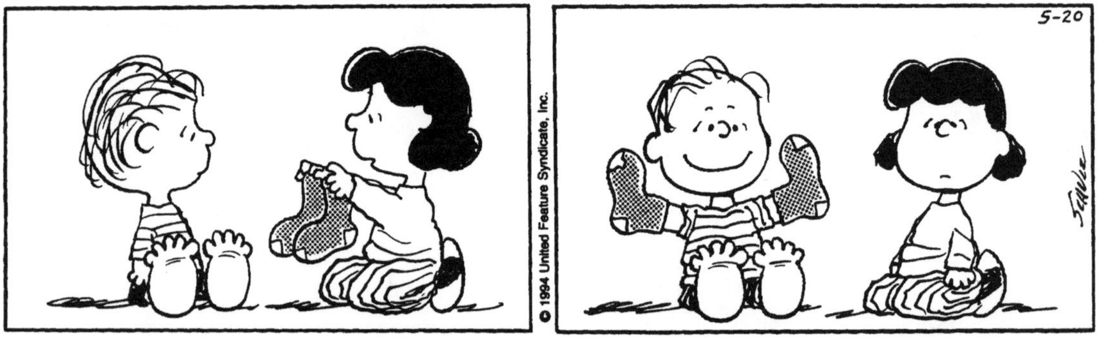
© 1994 United Feature Syndicate, Inc.
5-20

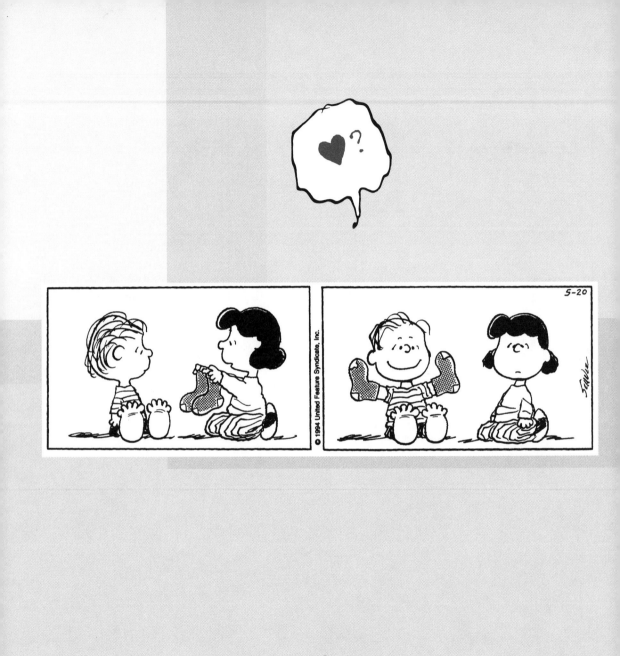

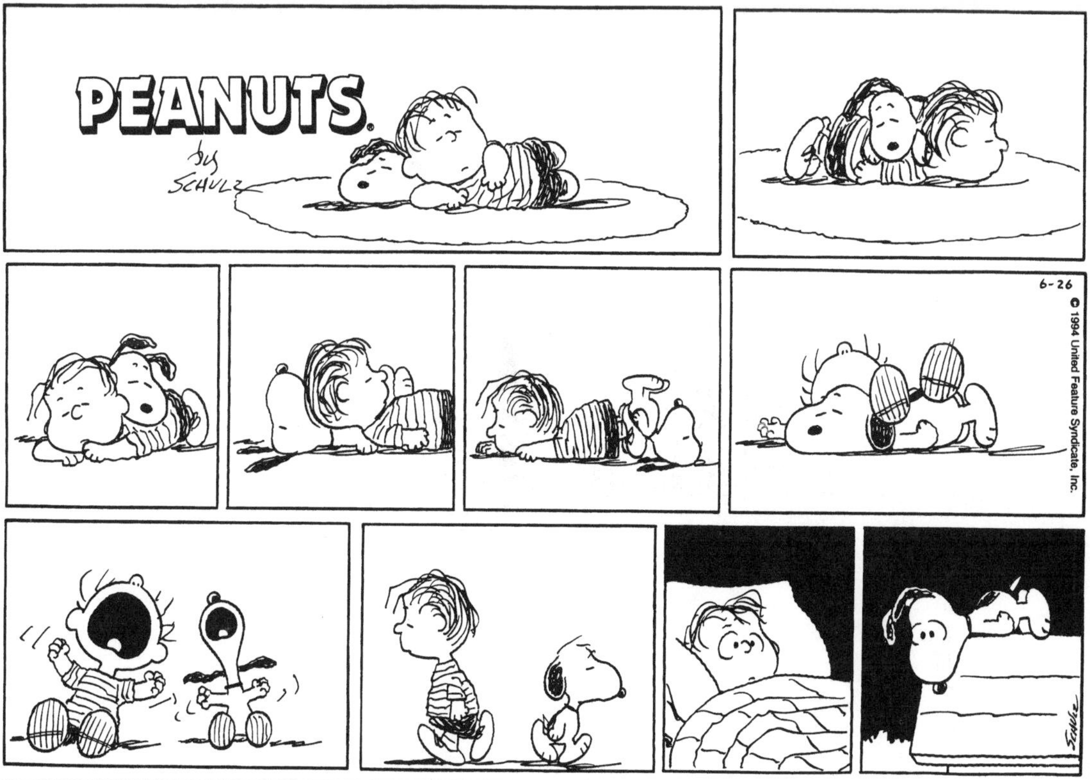
PEANUTS
by SCHULZ
6-26
© 1994 United Feature Syndicate, Inc.
SCHULZ

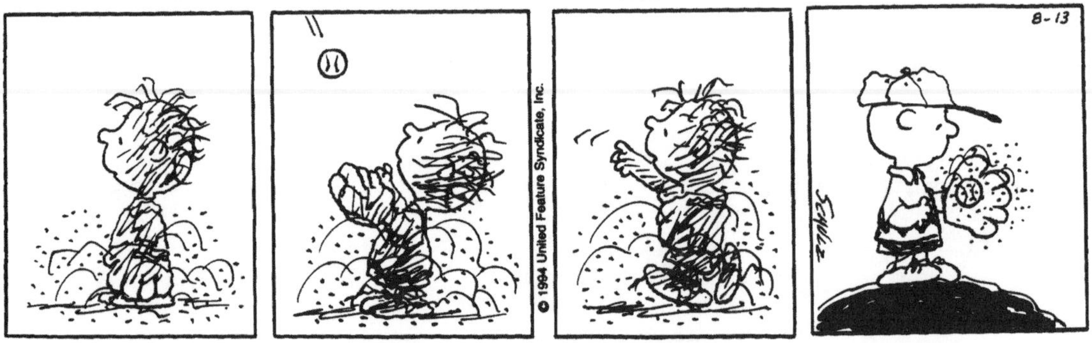
8-13
© 1994 United Feature Syndicate, Inc.
SCHULZ

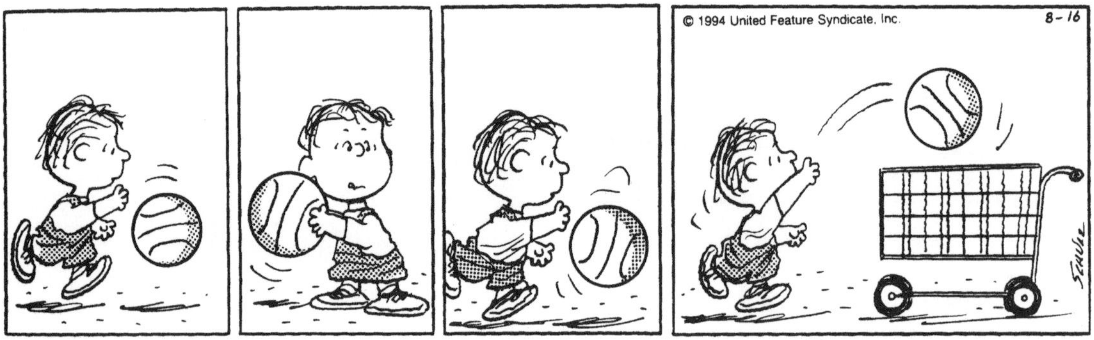
© 1994 United Feature Syndicate, Inc.
8-16
SCHULZ

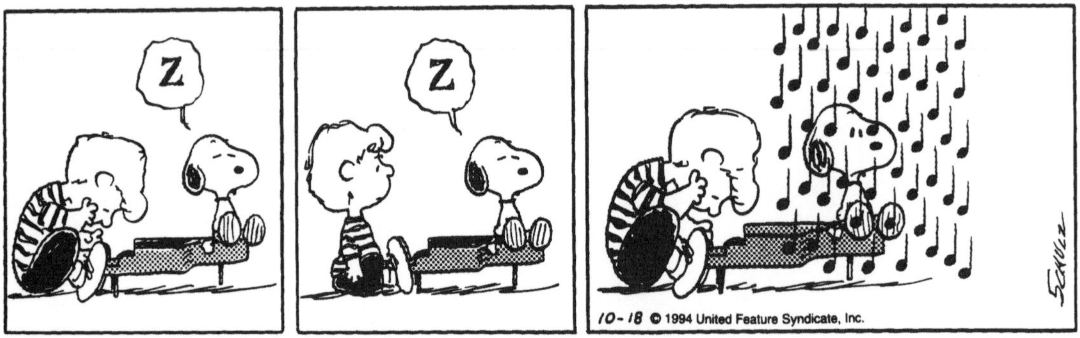
Z
Z
10-18 © 1994 United Feature Syndicate, Inc.
SCHULZ

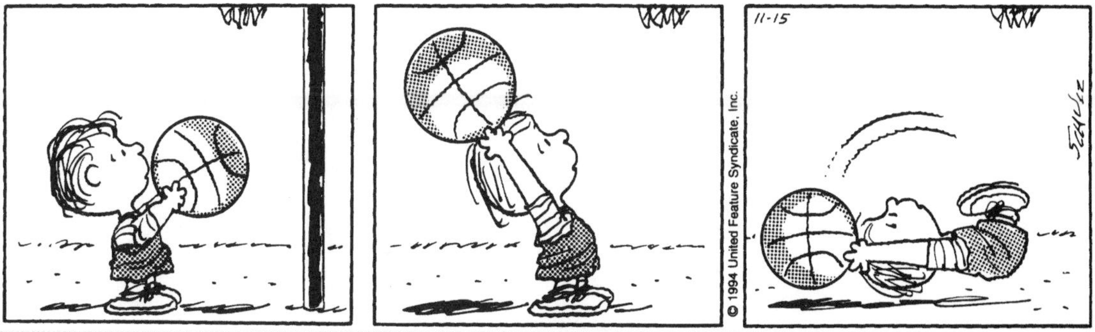
11-15
© 1994 United Feature Syndicate, Inc.
SCHULZ

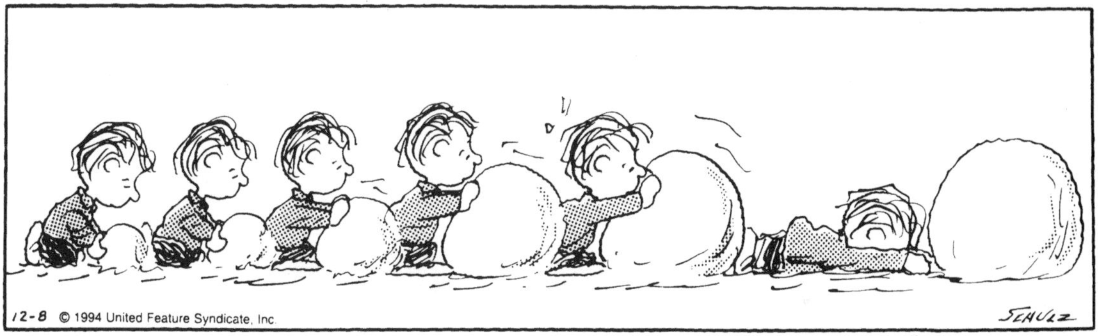
12-8 © 1994 United Feature Syndicate, Inc.
SCHULZ

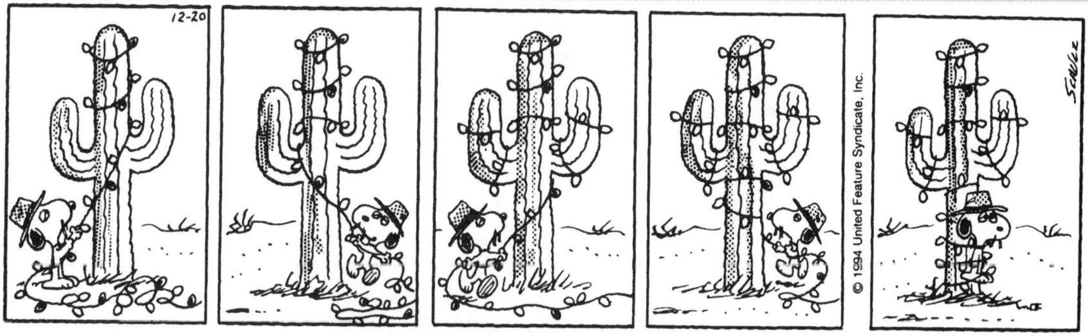
12-20
© 1994 United Feature Syndicate, Inc.
SCHULZ

1-31
© 1995 United Feature Syndicate, Inc.
SCHULZ

?

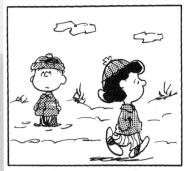

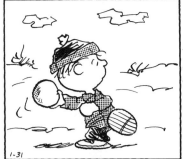

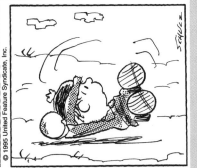

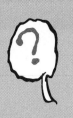

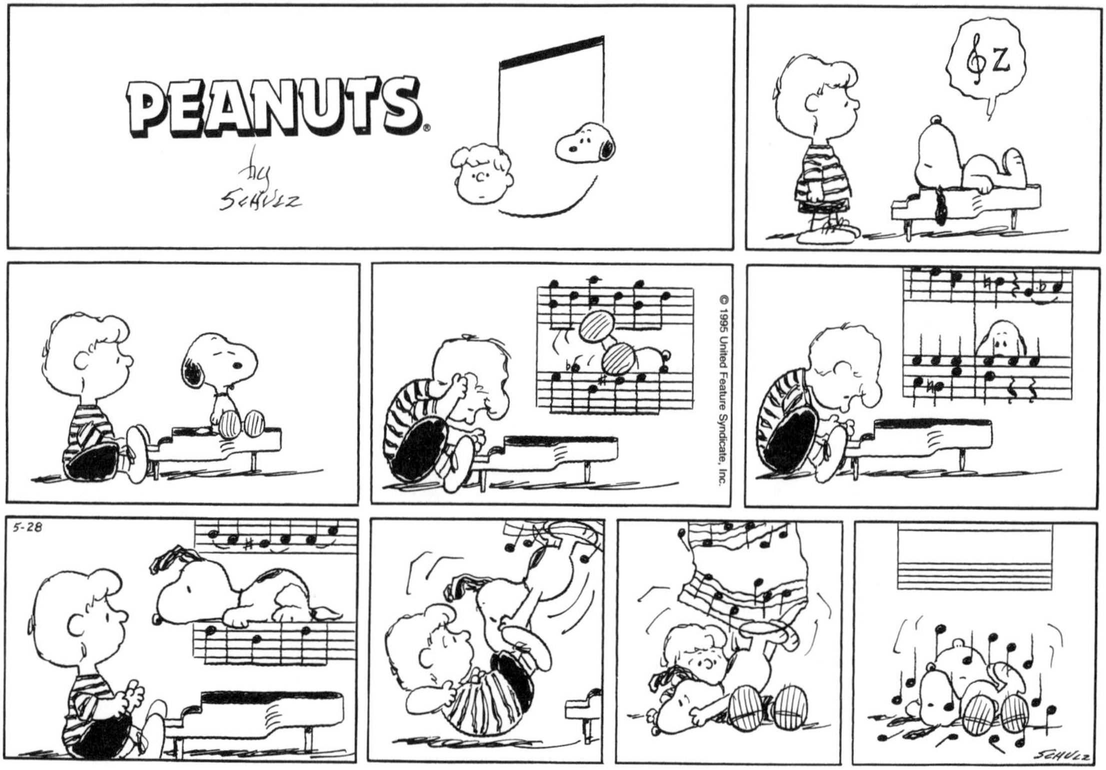
PEANUTS®
by SCHULZ
𝄞Z
© 1995 United Feature Syndicate, Inc.
5-28
SCHULZ

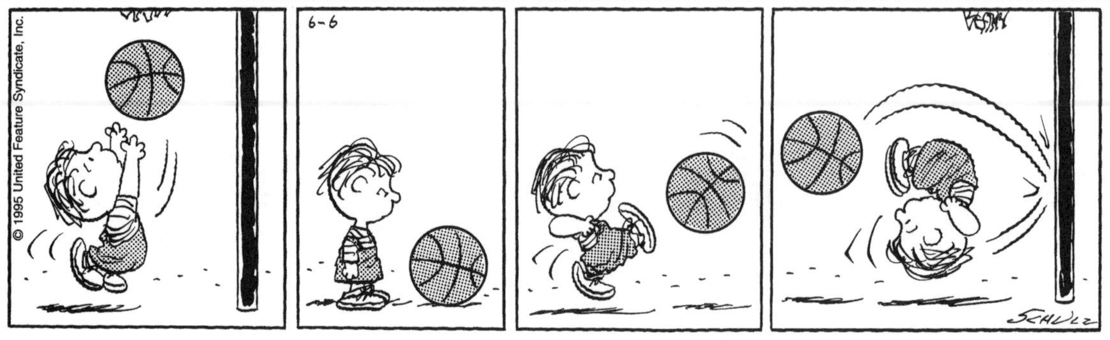
© 1995 United Feature Syndicate, Inc.
6-6
SCHULZ

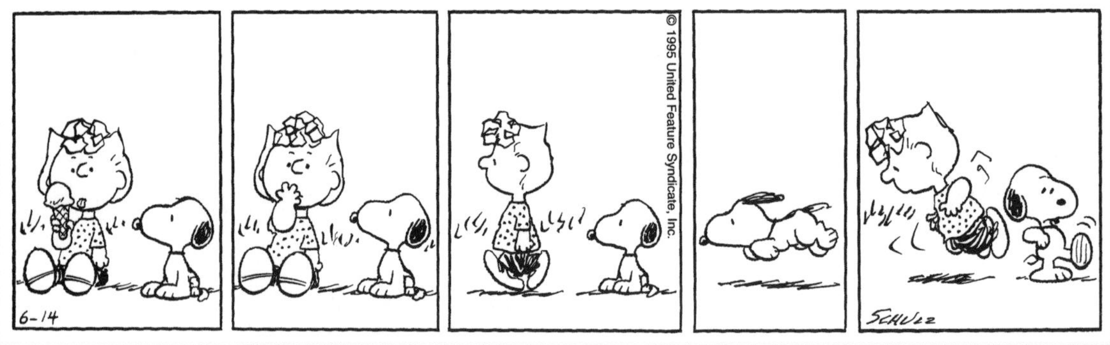
6-14
© 1995 United Feature Syndicate, Inc.
SCHULZ

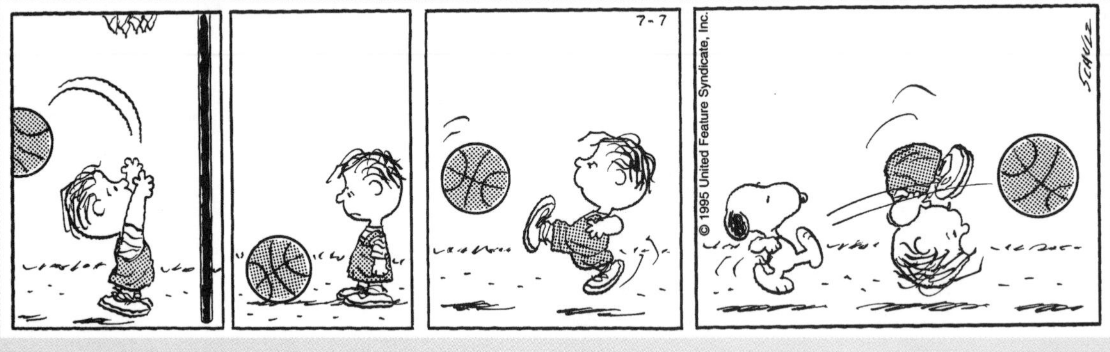
7-7
© 1995 United Feature Syndicate, Inc.
SCHULZ

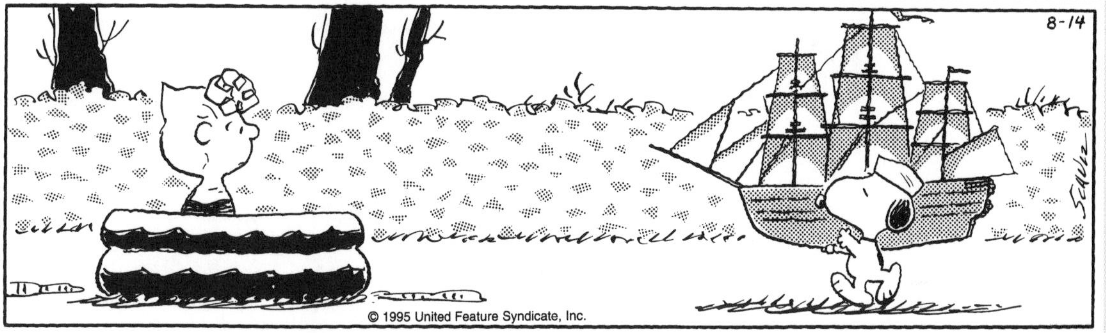
8-14
SCHULZ
© 1995 United Feature Syndicate, Inc.

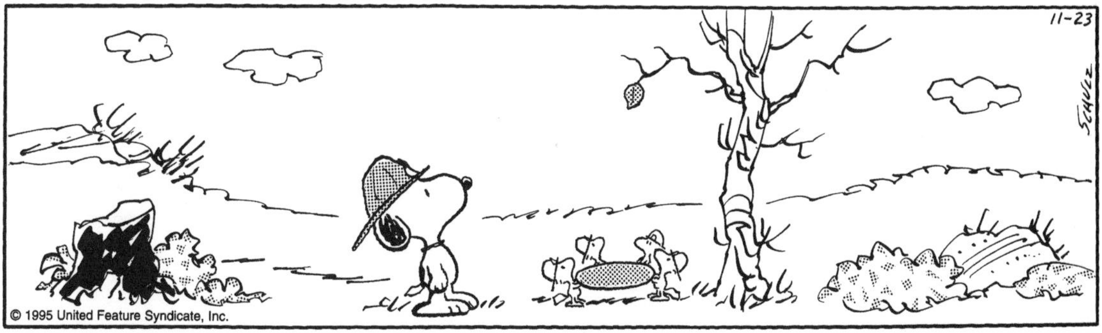
11-23
SCHULZ
© 1995 United Feature Syndicate, Inc.

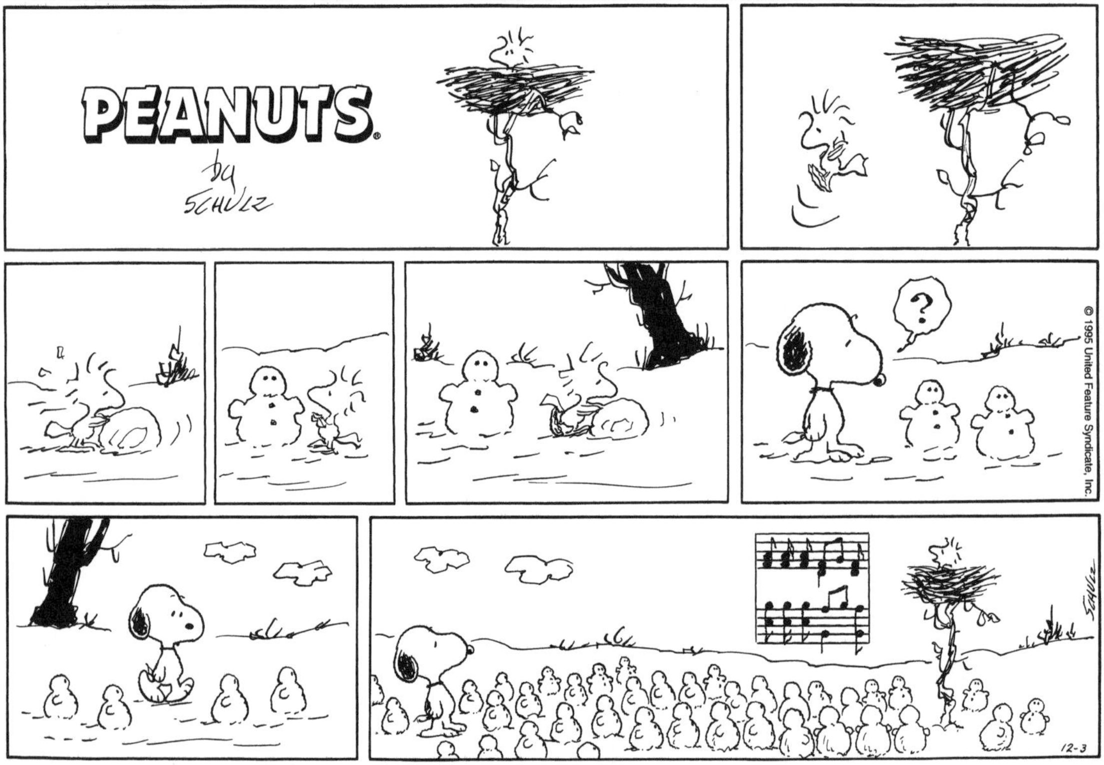
PEANUTS
by SCHULZ
?
© 1995 United Feature Syndicate, Inc.
SCHULZ
12-3

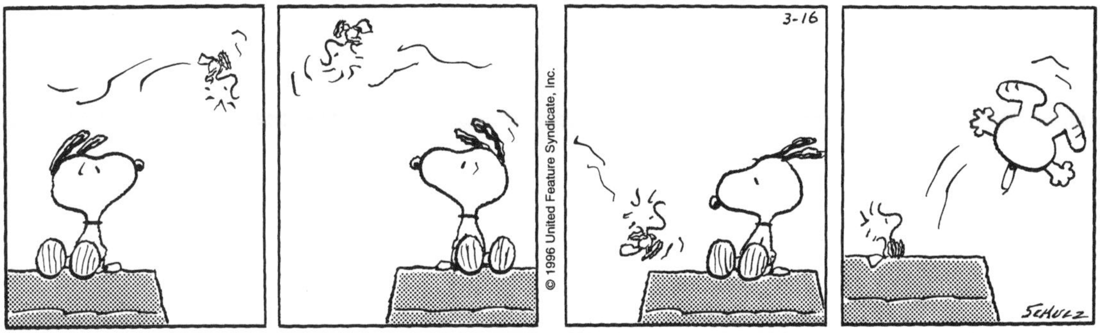
3-16
© 1996 United Feature Syndicate, Inc.
SCHULZ

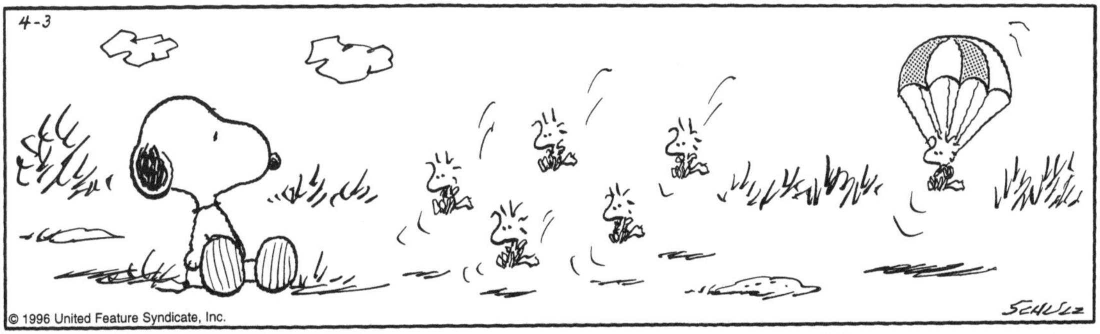
4-3
© 1996 United Feature Syndicate, Inc.
SCHULZ

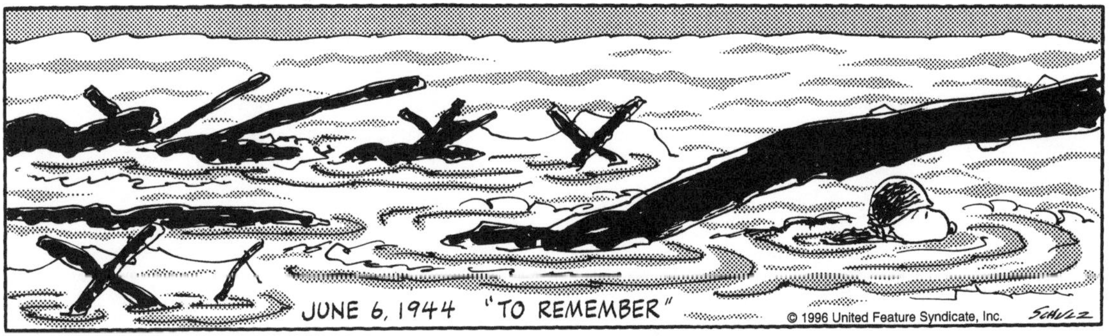
JUNE 6, 1944 "TO REMEMBER"
© 1996 United Feature Syndicate, Inc.
SCHULZ

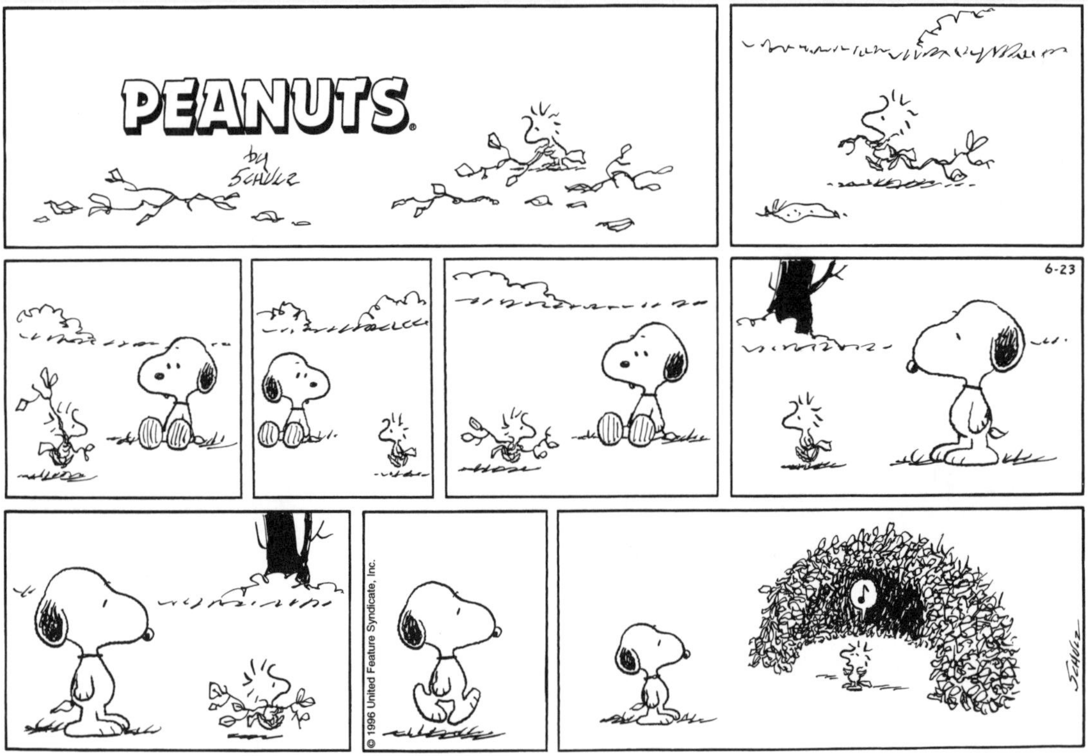
PEANUTS
by SCHULZ
6-23
© 1996 United Feature Syndicate, Inc.
SCHULZ

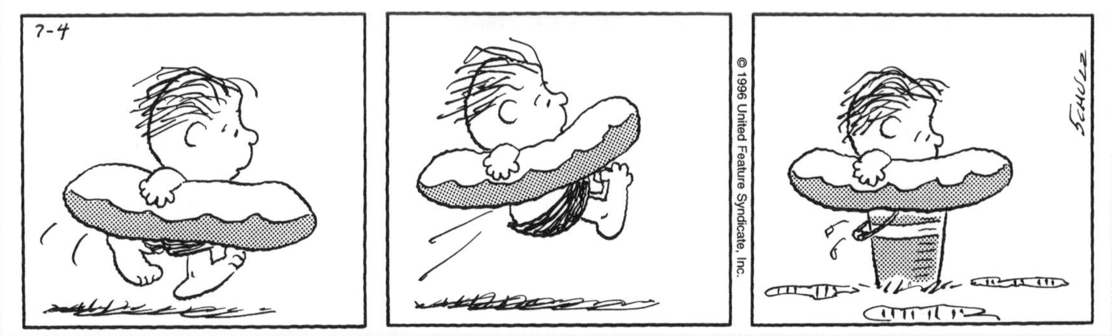
7-4
© 1996 United Feature Syndicate, Inc.
SCHULZ

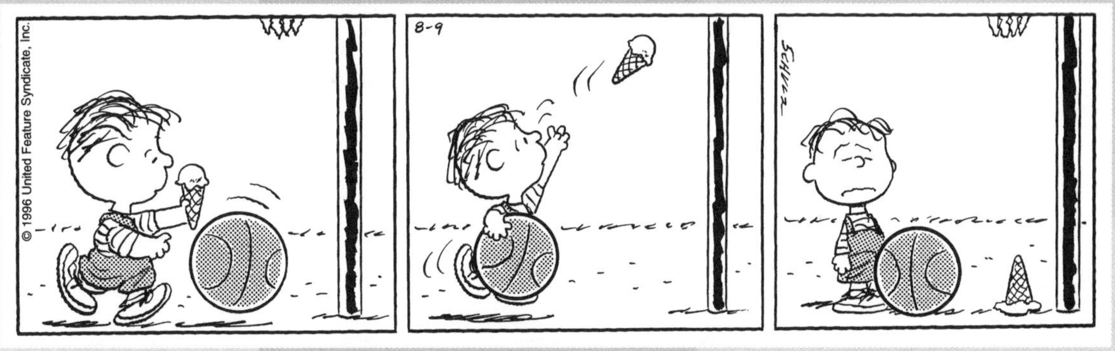
© 1996 United Feature Syndicate, Inc.
8-9
SCHULZ

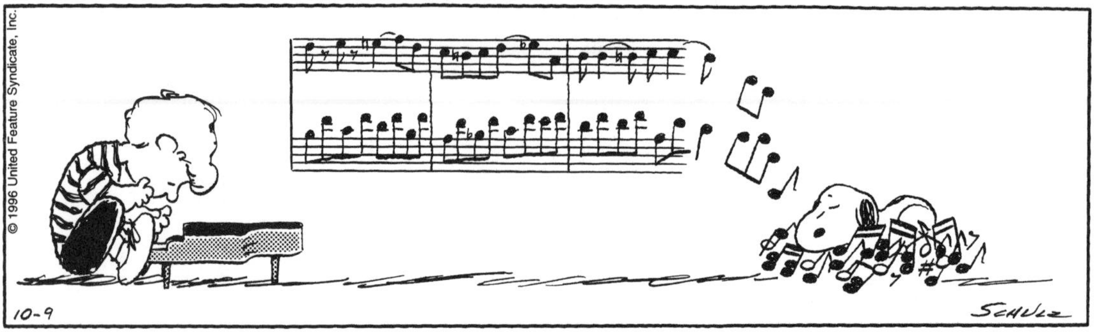
© 1996 United Feature Syndicate, Inc.
10-9
SCHULZ

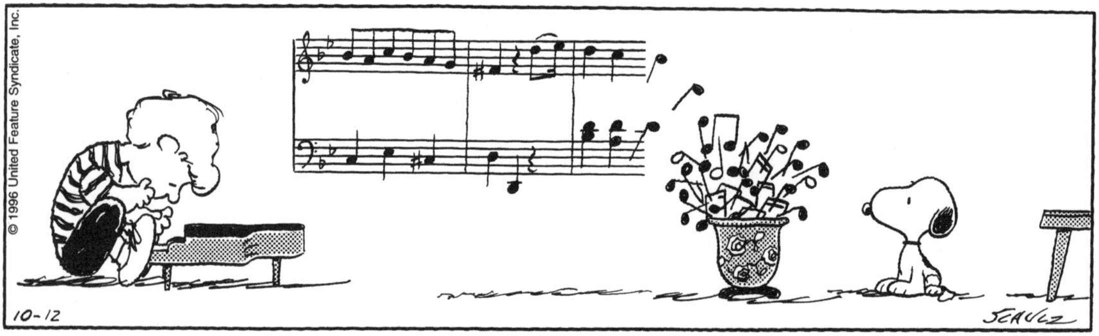
© 1996 United Feature Syndicate, Inc.
10-12
SCHULZ

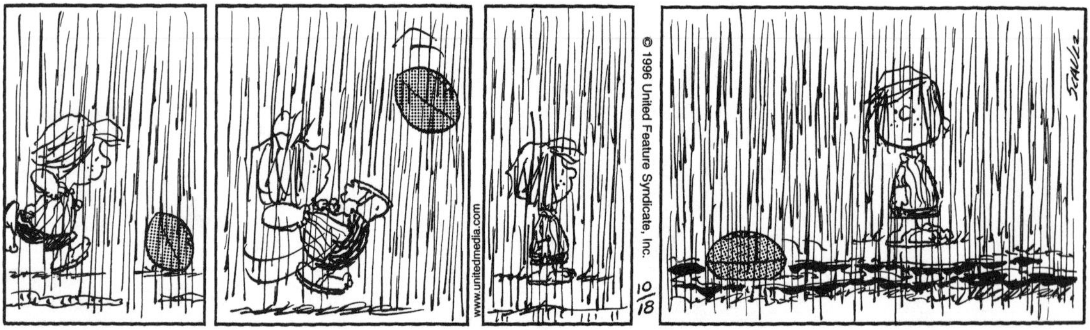
www.unitedmedia.com
© 1996 United Feature Syndicate, Inc.
10/18
SCHULZ

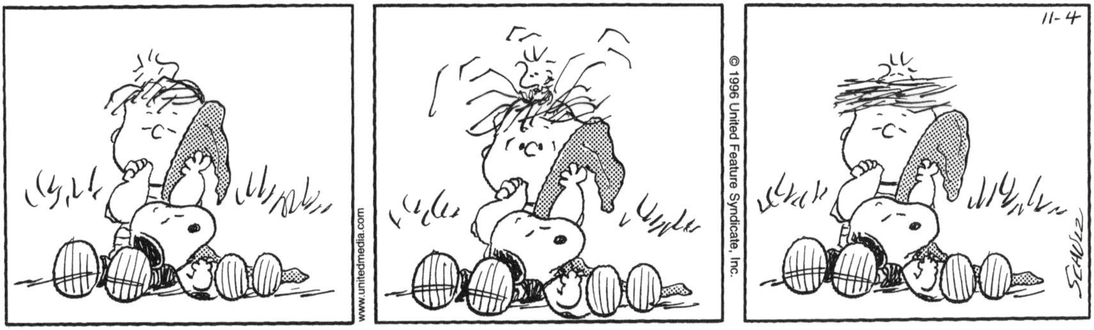
www.unitedmedia.com
© 1996 United Feature Syndicate, Inc.
11-4
SCHULZ

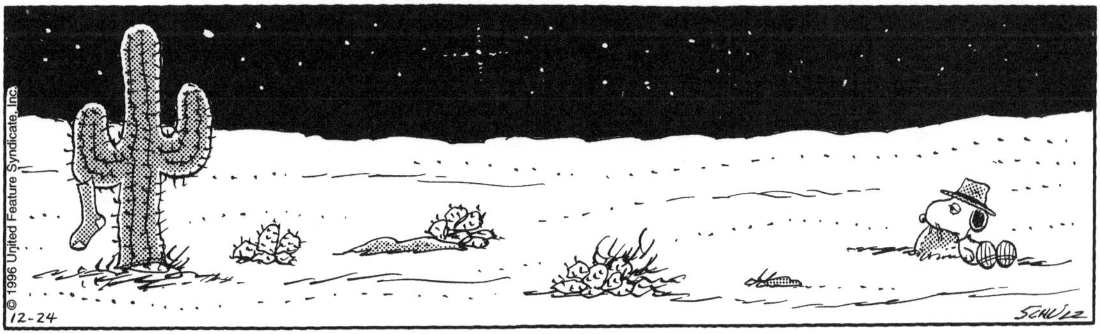
© 1996 United Feature Syndicate, Inc.
12-24
SCHULZ

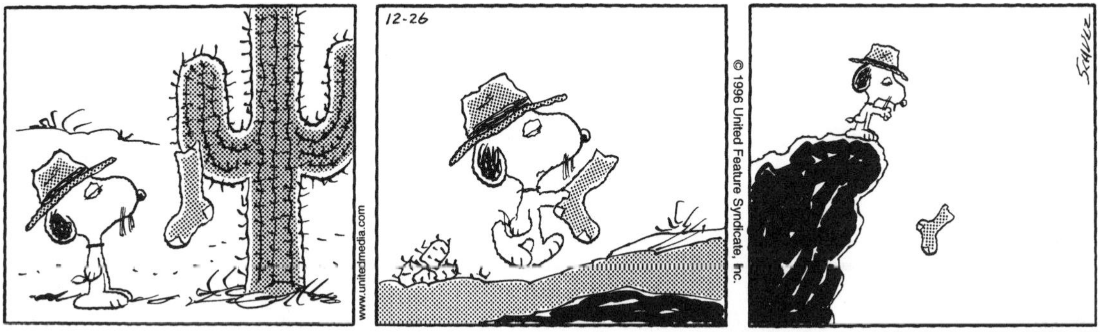
www.unitedmedia.com
12-26
© 1996 United Feature Syndicate, Inc.
SCHULZ

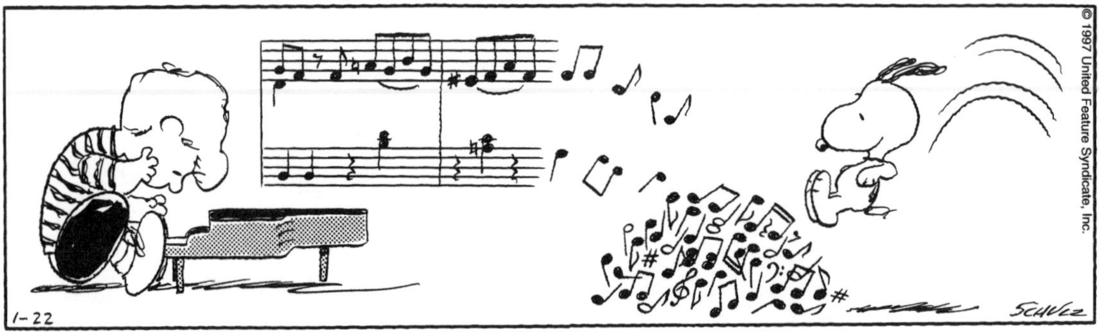
© 1997 United Feature Syndicate, Inc.
1-22
SCHULZ

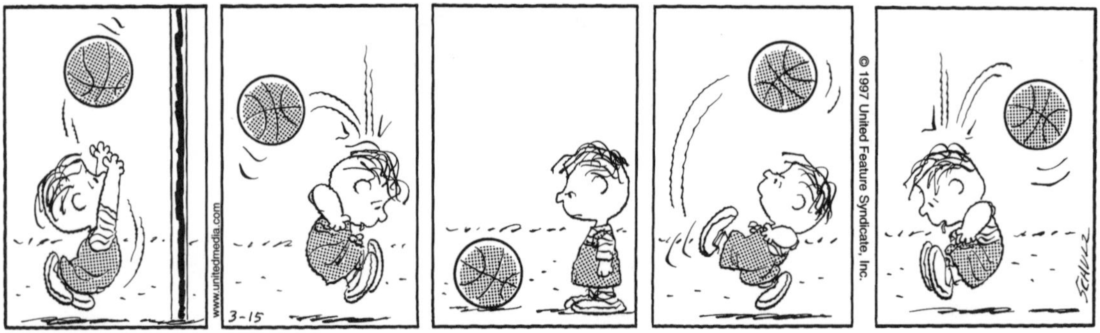
www.unitedmedia.com
3-15
© 1997 United Feature Syndicate, Inc.
SCHULZ

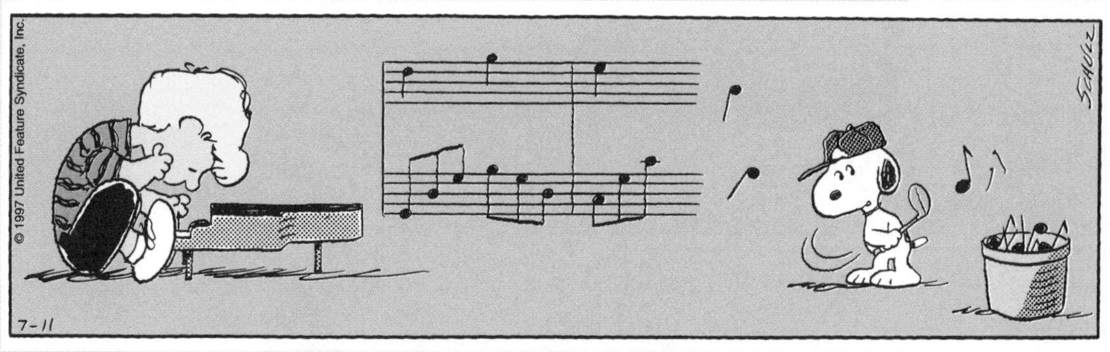
© 1997 United Feature Syndicate, Inc.
7-11
SCHULZ

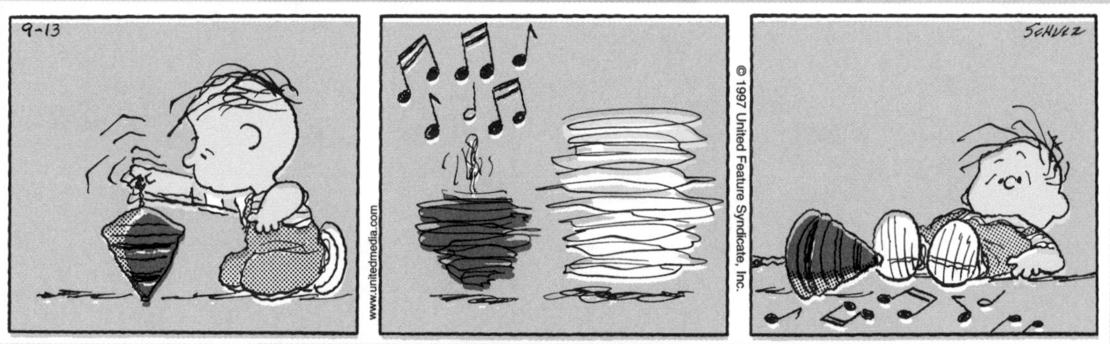
9-13
www.unitedmedia.com
© 1997 United Feature Syndicate, Inc.
SCHULZ

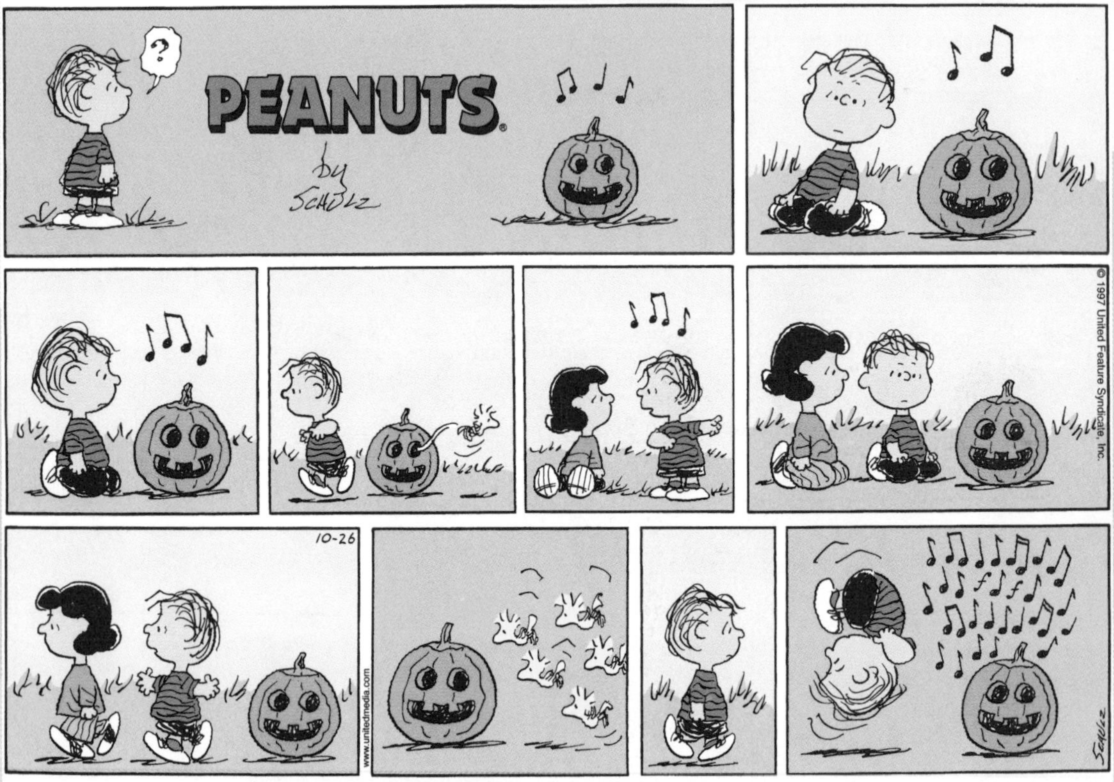
?
PEANUTS
by SCHULZ
© 1997 United Feature Syndicate, Inc.
10-26
www.unitedmedia.com
SCHULZ

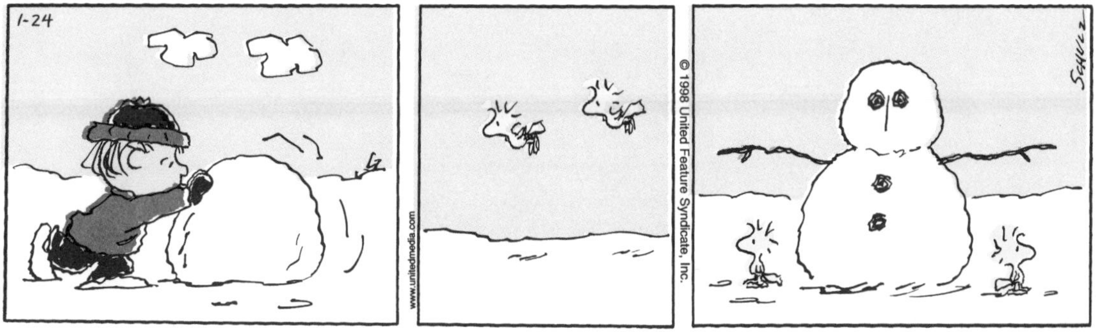
1-24
www.unitedmedia.com
© 1998 United Feature Syndicate, Inc.
SCHULZ

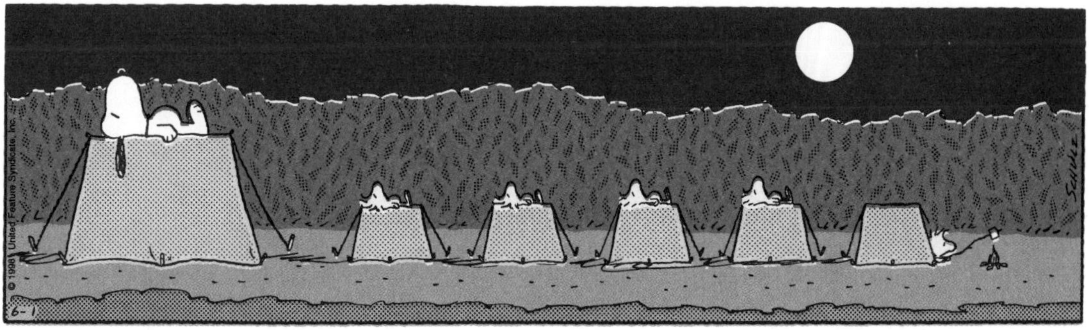
© 1998 United Feature Syndicate, Inc.
SCHULZ
6-1

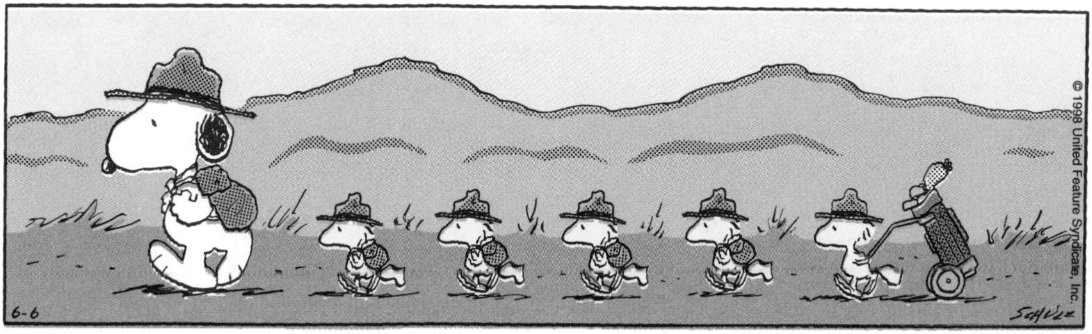
© 1998 United Feature Syndicate, Inc.
6-6
SCHULZ

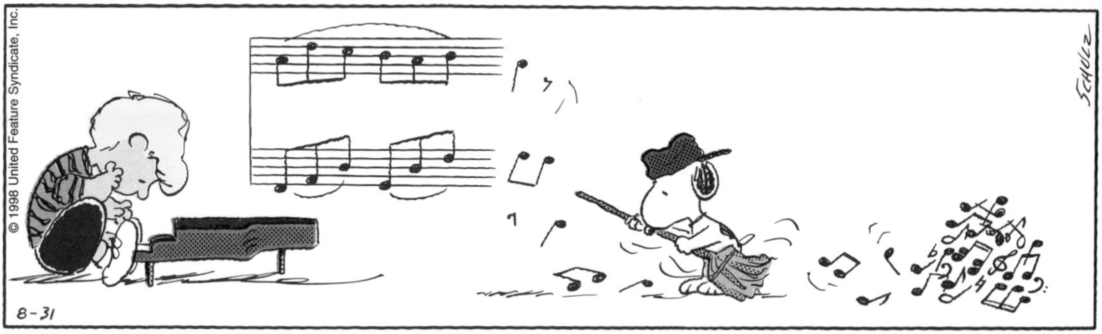
© 1998 United Feature Syndicate, Inc.
SCHULZ
8-31

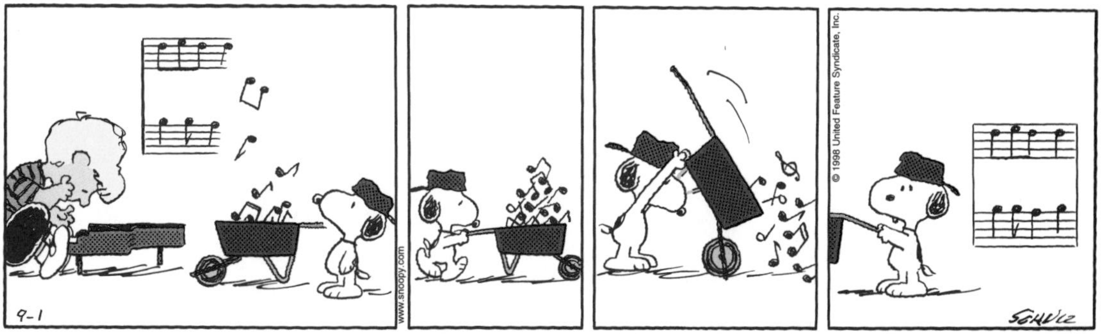
9-1
www.snoopy.com
© 1998 United Feature Syndicate, Inc.
SCHULZ

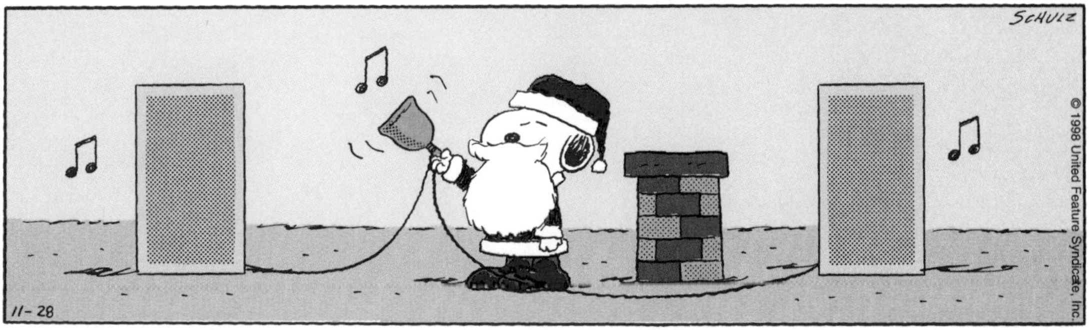
SCHULZ
© 1998 United Feature Syndicate, Inc.
11-28

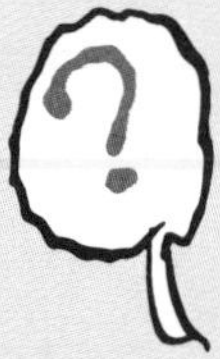
?

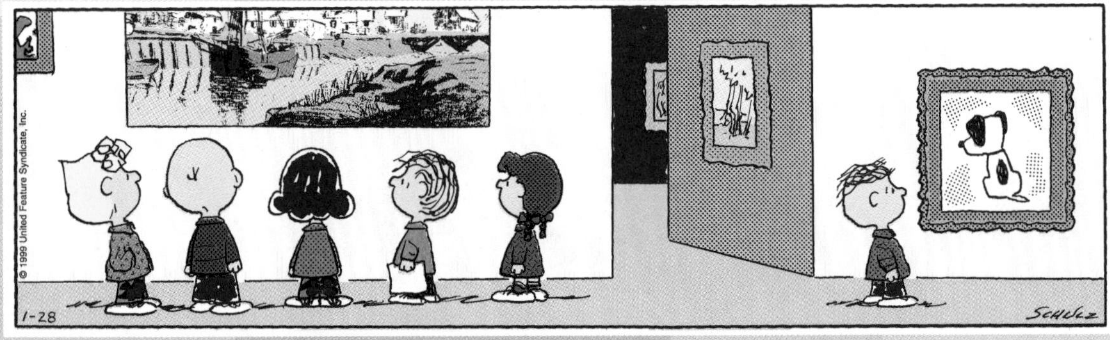
© 1999 United Feature Syndicate, Inc.
1-28
SCHULZ

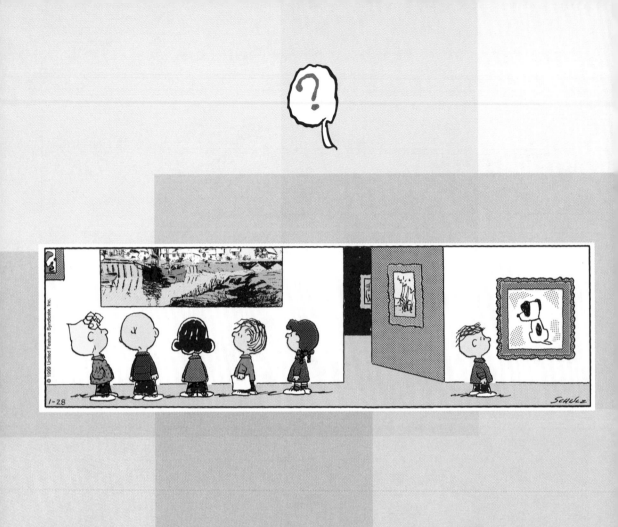

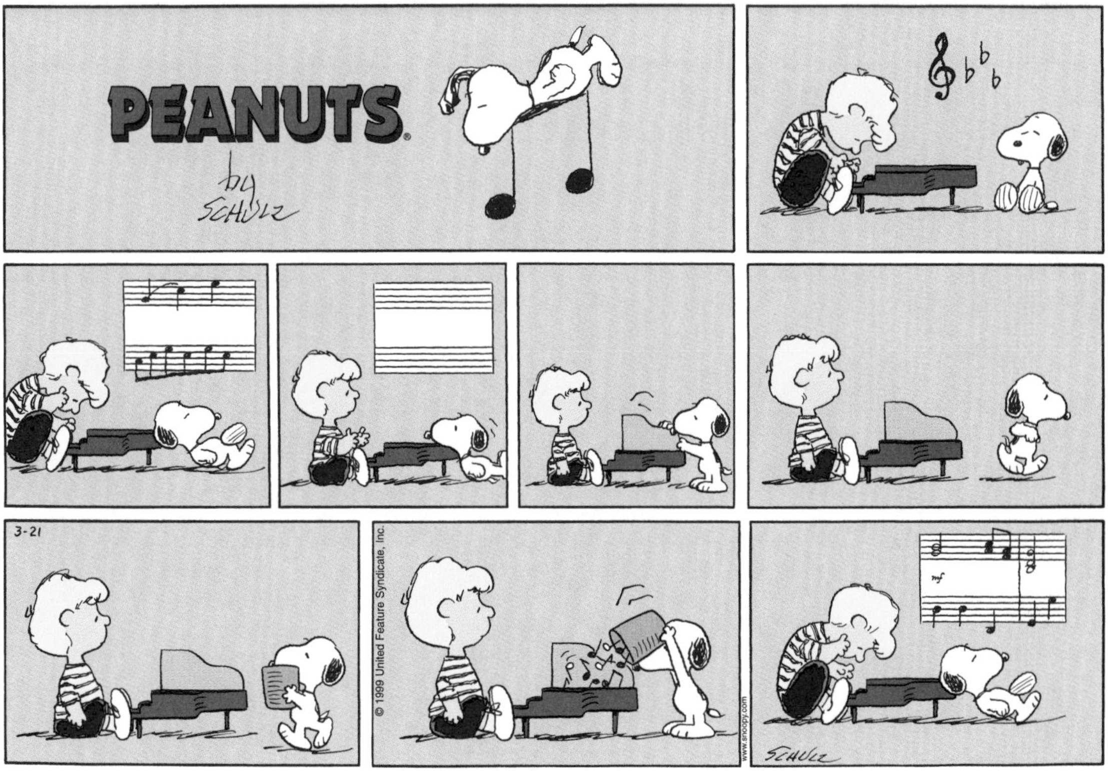
PEANUTS
by SCHULZ
3-21
© 1999 United Feature Syndicate, Inc.
www.snoopy.com
SCHULZ

© 1999 United Feature Syndicate, Inc.
SCHULZ
5-8

?

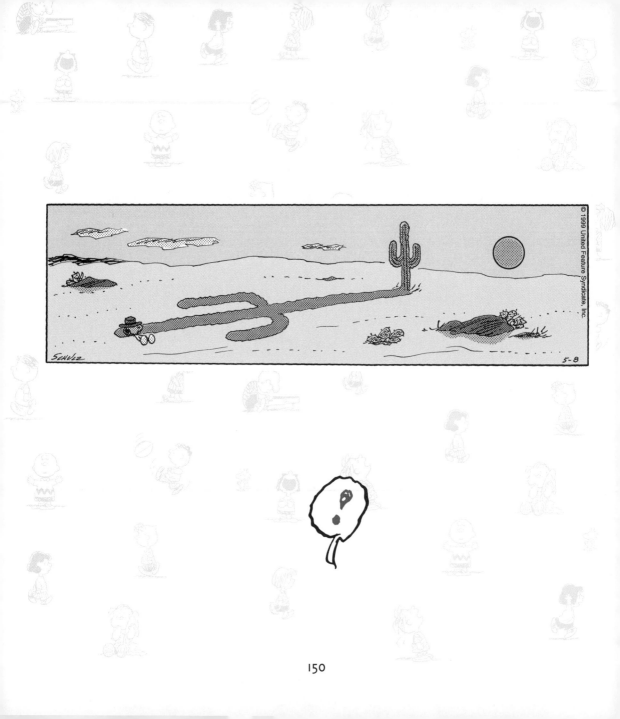

PEANUTS®
by SCHULZ
© 1999 United Feature Syndicate, Inc.
www.snoopy.com
5-9
SCHULZ

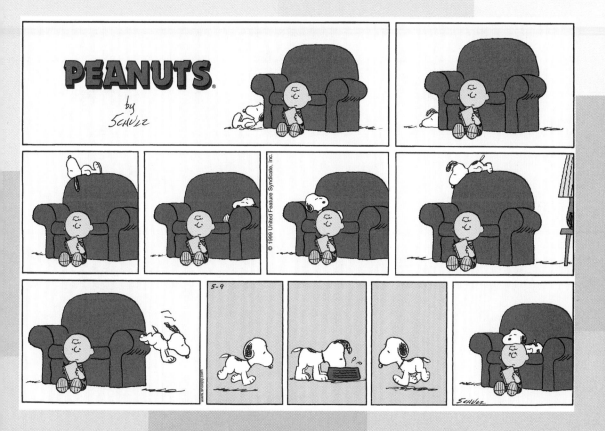

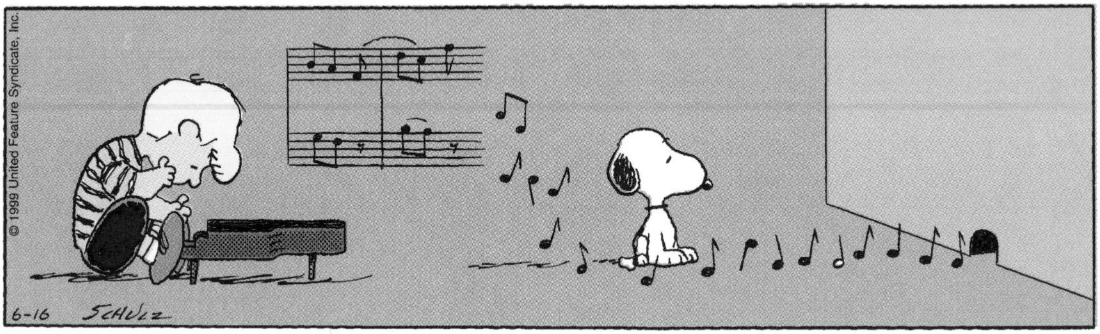
© 1999 United Feature Syndicate, Inc.
6-16
SCHULZ

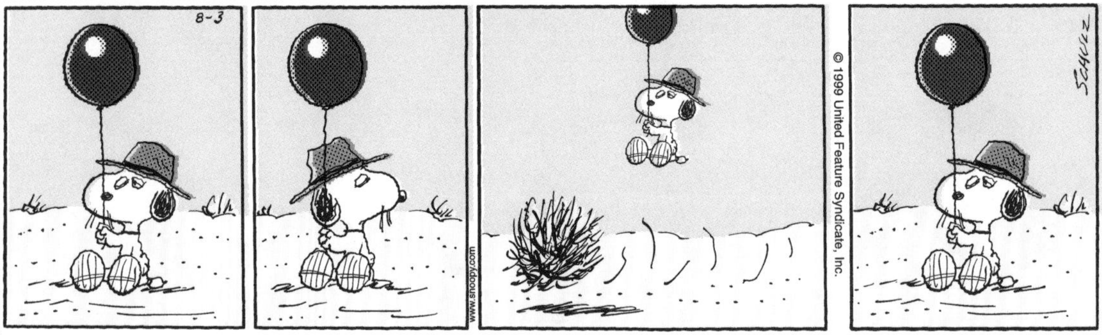
8-3
www.snoopy.com
© 1999 United Feature Syndicate, Inc.
SCHULZ

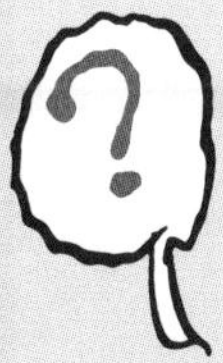
?

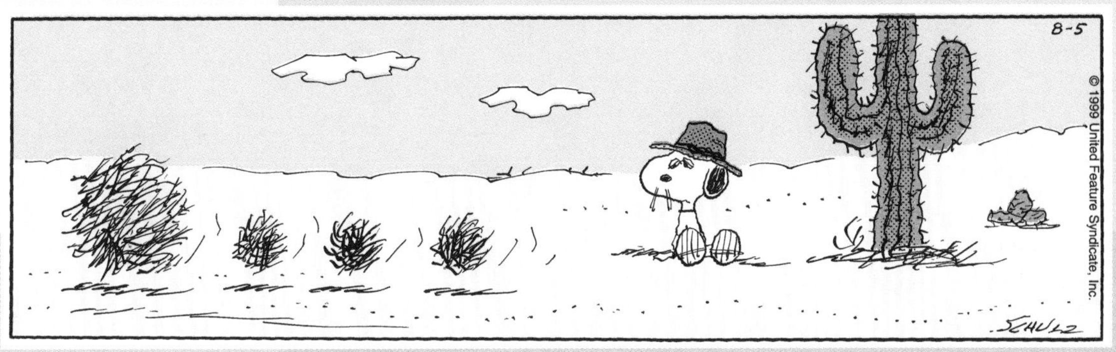
8-5
© 1999 United Feature Syndicate, Inc.
SCHULZ

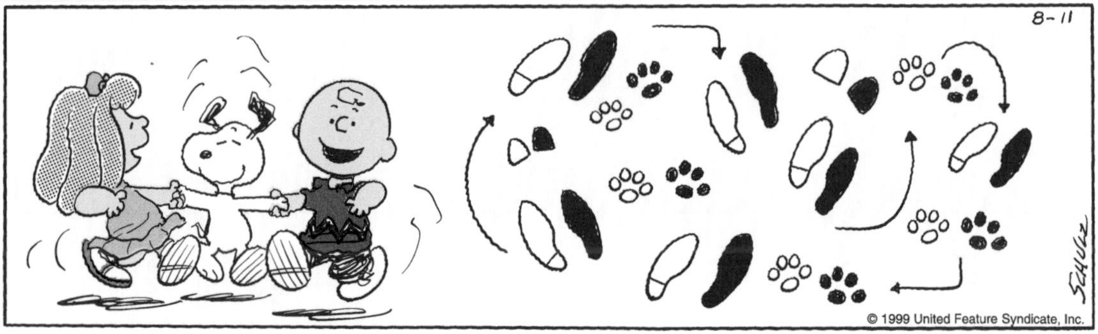
8-11
SCHULZ
© 1999 United Feature Syndicate, Inc.

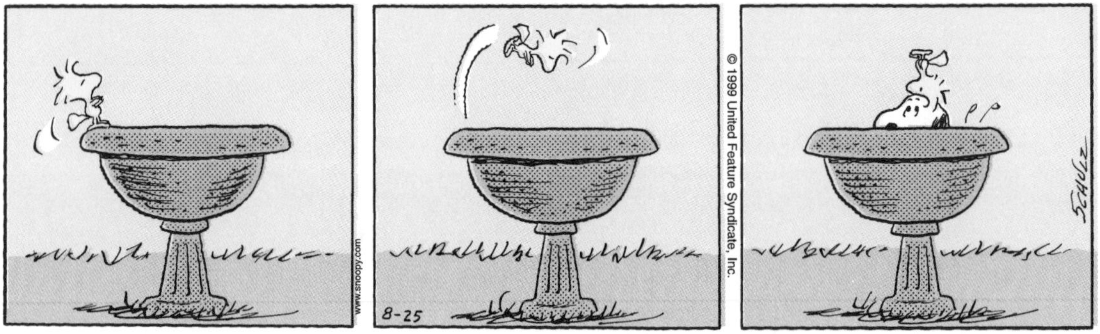
www.snoopy.com
8-25
© 1999 United Feature Syndicate, Inc.
SCHULZ

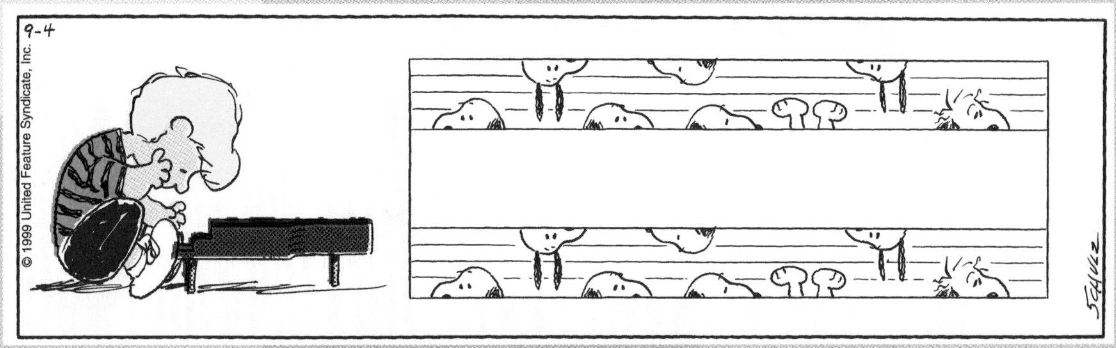
9-4
© 1999 United Feature Syndicate, Inc.
SCHULZ

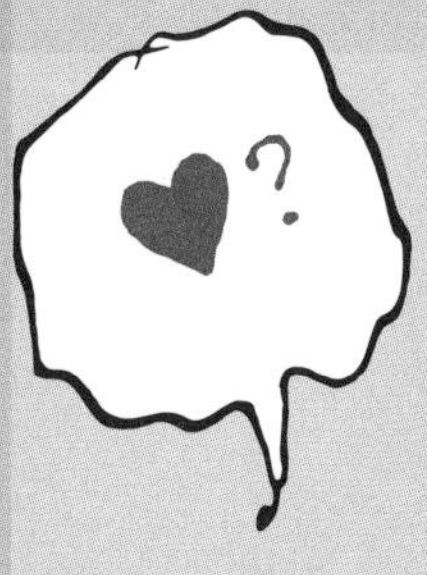

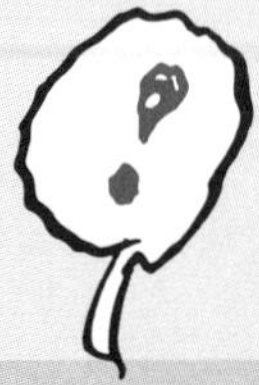
?

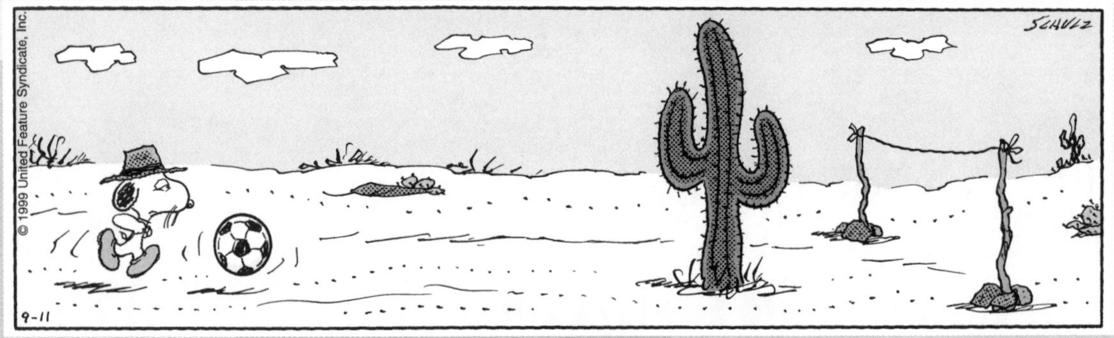
© 1999 United Feature Syndicate, Inc.
SCHULZ
9-11

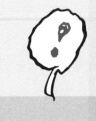

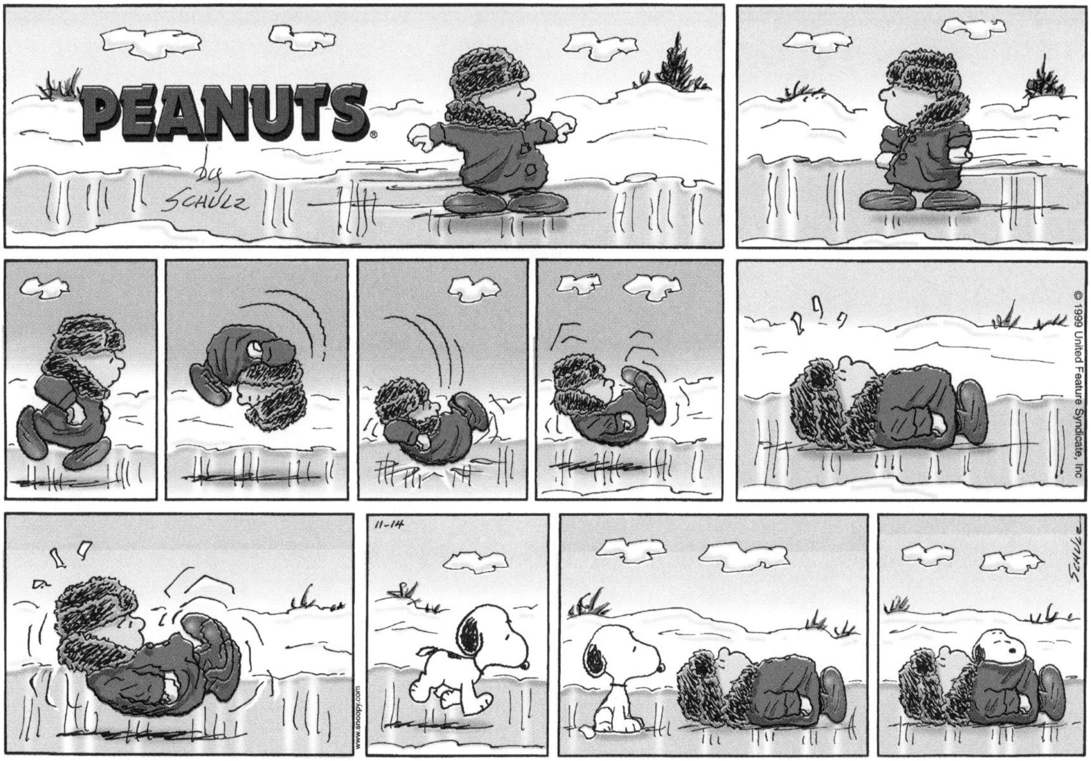
PEANUTS
by SCHULZ
© 1999 United Feature Syndicate, Inc
www.snoopy.com
11-14
SCHULZ

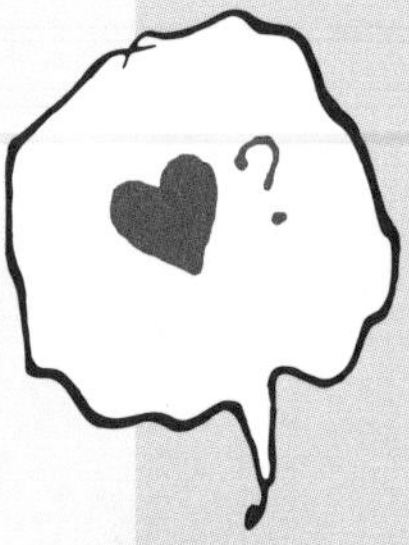
?

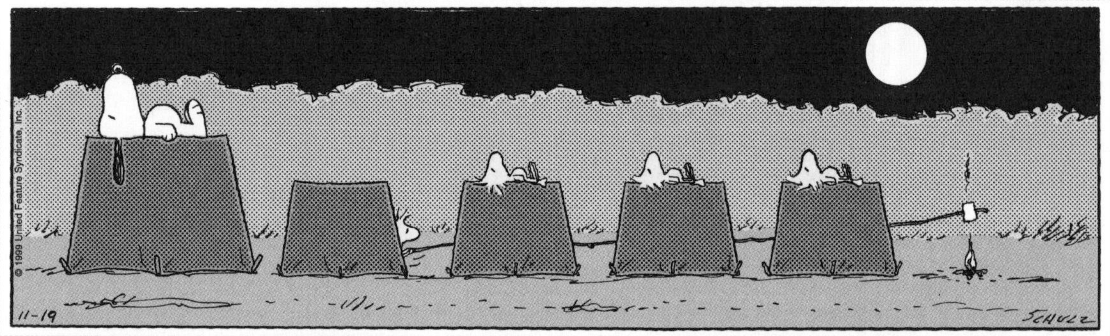
© 1999 United Feature Syndicate, Inc.
11-19
SCHULZ

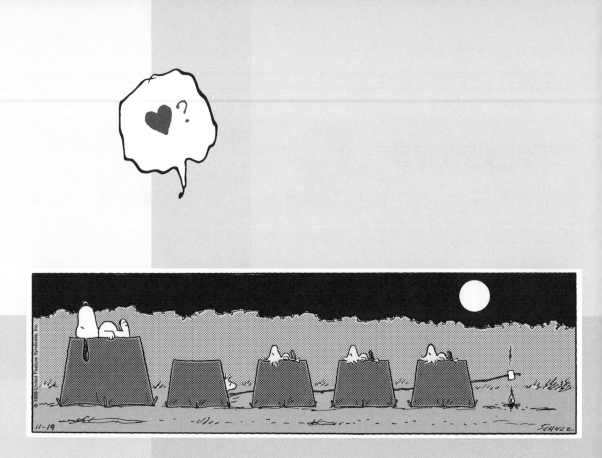

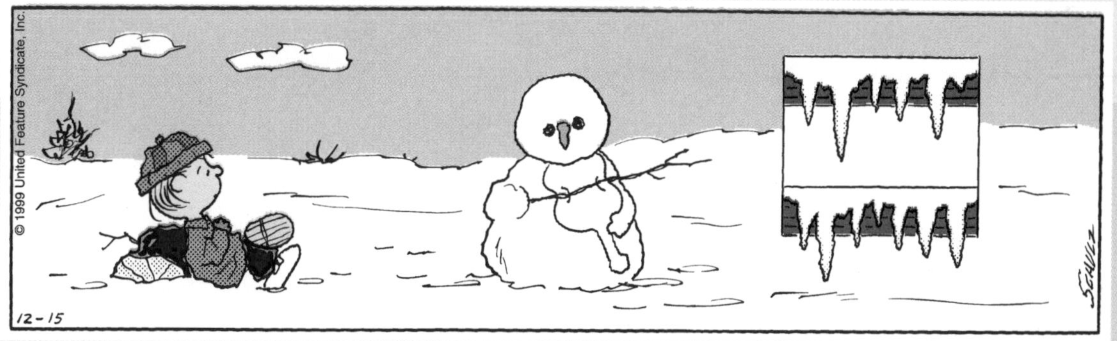
© 1999 United Feature Syndicate, Inc.
12-15
SCHULZ

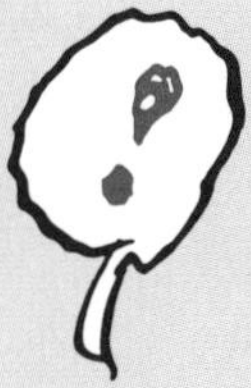

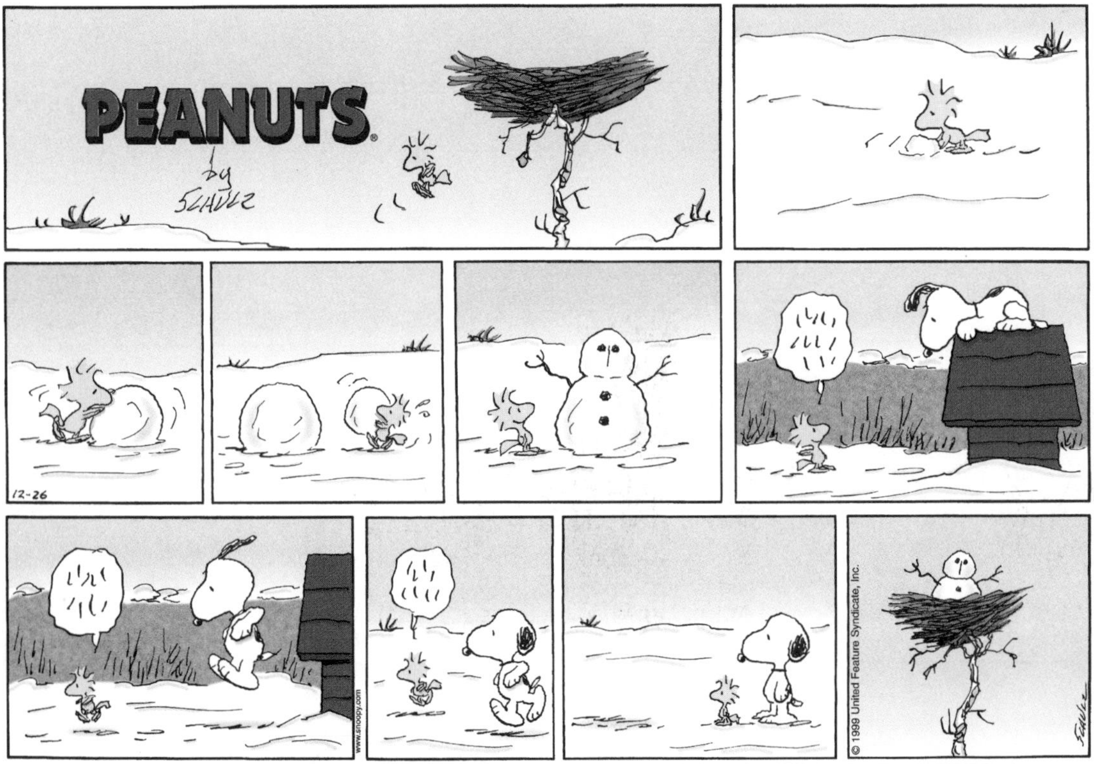
PEANUTS
by SCHULZ
12-26
www.snoopy.com
© 1999 United Feature Syndicate, Inc.